ENCYCLOPAEDIA OF INDIAN GOVERNMENT: PROGRAMMES AND POLICIES

ENCYCLOPAEDIA OF INDIAN GOVERNMENT: PROGRAMMES AND POLICIES

Vol. 1

Women and Child Development

Edited by

Satish Tiwari

ANMOL PUBLICATIONS PVT. LTD.
NEW DELHI - 110 002 (INDIA)

ANMOL PUBLICATIONS PVT. LTD.
4374/4B, Ansari Road, Daryaganj
New Delhi - 110 002

Encyclopaedia of Indian Government: Programmes and Policies

First Edition, 2000
ISBN 81-261-0515-1 (Set)

PRINTED IN INDIA

Published by J.L. Kumar for Anmol Publications Pvt. Ltd., New Delhi - 110 002 and Printed at Mehra Offset Press, Delhi.

Contents

Preface

Encyclopaedia of Indian Government: Programmes and Policies contains authoritative information on about fifty departmental policies and their future developmental programmes.

Organised to be completed in 40 volumes, this gigantic work covers Agriculture; Atomic Energy; Chemicals and Fertilizers; Coal; Commerce; Communication; Culture; Defence; Education; Environment and Forests; External Affairs; Finance; Food & Consumer Affairs; Food Processing Industries; Health and Family Welfare; Home Affairs and Internal Security; Human Resources; Industry; Information and Broadcasting; Labour; Law, Justice and Company Affairs; Non-conventional Energy Sources; Ocean Development; Parliamentary Affairs; Personnel, Public Grievances and Pensions; Petroleum and Natural Gas; Planning and Programme Implementation; Planning and Statistics; Posts and Telegraphs; Power; Rural Development; Science and Technology; Social Justice and Empowerment; Space; States Affairs; Steel; Steel and Mines; Sugar and Edible Oils; Surface Transport; Textiles; Tourism; Urban Development; Water Resources; Women and Child development etc.

Based on the information derived from authoritative sources, this work contains authentic facts and figures. I am deeply beholden to all the scholars whose writings are cited or substantially made use of in the present work. I am also thankful to Anmol Publications Pvt. Ltd. for undertaking publication of this encyclopaedia. I am solely responsible for shortcomings in presentation of matter.

Encyclopaedic in nature, this will prove a dependable reference work for scholars and academics besides those appearing for different competitive examinations.

—Satish Tiwari

1

Organisation

The department of women and child was, for most of the year under the minister for human resource development, Dr. Murali Manohar Joshi, who is of Cabinet rank. From 1st March 1999, it is under Ms. Uma Bharati, minister of state as an independent charge. Smt. Asha Das was the Secretary of the department of women and child development till Ist December,1998, thereafter Smt. Kiran Aggarwal took over charge. She is assisted by four Joint Secretaries, who head four bureaux, which are of child development, child welfare and nutrition, women's development and microcredit development.

The Department has 3 autonomous organisations viz. National Institute of Public Cooperation and Child Development (NIPCCD), Rashtriya Mahila Kosh(RMK) and the Central Social Welfare Board (CSWB) working under its aegis. NIPCCD and RMK are registered under the Societies Registration Act, 1860, whereas CSWB is a charitable company registered under Section 25 of the Indian Companies Act, 1956. These organisations are fully funded by the Government of India and assist the Department in its functions including implementation of some programmes/schemes. The National Commission for Women was constituted as a national apex statutory body in 1992 for protecting and safeguarding the rights of women.

The list of subjects allocated to the Department of Women and Child Development is as follows:

i. Family Welfare.
ii. Women and Child Welfare and coordination of activities of other Ministries and organisations in connection with this subject.
iii. Care of pre-school children,
iv. Coordination of National Nutrition Education of Women.
v. Charitable and religious endowments pertaining to subjects allocated to this Department.
vi. Promotion and development of voluntary effort on the subjects allocated to this Department.
vii. All other attached or subordinate offices or other organisations concerned with any of the subjects specified in this list.
viii. Administration of the Suppression of Immoral Traffic in Women and Girls Act, 1956 (10.4 of 1956).
ix. The Dowry Prohibition Act, 1961 (28 of 1961).
x. Coordination of activities of Cooperative for Assistance and Relief Everywhere (CARE).
xi. Planning, Research, Evaluation, Monitoring, Project formulation, Statistics and Training relating to the Development of Women and Children.
xii. References from the United Nations Organisations relating to traffic in Women and Children.
xiii. United Nations Children's Fund (UNICEF).
xiv. Central Social Welfare Board (CSWB).
xv. National Institute of Public Cooperation and Child Development (NIPCCD).
xvi. National Commission for Women (NCW).
xvii. Food and Nutrition Board (FNB).

xviii. Rashtriya Mahila Kosh (RMK).

xix. Mahila Samriddhi Yojana (MSY).

xx. National Nutrition Policy (NNP).

xxi. Indira Mahila Yojana (IMY).

Parlimentary standing committee

A meeting of the Parliamentary Standing Committee on Human Resource Development was held under the Chairpersonship of Shri S.B. Chavan on 19 June 1998 to examine the Demands for Grants of the Department of Women and Child Development for the year 1998-99. The Action Taken Report (ATR) on the 66th Report of the Standing Committee was submitted to the Rajya Sabha Secretariat on 28th January 1999.

Committee on empowerment of women

The Lok Sabha constituted a Committee on Empowerment of Women during March 1997 to consider the report of NCW and to report on the measures required by the Union Government for Empowerment of Women. Two sittings of the Committee were held on 6th January 1999 and on 15th January 1999 at New Delhi, to take oral evidence of Secretary (WCD) on the subject of "Developmental schemes for Rural Women"

Financial allocation

The Plan and Non-Plan outlays for the year 1998-99 were fixed at Rs.1225.95 crore and Rs.48.28 crore respectively. The outlays have been revised to Rs. 1134.48 crore under Plan and Rs.45.45 crore under Non-Plan during the year 1997-98.

Women's component plan

The Planning Commission, with a view to converge the benefits in the social and economic development sectors for women in the 9th Plan had requested all the Secretaries of the various Departments of the

Government to draw up a women's component plan to identify allocation in all the sectors at the Centre by aggregating them in an integrated manner in this context, the Minister for Human Resource Development had requested all the Ministers for their personal intervention in the matter of inclusion of an identifiable women component plan in the programmes of the respective Ministries/Departments right from the planning process and thereafter to monitor allocations and implementation of programmes to ensure the reach of benefits to women. The Cabinet approved one of the recommendations of the National Perspective Plan for Women (19982000), which says that the Planning Commission and all the Ministries/Departments should have a women cell and the Annual Reports of the Ministries/Departments at the Central and State levels should document and review the work done concerning women. The Department, accordingly, requested all the Ministries/Departments to set up advisory committees for women in each sector to help in the preparation, monitoring, and implementation of the women component plan, to set up a women's cell, and to include a chapter on women component plan in their annual reports.

Special Component Plan (SCP) for Scheduled Castes and Tribal SubPlan (TSP) for Scheduled Tribes

Programmes for women and children implemented by the Department, though not exclusively for SC/ST, are primarily directed towards the most disadvantaged groups of population like Scheduled Castes and Scheduled Tribes and other economically backward classes living in backward rural, tribal and urban slum areas.

About 80% of the Department's Annual Plan outlay is earmarked for ICDS. Selection of these projects are made in areas inhabited predominantly by SCs/STs and other disadvantaged/vulnerable groups in both rural and urban areas. Of the A200 ICDS Projects operational in the country, 750 are tribal projects, located in areas predominantly inhabited by tribes.

In addition, the World Bank assisted ICDS projects are being implemented exclusively in the predominantly backward/ tribal areas of the 4 States of Andhra Pradesh, Orissa, Madhya Pradesh and Bihar. In these projects certain additional services, like functional literacy for women, skill development training for empowerment of women, interventions for adolescent girls, rehabilitation of the severely malnourished, strengthened inputs in the spheres of communication, monitoring, and so on are provided.

A With a view to provide a sharp focus, the ICDS monitoring formats have been revised to include caste-specific information on beneficiaries. All the States/ Union Territories have been requested to ensure transmission of the said information on prescribed formats to facilitate the review of coverage of SC/ST population under the ICDS Scheme.

The Central Social Welfare Board made the following stipulations under its grant-in-aid rules to encourage voluntary action in tribal areas:

Normally, only suck institutions are eligible for grant-in-aid from the Board which are engaged in social welfare activities for a minimum period of three years; this condition is relaxed in the case of institutions located in tribal areas.

Institutions are normally given assistance under the grant-in-aid programme on an equal matching basis (50% grant from the Board and the other 50% raised by the institutions). In regard to the institutions in tribal areas, the Board allows grants upto 75% of the approved expenditure and in certain deserving cases, grants even upto 95%.

Further, the Central Social Welfare Board has been implementing the scheme of Socio-economic programme providing work and wages to women belonging to the weaker sections of the society. The beneficiaries under the programmes include, mostly, the members belonging to SC and ST communities. Specific instructions have also been issued to maintain separate records of the number of beneficiaries belonging to SCs and STs.

Similarly, under the scheme of Condensed Courses of Education for Adult Women, the institutions are required to make efforts to enroll Scheduled Caste and Scheduled Tribe women for the courses. In the case of SC and ST candidates, conditions regarding educational qualifications for admission to the courses are relaxed wherever necessary. Records are kept of the SC and ST candidates admitted to these courses.

Under the Scheme of Hostels for Working Women implemented by the Department, there are stipulations that 15% of the seats in hostels will be reserved for SCs and 7.5% for STs.

The schemes of the Food and Nutrition Board (FNB) are aimed at improving the nutritional status of people, in general, and of the vulnerable sections of the population including SCs and STs, in particular. The major thrust of the programmes of the Board is on the rural and tribal areas and urban slums.

Efforts are made to encourage more voluntary organisations to come forth with proposals to start welfare programmes in tribal and backward rural areas by extending special concessions and relaxation under grant-in-aid rules.

Annual action plan

The Department, at the instance of the Cabinet Secretariat, prepared the Annual Action Plan (AAP) for the schemes and activities of the Department, setting out the targets, both financial and physical, for the four quarters of the year. This AAP was monitored on a quarterly basis in the Department to review the financial and physical achievements as per the targets fixed at the beginning of the year.

Implementation of programmes the north-east

At the instance of the Prime Minister, the Ministry of Home Affairs vide their Order No. 9/19/97-T, dated 9th October, 1997 constituted a Committee of Secretaries under the Chairpersonship of the Home Secretary to look into the development programmes of the Central Government in the North-East (in which Secretary, Ministry of Human Resource Development is a member). The Department under the scheme of Integrated Child Development Services (ICDS), National Creche Fund (NCF), Assistance to Voluntary Organisations for Creches for the Children of Working and Ailing Mothers, Hostels for Working Women, Support to Training-cum- Employment Programme (STEP), Socio-Economic Programme (SEP), Condensed Courses of Education and Vocational Training for Women, Awareness Generation Projects for Rural and Poor Women, Food and Nutrition Board, National Institute of Public Cooperation and Child Development and other schemes of the Department allocated 10% of the budget available during the year for implementation of programmes in the North-East.

Reservation for SCs and STs

The reservation Policy of the Government of India is being followed by this Department. Out of the 30 Group "A" officers, 5 belong to the Scheduled Caste and 2 belong to the Scheduled Tribe category. Similarly, out of

95 Group 'B' officers, 17 officers belong to the SC community and A belong to the ST community. In respect of 69 Group 'C' posts, 12 officers belong to SC community and 4 belong to ST community. Out of 54 Group 'D' posts 25 officials belong to SC community and 3 belong to ST community.

Use of Hindi in official work

During the period under report, efforts were made to achieve the targets for the use of Hindi fixed by the Department of Official Language in their Annual Programme for 1998-99. Article 3(3) of the Official

Language Act, 1963 is being complied with in the Department. Letters received in Hindi were replied to in Hindi. Check points were strengthened to ensure better compliance of the provisions of the Official Language Act and Rules framed thereunder.

Quarterly Progress Reports received from the offices under the administrative control of this Department were reviewed. A representative of the Department has regularly been attending the meetings of the Official Language Implementation Committee of Central Social Welfare Board and National Institute of Public Cooperation and Child Development. Hindi Fortnight was celebrated from 1-15 September, 1998. During this period, debate, essay and noting and drafting competitions were held. In all, 40 officials appeared in these competitions, out of which 10 officials have been awarded prizes.

In addition to the routine work, the important material translated into Hindi relates to the Annual Report of the Department for the year 1997-98; Performance Budget, 1997-98; Parliament Questions; Cabinet Note on Rural Women's Development and Empowerment Project; Cabinet Note on Short Stay

Homes; Cabinet Note on ICDS Training; Papers for the Conference of State Ministers and Secretaries-in-charge of WCD; Parliamentary Consultative Committee; Parliamentary Standing Committee; and National Nutrition Week, National Children's Award for Exceptional Achievements, 1997; World Breast Feeding Week

2

Women's Development

The provisions of the Constitution of India granting equality to women in various spheres creates the legal framework within which the Department of Women and Child Development functions for women's development. At the same time, the paradigms for social development have been swiftly changing with greater attention to gender issues at the global and national levels. The Government of India has continuously been formulating strategies and initiating processes, to bring women into the mainstream. Women constitute half of the country's population (accounting for 407.1 million in absolute numbers as per the 1991 census), and it is abundantly clear that there can be no development unless their needs and interests are fully taken into account. In addition, the Government of India has brought about specific legislation to protect and safeguard the rights of women.

Although there have been various shifts in policy approaches in the last fifty years from the concept of 'welfare' till the '70's to 'development' in the '80's and now to 'empowerment' in the '90's, the Department of Women and Child Development, since its inception has been implementing special programmes designed to improve the socioeconomic status of women. The Bureau of Women's Development, and Micro Credit Development, in the Department play a major role in this national endeavour for the advancement and empowerment of women. In its nodal capacity, the Department also formulates policies and programmes, enacts/amends legislations affecting women and coordinates the efforts of both Governmental and Non-Governmental Organisations working to improve the lot of women in the country. Employment, credit facilities, training, awareness generation, income-generating activities have been major interventions for improving the position of women. In addition, provision is made for support services of various kinds, including help to the women of vulnerable groups. Capacity building through training, awareness generation and gender sensitisation also constitute a thrust area of the Department.

These programmes play the role of being both supplementary and complementary to the other general development programmes in the sectors of health, education, labour and employment, rural and urban development, etc.

In line with this integrated approach to the empowerment of women and enhancement of the status of the girl child, the, Department has sought to change attitudes in the family, the community and society towards women and the girl child and to mobilise these social units to play their rightful role in creating a conducive environment for women and girls. The interventions undertaken by the Department are directed to empower women and girl children legally, socially, economically and politically. The activities of the Department can be grouped under the following categories:

— Social and economic empowerment of women.

— Training, employment and education.

— Attitudinal change towards the girl child,

— Support services.

— Women's rights and the law.

The details of programmes and schemes implemented by the Department of Women and Child Development are briefly described below:

Social and economic empowerment

The Rural Women's Development and Empowerment Project has been sanctioned on 16 October 1998 as a Centrally-sponsored project for a period of 5 years in states of Uttar Pradesh, Madhya Pradesh, Bihar, Haryana, Karnataka and Gujarat with an estimated outlay of Rs. 186.21 crore. In addition, an amount of Rs. 5 crore will be provided over the project period, but outside the project outlay, for facilitating setting up, in the project states, of Revolving Funds for giving interest-bearing loans to beneficiary groups primarily during their initial formative stage. The overall objective of the project is to strengthen the processes, and create an environment for empowerment of women. Its specific objectives are:

— Establishment of between 7400 and 12000 self-reliant women's Self-Help-Groups (SHGs) having 15-20 members each, which will improve the quality of their lives, through greater access to, and control over, resources.

— Sensitising and strengthening the institutional capacity of support agencies to pro-actively address women's needs.

— Developing linkages between SHGs and lending institutions to ensure women's continued access to credit facilities for income generation activities.

— Enhancing women's access to resources for better quality of life, including those for drudgery reduction and time-saving devices.

— Increased control of women, particularly poor women, over income and spending, through their involvement in income generation activities which will indirectly help in poverty alleviation.

The implementing agencies will be the Women's Development Corporations of the concerned states in Bihar, Haryana and Karnataka, Gujarat Women's Economic Development Corporation in Gujarat, M.P. Mahila Arthik Vikas Nigam in Madhya Pradesh and Mahila Kalyan Nigam in Uttar Pradesh, who will actively associate NGOs in the implementation tasks. Funds needed by the implementing agencies will be provided by the Government of India in the form of grants-in-aid.

A substantial part of the outlay for the project will become available as soft-term loan/credit to the Government of India from the International Fund for Agricultural Development (IFAD) and International Development Association (IDA or World Bank). Almost the entire credit needs of the beneficiaries will be met from institutional sources. Roughly, sources of project funding would be as under:

(Rs. in crore)

Source of Funds	Combination as of total cost	presumptive Amount
IDA	36.43	67.84
IFAD	35.87	66.79
Institutional Finance	15.85	29.51
Government of India	6.82	12.70
Beneficiary women	5.03	9.37

Funds needed for setting up of the Revolving Funds in project states will be provided by the Government of India itself. The project, at the end of 5 years, is expected to bring about the following qualitative and quantitative benefits:

- Organisation of nearly 7,400 to 12,000 .Self -Help-Groups (SHGs) involving 2.14 lakh rural women and strengthening their ability to control their own affairs and to further their own development;
- Increased self-esteem, confidence and self-reliance of women to address the constraints which the society has imposed and is imposing on them;
- Improved management and technical skills for women;
- Improvement in the women's social status in both the family and the community;
- Increased mobilisation of various public and private sector services for women's benefit;
- Capacity building and strengthening of the support agencies, such as NGOs and Women Development Corporations, to enable them to be more effective in addressing women's needs.
- Orientation of financial institutions and line departments, to facilitate their sensitisation to gender issues and better services to women, especially rural women;
- Development of training modules and material which can be replicated and extensively used elsewhere, with such adaptations as may be warranted by local situations;
- Enhanced involvement of women in economic activities, additional income and control over it, thereby leading to upgradation of standards;
- Integration of women into the social mainstream, especially in the areas of control over and/or access to finance, including credit from institutional and other sources; and
- Improvement in women's well-being through

improved conditions of living, including drudgery-removal and time-saving devices.

During next 5 years, under the project Rs. 191.21 crore will be required out of which Rs. 5.00 crore will be required as revolving fund. For 1998-99, an amount of Rs. 8.00 crore will be required as the project was sanctioned on 16 October, 1998 by the Planning Commission.

Indira mahila yojana

The Indira Mahila Yojana (IMY) is a programme launched by the Government of India in August 1995 as a central sector project for the holistic empowerment of women. The vision of IMY is to develop empowered women who will:

— Demand their rights from family, community and the government;

— Have increased access to and control over material, social and political resources;

— Have enhanced awareness and improved skills; and

— Be able to raise issues of common concern through mobilisation and networking.

It is premised on recognition of the fact that empowerment is a multifaceted process. It seeks to achieve this by the following objectives:

— To generate awareness among women by disseminating information and knowledge, so as to bring about an attitudinal change;

— To help women achieve economic strength through micro-level income generating activities; and

— To establish convergence of various services such as literacy, health, non-formal education, rural development, water supply, entrepreneurship, etc.

The IMY is based on the idea of the strength of the Self-Help Groups. The development of Indira Mahila

Kendras (IMKs) at the Anganwadi level and also recognising other women's groups under the adult literacy programmes, health programmes, etc. and integrating, or associating them with the IMKs at the Anganwadi level would provide a grass-root level organisation for women to interact,

Achievements during the year

More than 37,000 small homogenous women's groups have been formed under the Scheme till December 1998, out of which 9000 women's groups have been formed during the period under reference.

For the purpose of sensitising implementors of IMY at the state/district level, a series of state/district level workshops are being conducted throughout the country with the assistance of National Institute of Public Cooperation & Child Development (NIPCCD). This process continued during the current year also. A total number of 2.4 state level workshops have been conducted so far, out of which 4 have been conducted this year.

Two training programmes of five days duration were organised at the Lal Bahadur Shastri National Academy of Administration (LBSNAA), Mussoorie for Chief Executive Officers, District Magistrates and District Officers of the concerned districts where Indira Mahila Yojana is implemented, to sensitise them towards IMY.

The third training programme for the child development project officers (CDPOs) and Non-Governmental Organisations (NGOs) under the collaboration of Department for International Development (DFID) and Department of Women and Child Development was organised this year. 26 persons took part in the Indian module held between November 2 and 14, 1998 at Bankers Institute of Rural Development, Lucknow. This Indian module was funded by Rashtriya Mahila Kosh

(RMK). 15 participants will be given intensive training at UK for 8 weeks and the other group will be taken on a study tour of 10 days duration to Bangladesh.

A teleconference inaugurated by Minister for HRD on IMY and group formation was organised from October 14-16-1998 covering six Hindi speaking states namely, Bihar, Gujarat, Haryana, Himachal Pradesh, Jammu and Kashmir, Madhya Pradesh and NCT of Delhi in collaboration with Indira Gandhi National Open University and Indian Space Research Organisation. Prior to this, a Master Trainers workshop was organised at NIPCCD by IGNOU between 6 - 7 October, 1998.

Resource material development

The main book on IMY has been translated into regional languages by some states. A Hindi version has also been brought out.

— Detailed guidelines for creation of a revolving corpus with Indira Mahila Block Society (IMBS) have been issued.

— A booklet on the Role of State Level Steering Committee (SLSC) and District Level Coordination Committee (DLCC) under Indira Mahila Yojana (IMY), has been compiled.

— A Handbook on IMY has been prepared with assistance of NIPCCD and with funding from the British Council and RMK.

— A project book on Micro-enterprise credit & Development Training (CREME) has been prepared by the IMY Desk and published by the British Council.

— All the important circulars of IMY and other related information has been compiled. A booklet containing this information will be published soon.

A new collaborative project "Training for Women Empowerment" has been launched in September 1998 in 21 IMY blocks of Maharashtra. A project launch workshop was held in Pune on 10-11 September, 1998 and the concerned Chief Executive Officers and Deputy Chief Executive Officers were sensitised.

An Aus-Aid assisted training-cum-workshop on micro-financing women's groups under India-Australia and capacity building project has been approved. Under this project, a training programme for senior/ middle level officials was conducted at BIRD, Lucknow from 14-18 December , 1998. Secretaries / Commissioners / Directors in charge of Women & Child Development of 8 states, 4 institutional faculty members and one official from this Department have been sent to Bangladesh, Indonesia, and Australia on a study tour from 8 - 31, January 1999, under this programme.

The DWCD and the Planning Commission conducted a rapid joint evaluation of the Scheme during 1997-98 and its report has been finalised this year. The evaluation study highlighted that although IMY had a potential to bring a major change in women's lives, the training requirements, resource material, personnel, etc. provided under the Scheme and its monitoring system should be strengthened. Based on the report and after further discussions with the Planning Commission, it has been decided to recast the Scheme incorporating provisions for removing the shortcomings. The recast Scheme is under finalisation. It is expected that the recast Scheme will be implemented in the next year.

Mahilla samriddhi yojana

Mahila Samriddhi Yojana, started in 1993 for the economic empowerment of women and to inculcate the habit of saving among rural women, is being recast and merged with Indira Mahila Yojana.

Women and structural adjustment

The department has taken up, in collaboration with International Labour Organisation, a project on 'National Network on Structural Adjustment, Women's Employment and Equality'. The project's objective is to ensure that women's needs in relation to employment and working conditions are fully incorporated and taken into account in Structural Adjustment Programmes and Policies.

A Tripartite Advisory Group headed by Secretary of the Department and comprising representatives of line Ministries, selected trade unions, National Commission for Women, employers organisations and leading NGOs and researchers has been set up to network with organisations interested in the subject focusing on labour market changes, etc. The project which started in January, 1997 has been successfully concluded in June, 1998. Under the project the following 4 studies have been conducted through reputed voluntary organisations:

i) Impact of Structural Adjustment Programme on Women's Employment in Unorganised Sector.
ii) Structural Adjustment Programme—Impact of Women's Work Participation.
iii) Structural Adjustment Programme—Impact on Women's Work.
iv) Impact of Structural Adjustment Programme on Women's Productive Work and Employment.

Haryana Integrated Women's Empowerment and Development Project

Haryana Integrated Women's Empowerment and Development Project with assistance from United Nations Fund for Population Activities (UNFPA) was under implementation from July 1994 to July 1998. The project areas were Mahendergarh district and 70 villages of Rewari district. The total cost of the project was Rs. 1382.00 lakh out of which UNFPA contribution was Rs. 812 lakh. The project comprised of components on (i) Empowerment, (ii) Health, (iii) Education, (iv) Adolescent Girl and (v) Economic Endowment.

Recently an independent evaluation was done for the Project. In view of the positive findings of the evaluation, 2nd phase of the Project in the same project area with assistance from UNFPA is about to begin.

Training employment and education

Self-Help Groups have emerged as one of the major strategies in group formation and various schemes of the Government of India have shown that strong women's, groups could contribute substantially to the development and convergence of services and activities. Experiences with various programmes and projects has highlighted the benefits of formation of women's groups for building confidence and focusing on developmental tasks. Different groups in various states all over the country have focused on skill development and awareness generation, promoting economic development through income generation activities, inculcating thrift, credit management activities among poor women.

The experience of running these schemes had shown that the sustainability of the majority of these groups was a major problem and one of the prime reasons for that was lack of a proper training strategy. Because of incomplete or ineffective training, full potential of women's groups formed in different states could not be realised. Many of the women's groups are neither homogenous nor sustainable. The vast geographical canvas also impedes transmission of messages in time and without distortion. The project called "Distance Education for Women's Development & Empowerment" aims to address some of these critical areas of concern. It is the first such programme of its kind in the country.

The scheme proposes to launch a certificate course by IGNOU to train a large mass of trainers from amongst village level implementors of the projects, their supervisors and district level functionaries. Such trainers after their successful participation in the project would be able to guide sustainable group formation work in their areas. Such an approach will also speed up the whole training process since a large number of centres could be activated simultaneously and the grass-root level trainers could be directly accessed. Considering about 7 lakh Government supported women's groups in the country at present, there will be a need of about 2.30 lakhs facilitators and 11,600 supervisory level functionaries who will require training on a best case scenario,

The implementation of the project is being jointly undertaken by the Department of Women & Child Development, Indira Gandhi National Open University (IGNOU) and Indian Satellite Research Organisation (ISRO). The Department of Women & Child Development would provide support of policy direction, sharing of available material and funds for the programme. The scheme would use IGNOU's experience in development and accreditation of software so that a standardised package consisting of self-instructional print, audio and video material with tutorial support through tele-conferencing could be developed. ISRO will provide the satellite linkage for at least 80 hours per year for the programme and will arrange some of the hardware related support. There would be 7 training cycles in English and 5 cycles in Hindi during the next 5 years.

The total cost of the project is about Rs. 3.90 crore consisting of Rs.105 lakh towards hardware, Rs. 166 lakh for software preparation and rest for printing, distribution and support services. The project also covers the installation of 150 units of receiving terminals with T.V. facilities and 250 new telephone connections at the identified centres.

The Programme will be open to employees of various Government bodies, NGOs and students.

Support to training and employment programme for women (STEP)

This programme launched in 1987, seek to provide updated skills and knowledge to poor and assetless women in the traditional sectors, such as agriculture, animal husbandry, dairying, fisheries, handlooms, handicrafts, khadi and village industries, sericulture, social forestry and wasteland development for enhancing their productivity and income generation. This would enhance and broaden their employment opportunities, including self employment and development of entrepreneurial skills. Women beneficiaries are organised into viable and cohesive groups or cooperatives. A comprehensive package of services such as, extension inputs, market linkages, etc. are provided besides linkage with credit.

Since the inception of the programme, about 4,16,000 women have been covered under 72 projects launched in the states of Andhra Pradesh, Bihar, Gujarat, Haryana, Himachal Pradesh, Kerala, Karnataka, Maharashtra, Manipur, Madhya Pradesh, Orissa, Tamil Nadu, Tripura, Uttar Pradesh and West Bengal. So far, women in the dairying sector have been receiving the maximum support. This is followed by handlooms, handicrafts, sericulture and poultry.

In the year 1997-98, 6 projects to benefit 53,325 women were sanctioned and an amount of Rs. 15 crore was released. During the year 1998-99, 5 projects have been sanctioned to benefit 31,320 women and an amount of Rs. 4.83 crore was released.

A sensitisation programme for the managers of new projects approved under the scheme of STEP during 1997-98 was organised in July, 1998 at the National Institute of Public Cooperation and Child Development (NIPCCD), New Delhi. This programme was attended by representatives from all new projects. Programme modules for legal literacy and health and nutrition education prepared earlier were finalised by the participants for use in the projects.

Trade-wise position of STEP projects sanctioned during 1997-98 and 1998-99 is given at Annexure V and trade-wise beneficiaries under STEP programme are as follows:

Setting up of employment-cum income generation-cum production units (NORAD)

The NORAD (Norwegian Agency for Development Cooperation) assisted programme launched in 1982-83 aims to improve the lives of poor women. Under this programme financial assistance is provided to Women's Development Corporations, Public Sector Corporations, Autonomous Bodies and Voluntary Organisations to train women, especially school drop-outs and semi-literates, in mostly non-traditional trades and to ensure their employment in these areas. Some of the trades are electronics, watch assembling, computer programming, garment making, secretarial practice, community health work, embroidery, weaving, etc. Financial assistance is also given to the grantee organisation for hiring of training-cum-production sheds, training costs, stipend to trainees and for training machinery and equipment.

The assistance under this Scheme is normally confined to Rs. 8000/- per beneficiary.

Since 1982-83 when the NORAD assisted programme was started, 1365 projects benefiting 1.99 lakh women have been approved. Since 1996-97 the assistance by NORAD has been supplemented with domestic resources. In 1997-98, out of an outlay of Rs. 17 crore, Rs. 12 crore was from domestic resources. During the year 1998-99, the Department has sanctioned 81 projects to benefit 6805 women and an amount of Rs. 3.01 crore has been released.

Since the inception of the Scheme the outlay has increased manifold, and the number of projects sanctioned so far has become large. Feeling a need for better monitoring of these projects, special emphasis has been given to monitoring during the current year. Desk (Monitoring) is looking after the monitoring work of the Projects sanctioned under the Scheme at Central Level. The projects functioning in the states of Andhra Pradesh and Uttar Pradesh have been inspected. On the basis of the inspection reports, appropriate action is being taken in each case.

An agreement was signed between the Government of India and Government of Norway on 13 November, 1997 for the extension of the assistance provided by the Norwegian Government for the next 5 years. As per the agreement, an amount of NOK 38 million (equivalent to about Rs. 20 crore) is to be provided by the Norwegian Government under the Scheme for the years 1997-2002. The contribution for the year 1997 and 1998 has been received from NORAD.

Attitudinal change towards the girl child

Balika samriddhi yojana

The scheme of Balika Samriddhi Yojana is under implementation since 199798. The main objective of the scheme is to raise the overall status of the girl child while changing family and community attitudes towards her and her mother. The lower status of the girl child is borne out by declining sex ratio, incidence of female foeticide and infanticide, lower nutritional intake, neglect of health as per hospital statistics, lower rates of literacy, enrolment and retention in schools, etc.

Under the scheme, an amount of Rs. 500/- is paid to the mothers of girl children born on or after 15 August 1997, in families below the poverty line. An amount of Rs. 60.00 crore has been released to the district level implementing agencies as identified by the State Governments/Union Territory administrations during 1997-98.

National Plan of Action for SAARC Decade of the Girl Child, 1991-2000 AD

National Plan of Action for the Girl-Child is under implementation since November, 1992.

Implementation of the Plan of Action is an inter-ministerial effort. The concerned Ministries/ Departments of Government are responsible for implementing the points of the Plan of Action through their girl-child specific or girl-child related programmes. In other words, targets/goals laid down in the NPA are to be achieved by different Ministries/Departments like Health, Education, Labour, etc. In view of this an Inter-Ministerial Coordination Committee of Secretaries was constituted in 1993 to review the progress of implementation of the National Plan of Action. The Committee meets at regular intervals for the purpose.

Support services

Working women's hostels

Many women—single, divorced, married, widowed—migrate to towns and cities, where employment opportunities are available. A large number of young women also migrate for purposes of technical training, or in pursuit of professional courses of various kinds.

One of the vital support services enabling enrolment of women in employment and work and in technical training is the provision of safe and inexpensive hostel accommodation. Besides promoting gender equity, these services are crucial to enhancing productivity and efficiency at work.

Catering predominantly to working women, the Scheme is implemented through voluntary organisations, registered societies, public trusts, women's development corporations, universities, schools/colleges of social work and local bodies, etc. State Governments and UTs are also eligible for assistance. Financial assistance is extended to the extent of 75% of the cost of construction of the hostel building and 50% of the cost of land. The income-ceiling for eligibility of hostel accommodation has been raised from Rs. 5,0001- and Rs. 4,5001- per month to Rs. 16,000/- and Rs. 15,000- p.m. in metropolitan cities and other cities and towns respectively w.e.f 14 July 1998. A resident is allowed to stay in the hostel for a maximum period of five years.

Tata Institute of Social Sciences, Mumbai was entrusted with a National level Research Study on the working of women's hostels. The Institute has since submitted its report entitled 'Working Women's Hostels in India'. The study covered the states of Maharashtra, Gujarat, Tamil Nadu, Delhi, Orissa, Rajasthan and Kerala. The study revealed that the majority of the boarders were satisfied with the safety, security, cleanliness and sanitary conditions afforded by the working women's hostels. In most of the hostels, Hostel Management Committees were functioning. There is an emergent demand for expansion of the hostel facilities for working women. The State Governments and Voluntary Organisations have been advised to take follow up action. The Master Plan of Operations (MPO) prepared by the Department in 1991-92 indicated a need to provide hostel accommodation to an estimated 1.35 lakhs working women all over the country. During the year 1998-99, 5 hostels have been sanctioned to provide accommodation to 614 working women. In four of these hostels, day care facilities for 110 children of working women have also been provided. Since the inception of the Scheme, 815 hostels have been sanctioned to provide accommodation to 57,683 working women. Day care facilities have been provided to 7528 children in 288 hostels. The State-wise/ UT-wise position of the hostels sanctioned and number of beneficiaries of the Scheme is at Annexure VII.

Short stay homes for women and girls

The Government of India launched a programme in 1969 in the Central Sector called the Short Stay Homes for Women and Girls to protect and rehabilitate those women and girls who are facing social and moral danger due to family problems, mental strains, social ostracism, exploitation or other causes. The services extended in these homes include medical care; psychiatric treatment; casework services; occupational therapy; education-cum-vocational training and recreational facilities.

The need for providing Short Stay Homes for women and girls has been due to the changing pattern of life, rapid urbanisation and industrialisation and the resulting migration from rural to urban areas. The break-up of social institutions like the Pint family, contributes considerably in creating problems of adjustment for women and young girls. Cases of marital conflict and emotional disturbance occur. This effort is made to help the women to rehabilitate themselves within a short period of time. These Short Stay Homes have been established by voluntary organisations.

At present, 272 Short Stay Homes receive grants from the Department, covering approximately 8160 beneficiaries. Under the scheme, the grant is being released at the existing financial norms on the recommendation of the State Governments, to the extent of Rs. 2,12,300 (Recurring and Non-recurring) when approved by the Government of India and subsequently, recurring grant of Rs.1,87,300 is given to the Home every year on the basis of 'C' Class city.

The Cabinet Committee on Economic Affairs has recently approved a proposal for revision of the norms and financial patterns of the scheme. The recurring cost as per the changed norms will now be Rs. 4,01,350 per Home per annum in 'C' class city and non-recurring cost would be Rs. 4,15,350. There is also a provision for some increase in subsequent years on the component of rent and the maintenance cost for residents. Provisions have also been made for upgrading skills and capacities of staff and residents as well as education of the children of residents. The implementation of the scheme will now be transferred to the Central Social Welfare Board.

During the year under report, a provision of Rs. 5.15 crore (Rs.4.00 crore under Plan and Rs. 1.15 crore under Non-Plan) (RE) has been made.

Women's rights and the law

Education work for prevention of atrocities on women

Linked with social advocacy and legal literacy issues, this programme started in 1982, provides financial support to research and academic institutions and voluntary organisations to conduct legal literacy camps, para-legal workers training, produce publicity materials, seminars, workshops, campaigns and to promote studies on gender and violence. The focus is on educating people on legislation and its enforcement to prevent social crimes against women. Assistance has been given to the Central Social Welfare Board to conduct legal literacy camps through voluntary agencies under the Scheme. Assistance has also been given to Women's Development Centres set up in colleges to take up activities under the Scheme.

In the year 1997-98, 7 projects were sanctioned and an amount of Rs. 30 lakh was released. In 1998-99, 3 projects have been sanctioned and Rs. 3.00 lakh were released.

National commission for women

The National Commission for Women, a statutory body, set up under the National Commission for Women Act, 1990 has a mandate to safeguard the rights and interests of women. The Commission continued to pursue its mandated activities, namely review of law, interventions into specific individual complaints of atrocities and remedial action to safeguard the interests of women, whatever appropriate and feasible. The Commission has accorded highest priority to securing speedy justice to women.

Smt. Vibha Parthasarathy has been appointed as Chairperson of the National Commission for Women, and assumed the charge on 18 January 1999. Smt. Vijay Daksh and Dr. Poornima Advani have been appointed as Members of the Commission w.e.f. 10 December 1998 and 28 December 1998 respectively.

Commissioner for Women's Rights

In the context of the rising trend of crimes against women, the need for establishment of an effective machinery to monitor the delivery of justice to women has long been felt, The National Perspective Plan for Women 1988-2000 AD has recommended the setting up of the Office of Commissioner for Women's Rights.

The Department has accordingly formulated a proposal for creation of a Cell in the National Commission for Women and similar Cells in the offices of State Secretaries in-charge of Women and Child Development/ Social Welfare in 5 States and in the office of District Magistrate in 50 selected districts.

The Department has requested the State Governments to set up District Committees for protection of Women's Rights to monitor and expedite disposal of cases of atrocities against women. The proposed Committees, would consist of the District and Session Judges, the District Magistrate, Superintendent of Police, Deputy Director of prosecution and others. The State Governments of Andhra Pradesh, Assam, Sikkim, Himachal Pradesh, Kerala, Madhya Pradesh and Maharashtra have set up such Committees.

National commission for women

The Department is examining a proposal to set up a National Resource Centre for Women (NRCW) and three State Level Resource Centres for Women (SRCW). The NRCW/SRCW will be an autonomous body to give technical backing to the draft National Policy for the Empowerment of Women by information dissemination, training, advocacy, policy support, research and documentation. This would be a nodal agency to mainstream gender issues in policies and programmes.

Laws affecting women

Under the Government's Action Plan for Effective and Responsive Government, the Women's Development Bureau of the Department initiated steps to review the following laws administered by the Bureau with the view to repealing and modifying procedures operating against the interests of women and to effect reforms:

i the Dowry Prohibition Act, 1961

ii) Indecent Representation of Women (Prohibition) Act, 1986.

iii) The Commission of Sati (Prevention) Act 1987 and

iv) The Immoral Traffic (Prevention) Act, 1956.

A Group of Experts was constituted in the Department to review the laws keeping in view the above objectives. The Group of Experts consists of representatives of the law enforcement machinery, consumers of the relevant laws and experts in laws affecting women. The Expert Group met on 5th February, 1998 and reviewed the Acts administered by this Department, including the four Acts mentioned above. The Expert Group took the view that none of the four Acts mentioned above need to be repealed. The Group also recommended codification of criminal laws concerning women mentioned in the Acts mentioned at (i) to (iv) above and inclusion of various substantive criminal offences against women in these Acts in the Indian Penal Code. The recommendations made by the Expert Group are being processed.

The Department of Women and Child Development is also reviewing the four Acts mentioned above with a view to make their provisions more stringent and to remove lacunae. The Department had entrusted the work of reviewing the Indecent Representation of Women (Prohibition) Act, 1986 and Immoral Traffic (Prevention) Act, 1956 to the National Law School of India University, Bangalore. The reports received from the National Law School in this regard have been sent to the NCW for comments. The comments of NCW with regard to the report of the National Law School of India relating to the Immoral Traffic Prevention Act have been received. The proposed amendments are being considered in consultation with the Ministry of Law & Justice. In respect of the other legislations namely, Dowry

Prohibition Act and Commission of Sati (Prevention) Act, inter-ministerial consultations are being held with a view to carry out the amendments.

SAARC regional convention on preventing and combating trafficking in women and children for prositution

India hosted an Expert Group meeting to negotiate the SAARC Regional Convention on Prevention and Combating Trafficking in Women and Children for Prostitution prepared by it, in New Delhi on 18-19 June, 1998. The Draft as approved at the Expert Group meeting was further deliberated at the XIIIth Meeting of the SAARC Technical Committee on Women in Development at Kathmandu from 28-30 June, 1998. The Regional Draft Convention has been endorsed by the SAARC Council of Ministers meeting held at the Xth SAARC Summit at Colombo from 29-31 July, 1998 for adoption by the SAARC countries and is awaiting ratification by the Government of India. The Convention is expected to be signed at the XIth SAARC summit.

The Convention would seek to take measures to prevent cross-border trafficking through proper international governmental coordination as well as harmonising of various laws and legal provisions relating to trafficking and rehabilitation of rescued victims.

In order to give greater teeth to the provisions relating to child prostitution in the Immoral Traffic (Prevention) Act, 1956, the Government is considering several amendments in the Act. These amendments were considered by the Central Advisory Committee on Child Prostitution on 16 October, 1998 and the recommendations are being consolidated for approval by the Government.

The Government has decided to involve Non -Governmental Organisations in the implementation of the Plan of Action prepared by the Government to combat trafficking and commercial sexual exploitation of women and children for prostitution. A meeting of NGOs active in this field was held on 2 December, 1998 to finalise the nature of help they expect from the Government to implement the Plan of Action. It has emerged that they would welcome financial support from the Government for rehabilitation of rescued victims as well as for awareness generation amongst the victims and their guardians.

3

Child Development

The Constitution of India emphasises the importance of improving the well-being of children. Article 39 deals with the Directive Principles of State Policy, which stipulates that the State shall, in particular, direct its policy to ensure:

— That health and strength of workers, men and women, and the tender age of children are not abused, and that citizens are not forced by economic necessity to enter into avocations unsuited to their age or strength;

— That children are given opportunities and facilities to develop in a healthy manner and in conditions of freedom and dignity and that childhood and youth are protected against exploitation and against moral and material abandonment.

Article 24 stipulates that no child below the age of 1,4 years shall be employed to work in any factory or mine or be engaged in any other hazardous employment. According to Article 45, the State shall endeavour to provide free and compulsory education for all children until they complete 14 years of age.

As per 1991 Census, India has around 1500 lakh children below the age of 6 years, constituting 17.5% of its population. A large number of these children live in economic and social environments which impede their physical and mental development. These conditions include poverty, poor environmental sanitation, disease, infection, inadequate access to primary health care, inappropriate child caring and feeding practices.

Present situation

While each crucial indicator including Infant Mortality Rate, Child Mortality Rate and levels of malnutrition have shown significant improvement, all of these are still considered abnormally high when viewed against the country's capabilities to protect and promote the development of children. Further, high population growth is also as much a cause for concern as infant and child mortality as we are still faced with human resource wastage of about 11% by the age of 5 years and most of it is avoidable. While significant success has been achieved in addressing vaccine preventable diseases and malnutrition, yet a large number of infants die each year. Inadequacy of care of women is also evident from prevailing high rates of low birth weight. Further, though the proportion of nutritional blindness has reduced drastically to 0.4% from 2% in 1973, sub-clinical deficiency of Vitamin 'A' is still prevalent.

Iron Deficiency Anaemia (IDA) is prevalent among women of child bearing age and preschool children. While over a period of time, use of iodised salt at the household level has significantly improved, yet no state in India is free from iodine deficiency.

To combat these problems, the Government of India in 1974 formulated a National Policy for Children which describes children as a supremely important asset. To look after the welfare and development of children, the Department of Women & Child Development is implementing various programmes, which are as follows:

Integrated child development scheme

The Integrated Child Development Services ICDS) Scheme aims to improve the nutritional and health status of vulnerable groups including pre-school children, pregnant women and nursing mothers through providing a package of services including Supplementary Nutrition, Pre-school Education, Immunisation, Health Check-UP, Referral Services, and Nutrition and Health Education. In addition, the Scheme envisages effective convergence of inter-sectoral services in the Anganwadi Centres.

The ICDS Scheme has now come to be regarded as the most viable vehicle for achieving the goals set in the National Plan of Action for Children, to be achieved by the year 2000 A.D. These, inter-alia, include reduction of Infant Mortality Rate (IMR) to less than 60 per thousand; reduction in Child Mortality Rate (CMR) to less than 10 per thousand; reduction in Maternal Mortality Rate (MMR) by at least 50 per cent; reduction in severe and moderate malnutrition among children under 5 years by at least 50 percent and universal enrolment and retention in primary schools.

Objectives

— Improve the nutritional and health status of children below the age of six years.

— Lay the foundation for the proper psychological, physical and social development of the child.

— Reduce the incidence of mortality, morbidity, malnutrition and school dropouts.

— Achieve effective coordination of policy and implementation among various departments to promote child development.

— Enhance the capability of the mother to look after the normal health and nutritional needs of the child, through proper health and nutrition education.

In addition to children below six years of age, ICIDS also takes care of the essential needs of pregnant women and nursing mothers residing in socially and economically backward villages and urban slums. The large network of ICIDS provides vital services in the disadvantaged areas to the most vulnerable groups.-

Services and beneficiaries

The programmes provide an integrated approach for converging basic services for improved child-care, early stimulation and learning, health and nutrition, water and environmental sanitation targeting young children, expectant and nursing mothers and women's/ adolescent girls groups. They are reached through well trained community-based Anganwadi Workers, an equal number of helpers and through the supportive community structure and women's groups. ICIDS provides increased opportunities for promoting early development, associated with improved enrolment and retention in the early primary stage and by releasing girls from the burden of sibling care, to enable them to participate in primary education. ICIDS today reaches out to 39 lakh expectant and nursing mothers and 203 lakh children (under six years of age), of disadvantaged groups. Of these, 114 lakh children (three to six years of age) participate in centre-based preschool education activities.

The following section deals with various aspects of the ICDS Programmes

- Nutrition
- Health
- Early Childhood Care and Pre-school Education

Nutrition

— Growth monitoring and promotion

- Supplementary feeding

— Nutrition and health education (NHED).

— Growth monitoring and promotion

Growth monitoring and nutrition surveillance are two important activities that are in operation at the field level in ICIDS. Both are important for assessing the impact of the health and nutrition related services.

Children below the age of three years are weighed once a month and children from three to six years are weighed quarterly. Fixed-day immunisation sessions on days when mothers come to take home rations for younger children (below two years of age) are used as opportunities for growth monitoring and promotion of younger children. In ICIDS, weight-for-age growth cards are maintained for all children below six years. Their growth is charted both to detect growth faltering and also to assess their nutritional status.

Growth monitoring and promotion helps the mother/family and AWW/ANM in taking timely, cost effective preventive action, to arrest any stagnancy or slipping down in weight, through early detection of growth faltering. Through discussion and counselling, growth monitoring also increases the participation and capabilities of mothers in understanding and improving child-care and feeding practices, for promoting child growth. It helps families understand better, the linkages between dietary intake, health-care, safe drinking water, environmental sanitation and child growth. Growth monitoring and promotion can thus also be an effective entry point for primary health-care.

Recently, the concept of community-based nutrition surveillance has been introduced in ICDS. A community chart for nutrition status monitoring is maintained at each Anganwadi. This chart reflects the nutritional status of all children registered with the Anganwadi, at any given point of time, helping the community in understanding what the nutrition status of its children is, why it is so and what can be done to improve it. This mobilises community support in promoting and enabling better child-care practices, contributing local resources and in improving service delivery and utilisation.

Supplementary feeding

All families in the community are surveyed, to identify low income families and deprived children below the age of six years, pregnant and nursing mothers and adolescent girls. They avail of supplementary feeding support for 300 days in a year. By providing supplementary feeding., the Anganwadi attempts to bridge the caloric gap between the national recommended and average intake of children and women in low income and disadvantaged communities. This pattern of feeding aims only at supplementing and not substituting for family food. It also provides an important contact opportunity with pregnant women and mothers of infants and young children, to promote improved behavioural actions for the care of pregnant women and young children. Specifically, it serves to reinforce the key message to promote appropriate and timely complementary feeding at home, starting among infants who are four to six months of age, with a full diet for young children by one year, and continued breast feeding up to two years.

The type of food varies from State to State, but usually consists of a hot meal cooked at the Anganwadi, containing a varied combination of pulses, cereals, oil, vegetables and sugar. Some States provide ready-to eat meals containing the same basic ingredients. There is flexibility in the selection of food items, to respond to local needs. The expenditure towards supplementary feeding is met by the State under the Plan budget available for Minimum Needs Programme. Special care is also taken to reach children below the age of two years, and to encourage parents and siblings to either take home ration for them or to bring them to the Anganwadi for supplementary feeding. The take-home ration is a contact opportunity for growth monitoring and promotion of children under two years of age and nutrition counselling of mothers, for improved childcare and feeding practices.

The national prophylaxis programme for prevention of blindness caused by vitamin A deficiency, and control of nutritional anaemia among mothers and children, are two direct interventions integrated in ICDS. Dietary promotion is an important part of nutrition health education and targetted supplementation is also provided. At nine months of age, 100,000 International Units (IU) of vitamin A solution is administered to infants, along with immunisation against measles, Children in the age group of one to five years receive 200,000 IU of vitamin A solution every six months, with priority to children under three years of age.

Tablets of iron and folic acid are administered to expectant mothers for prophylaxis and treatment and to children with anaemia. These supplements are distributed in Anganwadi Centres, and their utilisation is monitored by them. The usage of iodised salt is promoted, especially in the food supplement provided.

Nutrition and Health Education

Nutrition, Health and Education (NHED) is a key element in the work of the Anganwadi Worker. This has the long term goal of capacity building of women -especially in the age group of 15-45 years -so that they can look after their own health and nutrition needs as well as that of their children and families. All women in this age-group are expected to be covered by this component.

Anganwadi Workers use fixed-day immunization sessions, mother-child days, growth monitoring days, small group meetings of mothers/Mahila Mandals, community and home visits, village contact drives and other women's groups meetings (DWCRA, Mahila Samakhaya, etc.), local festivals and gatherings, for nutrition and health education. Presently there are nearly 1,00,000 Mahila Mandals which are actively involved in extending nutrition and health education activities.

All efforts are made to reach out to women, including pregnant women and nursing mothers. Sustained support and guidance has to be provided in the period spanning pregnancy and early childhood, to mothers of young children, building upon local knowledge, attitudes and practices. This helps promote antenatal care, maternal nutrition, exclusive breast-feeding of infants upto four to six months of age, timely immunisation, introduction of timely and appropriate complementary feeding at home of infants at four to six months of age with a full diet by 12 months of age and continued breast-feeding up to two years. NHED also promotes appropriate prevention and management of diarrhoeal diseases (through ORT and continued feeding) and management of acute respiratory infections, to promote proper growth of the child.

Health

— Health Care

— Immunisation

— Referral Services

— Treatment of minor illness

Health Care

This includes

- Ante natal care of expectant mothers;
- Post natal care of nursing mothers and care of new born infants; and
- Care of children under 6 years of age.

The various health services provided for children by AWWs and PHC staff include regular health check-ups, recording of weight, immunisation, management of malnutrition, treatment of diarrhoea, deworming and distribution of simple medicines, etc.

At the Anganwadi, children, adolescent girls, pregnant women and nursing mothers are examined at regular intervals by the Lady Health Visitor (LHV) and Auxiliary Nurse Midwife (ANM) who also diagnose minor ailments and distribute simple medicines. They provide a link between the village and the Primary Health Care Subcentre. Maternal and child health facilities are geared towards providing adequate medical care during pregnancy, at the time of childbirth and subsequently. It is aimed at reducing complications during pregnancy and reducing perinatal mortality.

Immunisation

Immunisation of pregnant women against tetanus and immunisation of infants against six vaccine- preventable diseases -poliomyelitis, diphtheria, pertussis, tetanus, tuberculosis and measles - protects children from these diseases. These are major preventable causes of child, mortality, disability, morbidity and related malnutrition. Immunisation of pregnant women against tetanus also reduces maternal and neonatal mortality.

PHC and its subordinate health infrastructure carries out immunisation of infants and expectant mothers as per the national immunisation schedule. Children are also given booster doses. The AWW assists the health functionaries in coverage of the population for immunisation. She helps in the organisation of fixed-day immunisation sessions. She maintains immunisation records of ICDS beneficiaries and follows up to ensure full coverage.

Referral services

During health check-ups and growth monitoring, sick or malnourished children in need of prompt medical attention are provided referral services through ICDS. The AWW has also been oriented to detect disabilities in young children. She enlists all such cases in a special register and refers them to the medical officers. The effectiveness of this service depends on timely action, cooperation from health functionaries and the willingness of families to avail of these services. The Health Department in States/UTs identifies one hospital at the district level, which attends to the referral cases coming from the ICDS areas.

Early childhood care and pre-school education

— Early Childhood Care

— Early Childhood Education

Early Childhood Care and Pre-School Education under ICDS-non-formal pre-schooi education is a crucial component of the package of services envisaged under ICDS scheme, aims at universalisation and qualitative improvement of primary education in remote and socio-economically backward areas with primary attention being given to the girl child. The Early Childhood Care and Pre-school Education (ECCE) component of the ICDS may well be considered the backbone of the ICDS programme, since all its services essentially converge on the AW. This is also the most joyful play-way daily activity, visibly sustained for three hours a day. It brings and keeps young children at the Anganwadi Centre - an activity that motivates parents and communities. ECCE, as envisaged in the ICDS, focuses on the total development of the child, in the age range of up to six years, from the underprivileged groups. It includes promotion of early stimulation of the under-threes through intervention with mothers/ caregivers. Child-centred play-way activities which build on local culture and practices, using local support materials developed by Anganwadi workers, through enrichment training, are promoted. The early-childhood, pre-school education programme, conducted through the medium of play, aims at providing a learning environment for the promotion of social, emotional, cognitive, physical and aesthetic development of the child. Through ICDS, 11 A lakh children (3-6 years of age), from disadvantaged groups, are participating in centre-based, pre-school, play-way activities.

The ECCE component of the ICDS is a significant input for providing a sound foundation for development. It also contributes to the universalisation of primary education, by providing to the child the necessary preparation for primary schooling and offering substitute care to the younger siblings, thus freeing the older ones -especially girls - to attend school.

For this, improved coordination between the Anganwadi Centres and primary schools, in terms of timings, location and supportive linkages between the Anganwadi Worker and primary school teacher - are being promoted.

Convergence

ICDS scheme supports convergence with other supportive services, such as safe drinking water, environmental sanitation, women's empowerment programmes, nonformal education and adult literacy, and health and nutrition.

Targetted beneficiaries

The Scheme targets the most vulnerable groups of population including children upto 6 years of age, pregnant women and nursing mothers belonging to poorest of the poor families and living in disadvantaged areas including backward rural areas, tribal areas and urban slums. The identification of beneficiaries is done through surveying the community and identifying families living below the poverty line.

The ICDS team

The ICDS team comprises the Anganwadi helpers/ Anganwadi Workers (AWWs), the supervisors and the Child Development Project Officers (CDPOs). In larger rural and tribal projects, Additional Child Development Project Officers (ACDPOs) are also a part of the team. The medical officers, the lady health visitors and female health workers from nearby primary health centres and sub-centres form a team with social welfare/women and child development department functionaries to implement ICDS.

The AWW is a community-based voluntary frontline worker of the ICDS programme. Selected from the community, she assumes a pivotal role due to her close and continuous contact with the people, especially women she works with. As a crucial link between the village population and the Government administration, she becomes a central figure in helping the community identify and meet the needs of their children and women. The AWW is expected to monitor and promote the growth of children, with the active participation of community/ mothers. She enhances their capability for preventive and promotive action for child growth -

through improved childcare and feeding practices. She also enables them to prevent disease infection. The AWW organises supplementary feeding, helps organise immunisation sessions, distributes vitamin A supplements and iron and folic acid tablets, treats minor injuries and ailments, and refers cases to medical services. The more visible aspects of her role is in making the Anganwadi literally a courtyard play centre - nurturing and joyful -with play-way activities attracting and sustaining the participation of children and families. Considering the valuable services provided by the Anganwadi Worker and Anganwadi Helper, their honoraria has been increased by 25% and 30% respectively.

The Supervisor (Mukhya Sevika) is responsible for 17-25 Anganwadis, depending upon the nature of the project. She supports and guides AWWs and assists in recording home visits, organising community meetings and visits of health personnel, and providing on-the-job orientation to AWWs. The CDPO provides the link between ICDS functionaries and the Government administration. This officer is also responsible for securing Anganwadi premises, identifying beneficiaries, ensuring supply of food to centres and flow of health services, and monitoring programmes and reporting to the State Government. At the community level, other frontline workers, including the Gram Sevika, primary school teachers, also link with the Anganwadi worker. Local women's groups, Mahila Mandals, youth clubs, local organisations, Panchayat Samitis and Bal Vikas Mahila Samiti members also support the Anganwadi Workers.

The ICDS team facilitates creation of partnerships between frontline workers and community/ women's groups, ensuring an integrated approach for improved childcare, health, nutritional well being and development at the Anganwadi Centre, literally a courtyard play centre, a childcare centre located within the village or the slum area itself. It is the focal point for the delivery of services at community level to children below six years of age, pregnant women, nursing mothers and adolescent girls. Besides this the AW is a meeting ground where women's groups can, come together, with other frontline workers, to promote awareness and joint action for child development and women's empowerment.

In addition to the job responsibilities of AWW originally envisaged, AWW is discharging additional activities in various sectors in different State and UT's. Throughout the country, the Anganwadi Worker and Helper have been utilized for schemes related to health and family welfare. Further her services are vital in implementation of the RCH (Reproductive Child Health) programme and National AIDS Control Programme during the Ninth Five Year Plan. Apart from this ' the Anganwadi Worker and Helper are significantly contributing in implementation of various other programmes and schemes of both Central Government and State Government.

Setting up of the National Committee for Reviewing benefits/facilities being provided to Anganwadi Workers and Helpers

During the conference of State Ministers and Secretaries of the Department of Women and Child Development held on 22nd and 23rd July, 1998, the Minister for HRD stated that a Committee will be constituted with definite terms of reference for going into the whole gamut of the issues affecting the service conditions of the Anganwadi Workers and Helpers and exploring the avenues for increasing the honoraria being paid to Anganwadi Workers and Helpers. It was, therefore, decided to set up a National Committee in the

Department of Women and Child Development in order to take stock of the service conditions and duties of the Anganwadi Workers and Helpers and to identify the Ministries/

Departments/States, etc. which can provide additional remuneration to the Anganwadi Workers and Helpers functioning under the centrally sponsored ICDS Scheme. Besides the representatives of the concerned central departments, representatives of some State Governments who have taken initiative to increase the honoraria of Anganwadi Workers have also been included in this Committee. The Committee set up under the chairpersonship of Joint Secretary, in the Department, is in the process of finalising its report.

Coverage and outreach

Started on an experimental basis during 1975-76 in just 33 blocks of the country, the Scheme has gradually expanded and till November 1998, 4200 projects are in operation with sanctioned strength of 5.92 lakh Anganwadi Centres. However, while approving the enhancement of honoraria to Anganwadi Workers and Helpers working under the Scheme in May 1997, Ministry of Finance imposed a freeze on further operationalisation of ICDS projects beyond 4200 and Anganwadi Centres beyond 5.92 lakhs (approx.).

An in-depth review with each State/LIT was undertaken in the month of July/August-to ascertain the macro-picture regarding ICDS. The review included reconciliation in the number of sanctioned ICDS blocks, operational blocks, number of sanctioned Anganwadi Centres and operational Anganwadi Centres besides financial review. The focus of the review was to firm up the number of operational blocks state-wise as also to identify these blocks. With the approval of HRM, reallocation of operational 4200 ICDS blocks was carried out during August 1998.

Financial resources and funding pattern under the ICDS Scheme

The ICDS Scheme is a centrally sponsored Scheme implying thereby a Central share and a State share in the total costs. While the Central Government bears the full cost of meeting the operational requirements, the States provide for funds for supplementary nutrition component.

In addition to mobilising domestic resources, significant contribution also comes from UN Agencies, bilateral donors and the World Bank. Swedish Industrial Development Agency (SIDA) was providing support to 47 ICDS projects in Tamil Nadu upto June 1997 which has been extended upto 31st December 1998. SIDA supported ICDS projects were evaluated by a joint evaluation team comprising of representatives of Government of India, Swedish Embassy and Government of Tamil Nadu who conducted various studies. The joint evaluation is now complete and report is awaited.

Expenditure on ICDS

Alongwith the gradual expansion of the Scheme, there has also been a significant increase in the Central Government's spending on implementation of the Scheme during the 8th Plan period. As against the expenditure of only Rs. 1190.21 crores during 17 years, i.e. 1975-76 to 767.1 98-99 (uptoFeb'99) 1991-92, the expenditure during the 8th Plan period was Rs. 2271.28 crore. During 1997-98 against the provision of Rs. 479. 40 crore in BE, the central expenditure was to the tune of Rs. 608.35 crore. During 1998-99, against a provision of Rs. 768.41 crore in RE, the expenditure incurred up to February 1999 has been to the tune of Rs. 767.1 A crore.

Monitoring and evaluation

Management Information System

The ICDS programme is characterised by a built-in

monitoring system for promoting assessment, analysis and action at different levels at which data is generated. A central cell established at the Department collects and analyses periodic work reports. Based on this, programme strategies are refined, and timely interventions made -ensuring effective programme planning, implementation and monitoring. A national ICDS Management Information System (MIS) working group facilitates this process. Each State Government also has a MIS coordination cell. Districts with more than five projects have a district level ICDS monitoring cell, to facilitate programme monitoring.

MIS ensures a regular flow of information and feedback between each Anganwadi and the project, between the ICDS project and the State Government, and between the State Government and the Government of India. The flow of information is not only upwards - it is a two-way process and constitutes the basis for discussion and improved action at the level at which it is generated. This is done through a Monthly Progress Report (MPR) and a Monthly Monitoring Report (MMR).

Under the National Plan to monitor ICDS, Anganwadi Workers compile standardised monthly and half-yearly reports based on their register data. These reports are forwarded through supervisors to Child Development Project Officers (CDPOs) who are responsible for forwarding the reports (MPRs) to the State and Central ICDS Cell at the Department of Women and Child Development. MPRs quantify the status of key input, process and output indicators pertaining to the major component of ICDS service delivery, which can be used to manage operations.

Through monthly review meetings of ICDS and health functionaries at various levels - block, district, division and state - both MMRs and MPRs are discussed, for Promoting joint action. Efforts are underway to strengthen this process further.

The Department compiles computerised quarterly monitoring reports from the CDPOs. A State level performance statement is prepared on 8 indicators, comparing the performance of each state with the national performance. Copies of these reports are also sent to the Planning Commission, Prime Minister's Secretariat, National Institute of Public Cooperation and Child Development (NIPCCD) and other Ministries/ Organisations involved in the ICDS Programme. Quarterly status reports and performance reports are sent to the State's nodal departments for faking necessary corrective action.

ICDS Scheme: Strengths and impact

The impact of ICDS, however, has been quite dramatic on the health of the participant families. As a service delivery programme, the ICDS has certain unique features which constitute its areas of strength as enumerated below:

— The programme is village based and conducted by workers (Anganwadi Workers & Helpers), who are normally residents of the same village;

— The Anganwadi Worker is supposed to maintain close contact with individual households of the village.

— The programme enlists the active help and participation of voluntary organisations, social activists, academic institutions and professionals;

— There is a built-in scope for convergence of Health, Nutrition and Childhood Education Services at the Anganwadi level;

— Two-third of the population covered by the ICDS programme comprise scheduled castes, scheduled tribes and other backward communities.

ICDS scheme has been subjected to intensive research since the beginning. The impact of the programme is evident from:

- Decrease in prevalence of malnutrition among pre-school children
- improvement in the nutritional status of the children
- Improved immunisation coverage
- Decrease in IMR
- Improvement in school enrolment and reduction in school dropout rate

The most important impact of the Scheme is clearly reflected in significant declines in the levels of severely malnourished and moderately malnourished children in the country as also in significant decline in Infant Mortality Rate. The percentage of children suffering from severe malnutrition have significantly declined from 15.3% during 1976-78 to 8.7% during 1988-90 (figures published by National Nutrition Monitoring Bureau). The Infant Mortality Rates have significantly declined from 80 per 1000 live births in 1991 to 73 during 1994 (Sample Registration System).

ICDS - Evaluation and Research -1975-88 conducted by Central Technical Committee highlighted that the impact of the ICDS on the decline in Infant Mortality Rate is extremely favourable.

Major initiatives

A number of new initiatives have been taken during recent years to strengthen the impact. These chiefly include the adolescent girls scheme for girls in the age group of 11-18 years, effective involvement of the NGOs, provision of income generating activities for women and monitoring. The scheme is viewed as a major national vehicle for achieving the goals of the health and family welfare sector, education and rural development. The provision of income generating activities for women under this scheme is a major step for mobilising women in the rural areas and ensuring their empowerment.

Improving nutrition levels

The monthly monitoring formats have been amended to include frequency aspect of delivery of supplementary nutrition and gender and age specific information. This has also helped in timely detection of interruptions in the nutrition component and in taking early corrective actions. The cost norms of nutrition have been revised upwards to provide minimum calories/proteins on each day and supervisors of the projects have been made directly responsible for monitoring the growth of severely malnourished children and mothers. Further, in order to enable the community to assess the nutritional status of their children on a regular basis, Community Growth Charts have been designed and supplied to all the States for use in the Anganwadi Centres. In addition, Food and Nutrition Board (F&NB) with its 43 Community Food and Nutrition Extension Units (CFNEU) located in 27 States/ UTs is being effectively used for dissemination of vital nutrition and health education to ICDS functionaries/ beneficiaries. Further, 43 CFNEUs are also being used in monitoring the quality and delivery of supplementary nutrition in Anganwadi Centres under the ICDS Scheme.

Pre-school education

Resource Centres have been located in the CDPO's Offices and the necessary tie up has been done with NCERT and SCERTs for development of pre-school material in the local languages for use in the Anganwadi Centres. In addition, instructions have been issued for coordinating the timings between the primary schools and Anganwadi Centres and for regular visits of primary school teachers to the Anganwadi Centres. This has been done to ensure enrichment of pre-school component and better enrolment and retention in the primary schools.

Community partnership

The 73rd and the 74th Constitutional Amendments have created vibrant new partnerships to reach the most disadvantaged and the most vulnerable young children. In some States, devolution of powers to Panchayati Raj institutions has also involved the transfer of some functions for managing and monitoring ICDS to district Zila Parishads, Block Panchayat Samitis and Gram Panchayats.

This constitutes a major opportunity for rooting development programmes more firmly in the community with the active participation of women. The Department has recently initiated steps for the constitution of Baal Vikas Mahila Samitis at village, block and district levels, with representations from women panchayat members, NGOs and ICDS functionaries. This is for integrated community-based monitoring of all programmes for women and children -especially ICDS.

Mobilising women for promoting their own health, nutritional well-being and self development as well as that of their children is an underlying principle of ICDS. This was furthered by the introduction of the ICDS adolescent girls' scheme in 507 blocks.

With the recently launched Indira Mahila Yojana (IMY), new possibilities are unfolding for ICDS to promote the process for women's empowerment. The Indira Mahila Yojana has three components: convergence of inter-sectoral services; awareness creation; and income generation activities. It has been initiated in 200 ICDS blocks during 1995-96.

Opening of Mini-Anganwadis to cover remote and low populated hamlets

Universalisation of the Integrated Child Development Service (ICDS) Scheme has been made in the country in 1995-96 by covering all the Community Development Blocks by the Scheme. There are, however, some small hamlets/villages in the country in Tribal Blocks having population of less than 300 and situated in far flung areas where the actual beneficiaries might be deprived of the benefits of the Scheme. To make full use of the ICDS Scheme and provide benefits of the Scheme to each and every child who is entitled to it, it has been decided by the Department to open Mini-Anganwadis in small hamlets/pockets in Tribal Blocks which are in far flung and remote areas. The guidelines to open Mini-Anganwadis in an ICDS project for such hamlets/pockets are as follows:-

10 Mini Anganwadi Centres can be opened in lieu of a full fledged Anganwadi. There may be one main Anganwadi out of 10. A Mini Anganwadi can be opened with a population of 150 in a village/hamlet. It should be located within 1 km. from the main Anganwadi and there should be 15 to 20 beneficiaries therein. A woman/adolescent girl is made responsible for distribution of nutrition diet to beneficiaries. An honorarium of Rs.50 is to be paid to the Mini Anganwadi Worker who provides cooked hot food to the Anganwadi beneficiaries. The maintenance of 10 Mini Anganwadis is managed within the cost of an Anganwadi norm of Rs. 11,200 per annnum. The provision of nutrition is to be ensured by the State Government from their own resources, being provided by them under ICDS Scheme as per norms. Uptil now, 1881 Mini-Anganwadi Centres have been sanctioned in tribal blocks of Maharashtra, 25 Mini-Anganwadi centres in Andhra Pradesh, 1708 in the tribal blocks of Orissa and 2878 Mini-Anganwadi Centres

were sanctioned in Madhya Pradesh with World Bank Assistance.

Integration of ayurveda and Indian system of medicines in ICDS scheme

The issue of inclusion of Ayurvedic medicines in Medicine Kits given to Anganwadis under ICDS Scheme was undertaken during this year. Instructions have been issued to State Directors of Ayurveda to further instruct ISM&H doctors to regularly visit AWCs in rural and remote areas. A list of simple home remedies for common ailments and a list of Ayurvedic medicines to be included in the Medicine Kits is being procured by this Department to be supplied to AWCs. A training module for AWWs in Ayurveda and Ayurvedic concept of life style is being developed which can be accommodated in the basic training course meant for AWWs. Department of ISM&H has been requested to forward a proposal with area-specific intensive intervention for meeting full integration of Ayurveda and ICDS Scheme.

Convergence strategy of intersectoral services in the anganwadi centres

Recognising the need for securing convergence of various services in the Anganwadi Centres so as to improve the efficiency of sectoral programmes and to ensure that the services are provided to the beneficiaries in a cost effective manner, the Department of Women and Child Development has identified specific thrust areas relating to various Departments including Ministry of Health & Family Welfare, Rural Development, Education, Urban Development. Welfare and this Department for convergence. These thrust areas were communicated to all concerned for taking necessary action towards integration and convergence of services of this Department.

World Bank assisted ICDS projects

The World Bank provided credit for the Centrally sponsored ICDS Projects, viz. ICDS-I Project in Andhra Pradesh and Orissa, and ICDS-11 Project in Bihar and Madhya Pradesh. Apart from providing normal ICDS services the Project also includes additional components like construction of AW buildings and CDPOs office cum godowns on a selective basis, strengthening training and communications components, improved health facilities, income generation activities for women and Women's Integrated Learning for Life.

ICDS-1 Project

The Project in Andhra Pradesh and Orissa became operational in January, 1991 initially for a period of 6 years i.e. upto 31st December, 1997.

The Project covered 191 blocks in Orissa and 110 blocks in Andhra Pradesh. The Project covered tribal areas, dominated by schedule castes and other backward classes.

The approved provision for the Project was Rs. 303.22 crore (Rs. 130.79 crore for Andhra Pradesh and Rs. 172.43 crore for Orissa) exclusive of the cost of the supplementary nutrition. This was subsequently revised to Rs. 343.69 crore (Rs. 1 59.40 crore for Andhra Pradesh and Rs. 184.29 crore for Orissa).

All the blocks covered under the Project in both the States have become operational. The available credit for the project was of the order of US $ 740 lakh which was fully disbursed.

ICDS-11 Project

The World Bank assisted ICDS-11 Project in Bihar and Madhya Pradesh became operational in September 1993 for a period of seven years, i.e., upto ' March 2000. The Project covered 210 blocks in Bihar and 244 blocks in

Madhya Pradesh in predominantly tribal and difficult areas, in a phased manner.

Additional inputs

In addition to the normal six ICDS services, the additional input being given in the project is as follows:

— Construction of Anganwadi buildings at village level and godown-cum-CDPO's office building at Block level in the most needy areas.
— Experimentation with Nutritional
— Rehabilitation Centres
— Schemes for Adolescent girls
— Skill upgradation / development for women
— Income Generation Schemes for Women
— Strengthening health and nutrition, awareness generation, community participation, communications, training, supervision, operations research, monitoring and evaluation components.

The Government of India has released an amount of Rs. 322.69 crore to the States of Bihar and Madhya Pradesh upto 31st March, 1998.

The approved provision for the Project is Rs. 596.23 crores out of which Rs. 257.13 crore for Bihar, and Rs. 339.10 crore for Madhya Pradesh. So far Rs. 133.38 crores have been released for the Government of Bihar, and Rs. 223.41 crores have been released to the Government of Madhya Pradesh. State Government of Bihar has reported an expenditure of Rs. 92.85 crores and Government of Madhya Pradesh has incurred expenditure worth Rs. 184.80 crores.

The approved IDA credit for the project is US $ 1910 lakh out of which US $ 630 lakh (approx.) has been disbursed.

ICDS-111 Project

The third phase of the World Bank assisted ICDS (ICDS-111) Project has been approved by the World Bank. The project would cover the States of Kerala, Tamil Nadu, Maharashtra/ Rajasthan and Uttar Pradesh including the training component of ICDS Programme being implemented in the country.

The total cost of the Project as approved by the Expenditure Finance Committee is around Rs. 1600 crore; Rs. 1000 crore for the Project in five states and Rs. 600 crore for the training component in the entire country for a period of five yea rs. The IDA has committed US $ 3000 lakh (including US $1000 lakh for the training component) for the project.

Andhra Pradesh Economic Restructuring Project (APER)

The Project proposal for World Bank assisted ICDS component of Andhra Pradesh Economic Restructuring (APER) Project in Andhra Pradesh, a Centrally Sponsored Project, is under process in this Department.

The Project proposes to cover 251 blocks at a total cost of about Rs. 392 crore for a period of five years. The project would form a part of the US $ 543.2 million assistance package committed by the World Bank for APER project.

World food programme (WEP) project 2206

World Food Programme (WFP), a United Nations agency, extends food aid under its Project 2206 for supplementary nutrition to children below 6 years of age and to expectant and nursing mothers under the Integrated Child Development Services (ICDS) programme. The WFP Project 2206 has completed 5 phases from March 1976 to June, 1995.

The Plan of Operations for Expansion Phase VI of

WFP Project 2206 was signed between the Government of India and the WFP on 4 July, 1995 for a period of three years to cover 22 lakh beneficiaries (including 80,250 Anganwadi Workers / Helpers / adolescent girls) in the five states of Assam, Kerala, Madhya Pradesh, Rajasthan and Uttar Pradesh. There is a Country Programme (CP) for India for the five year period from Ist April, 1997 to 31st March, 2001. As resources are limited, the WFP has reduced its food assistance for India to 70,000 MTs out of which 40,000 MTs is earmarked for Project 2206 (ICDS) annually. As a consequence WFP was able to cater to 16.8 lakh beneficiaries under ICDS w.e.f. 1st September, 1997. Due to carry over stocks and outstanding deliveries, 50,667 MTs of food is available w.e.f. I April, 1998. In addition to this, 3500 MTs of food is also available from Canandian International Development Agency (CIDA) assistance through WFP for the state of Rajasthan which will cover an additional 2.30 lakh beneficiaries. Accordingly the revised allocation of 54,167 MTs of food for a total of 25.98 lakh beneficiaries has been distributed amongst the WFP assisted states upto 31 March 1999 as under:

Revised allocation
during 1st June 1998 to 31st March 1999

Sl. No. Name of State	No. of Beneficiaries (in lakhs)	Food Commodity (in MTs)
1. Assam	1.72	2750
2. Kerala	4.22	9260
3. Madhya Pradesh	6.20	12000
4. Rajasthan	6.58	13807
5. Uttar Pradesh	7.26	16350
Total	25.98	54167

It includes 3500 MTs Canadian International Development Agency (CIDA) assistance for the State of Rajasthan which will cover 2.30 lakh beneficiaries.

WFP is providing a single micro-nutrient fortified blended food-either Corn Soya Blend (CSB) or locally produced 'Indiamix'. CSB is being imported through the Ports of Cochin, Calcutta and Jamnagar and can be cooked with jaggery and condiments to suit local tastes. The WFP Project 2206 is being reviewed by the Department of Women and Child Development, Government of India biannually in the meetings of the Food Aid Advisory Sub-Committee (FAASC).

WFP assistance for non-food programmes

The Better Health and Nutrition (BHN) Project (with a total cost of Rs. 175.67 lakhs) in Sirohi and Udaipur districts in the State of Rajasthan for a period of two years starting from March, 1997. The project is in collaboration with CARE India. The project's aim is to improve the nutritional status of women and children and reduce the rates of malnutrition and mortality.

Improving Child Survival through the ICDS (with a total cost of Rs. 81.65 lakhs) in Banswara district of Rajasthan for a period of two years w.e.f. December, 1996. The project mainly aims to reduce the extent of childhood malnutrition through a campaign on timely initiation of complementary feeding and increased convergence of on going women and child development programmes.

CARE - India assisted programmes

Government of India signed an agreement with CARE (Cooperative for Assistance and Relief Everywhere) on 6th March, 1950. The primary purpose of this agreement is to facilitate and maximize voluntary gifts of food and other urgently needed commodities by individuals and organisations outside India. The Department of Women ' and Child Development, Government of India is the nodal Department for implementation of CARE-India's programmes. CARE-India assisted programmes have been broadly classified in two parts (1) Food Programme, and (ii) Non-Food Programmes.

Food Programme

CARE-India extends food aid for supplementary nutrition to -children below 6 years of age and pregnant and nursing mothers in the ICDS programme. In accordance with the List of Provisions (LOP) approved for 1998-99, CARE-India has supplied food aid to 66.05 lakhs beneficiaries distributed in the States of Andhra Pradesh, Bihar, Madhya Pradesh, Orissa, Rajasthan, Uttar Pradesh and West Bengal. The food commodities include vegetable oil and a highly nutritious blend of corn and soya. These are cooked with other food items such as jaggery and condiments to make the food tasty and acceptable. CARE food is received in India at the ports of Calcutta, Vishakapatnam, Jamnagar and Paradeep.

Non-Food Programmes

The Integrated Nutrition and Health Programme (INHP) has been approved by this Department for a period of 5 years w.e.f. April 1996 to March 2001 A.D. with a total budget of Rs. 1,13,16,35,505. The INHP seeks to improve the health and nutritional status of women and children by directing resources and efforts to achieve those changes in health behaviour which lead to a reduction in mortality and malnutrition. The INHP is being implemented in the seven states where CARE is presently functioning in collaboration with the State Governments. State level advisory groups have also been set up in each of the seven states to facilitate implementation.

Improving Women's Reproductive Health & Family Spacing Project in the State of Uttar Pradesh for a period of five years with a total budget of Rs. 32,251,014 The project is in two districts of Uttar Pradesh namely, Sitapur and Shahjahanpur. The project aims to empower women to take informed decisions about their reproductive health including the number and spacing of children.

Improving Women's Health in Urban Slums Project in Allahabad, Uttar Pradesh for a period of six years with a total budget of Rs. 89,64,879. The project aims to significantly reduce mortality among 28,000 women (15-45 years) in 65 of the neediest authorised slums of Allahabad. Community based women's reproductive health care services are - created and extended, along with increased proficiency of Private Medical Practitioners (PMPs) and public sector personnel in providing reproductive health care,

Improved Health Care for Adolescent Girls in Urban Slums Project in Jabalpur, Madhya Pradesh for a period of six years with a total budget of Rs. 2,22,43,210. The project aims at a significant reduction in the morbidity and mortality associated with reproductive health among adolescent girls, both unmarried and married, in the slums of Jabalpur.

Girls Primary Education (GPE) Project for a period of five years with a total budget of Rs. 6,80,01,325/- in the States of Rajasthan and Uttar Pradesh. The project's aim is to increase girls' access to education in collaboration with local NGO's and community groups.

Credit Rotation for Empowerment and Development through Institution Building and Training (CREDIT) Project for a period of 5 years at a total cost of Rs. 11,22,05,790. The proposal is a joint venture of the WFP and CARE-India. The project proposes to expand the savings and credit portfolio of rural women in partnership with local NGOs in the States of Orissa and Bihar, Maternal and Infant Survival Project with Canadian International Development Agency (CIDA) assistance in the State of Madhya Pradesh. The total cost of the project is estimated at Rs.19,65,80,762/- for a period of two years and six months. The aim of this project is to improve the health and nutritional status of women and children of 5 Blocks in Hoshangabad Division and 6 Blocks in Bhopal Division.

CARE-India assisted programmes (Food Programme and Non-Food Programmes) are being reviewed by this Department with the State Governments and CARE-India biannually.

ICDS training programme

Training is the most crucial element in ICDS, since the achievement of programme goals depends upon the effectiveness of frontline workers in improved delivery of packages under ICDS. Recognising this, from the inception of the ICDS Scheme itself, the Department of Women and Child Development formulated a comprehensive training strategy for different functionaries involved in the ICDS, such as the Anganwadi Workers, Supervisors, Additional Child Development Project Officers (ACDPOs) and Child Development Project Officers (CDPOs).

Training is imparted to these functionaries through the National Institute of Public Cooperation & Child Development (NIPCCD) through its three Regional Centres at Lucknow, Guwahati and Bangalore, 36 Middle Level Training Centres (MLTCs) and 392 Anganwadi Workers Training Centres (AWTCs).

Training of Anganwadi Workers

For imparting training of Anganwadi Workers, the grass-root level functionaries, there are 392 Anganwadi Workers Training Centres (AWTCs) in the country. AWWs are given job training immediately on their joining which is followed by a refresher training on completion of two years. During 1997-98, 41,193 Anganwadi Workers were trained. During 1998-99, 15,000 Anganwadi Workers have been trained upto November, 1998.

Training of Supervisors

For imparting training to Supervisors, who are the middle level functionaries of the ICDS, there are 36 Middle Level Training Centres (MLTCs) in the country. They function under the administrative control of NIPCCD and also include the three Regional Centres of NIPCCD, located at Lucknow, Guwahati and Bangalore, which act as MLTCs. Training is imparted to Supervisors to help them acquaint themselves with various components of the scheme, and to develop appropriate skills in supervision an programme management. Refresher training is imparted to Supervisors on completion 0 one and a half years of service. During 1997-98, 921 Supervisors were trained. During 1998-99, 234 Supervisors have been trained upto November, 1998.

Training of CDPOs/ACDPOs

Training of Child Development Project Officers (CDPOs) and Additional Child Development Project Officers (ACDPOs) is conducted by NIPCCD at its headquarters and its three regional centres. On joining service, CDPOs/ACDPOs are given job training followed by a refresher training on completion of two years' service. During the training, efforts are made to familiarise them with various aspects of the Scheme, including, organisational and administrative structures. During

1997-98, 386 CDPCs/ACDPCs were trained. During 1998-99, 265 CDPC)s/ ACDPC)s have been trained upto November, 1998.

Hundred per cent grant-in-aid is provided by this Department to State Governments, NIPCCD and NGCs for conducting various training courses. The entire expenditure on training, except non-recurring expenditure, capital expenditure and rent component, is reimbursed by UNICEF. During 1996-97 and 1997-98, an amount of Rs. 9.94 crore, Rs. 4.29 crore respectively were released under the ICDS Training Programme. During 1998-99, an amount of Rs. 3.97 crore has been released upto November, 1998.

During the last 2 years, the Training Division of the Department - of Women & Child Development and NIPCCD have carried out a comprehensive review of the ICDS Training Programme. Based on this, a new, dynamic, programme called Project UDISHA has been envisioned.

ICDS Training Programme - Project UDISHA

Salient features of the craft proposal - Project Udisha

— Decentralised training

— Concept of 'Training Teams' has been introduced

— Joint training will be held with officials of other departments e.g. health, education and rural development

— Training will be imparted to other groups, e.g. Panchayati Raj members, the community etc.

- There will be an emphasis on advocacy and IEC activities
- There will be a new syllabus and curriculum
- There will be more flexibility, innovations and dynamism in the training programme NIPCCD has

been given a very prominent role. It is hoped that it will be the premier institute of child development in the world in the next few years.

— Professional training will be given to all trainers including NIPCCD faculty.
— Each Anganwadi Worker will be given a comprehensive Training Kit which will be in her local language or dialect and will be AWW-friendly.
— All Institutes (NIPCCD, MLTCs, AWTCs) will be upgraded.
— Innovative methodologies for refresher training is being suggested.

Balsevika Training Programme

Balsevika Training Programme was started in 1961-62 to meet the requirements of trained personnel in the institutions implementing welfare programmes for pre-school children. With increased coverage of ICDS, the programme of Balsevika Training was discontinued from 1998-99. During the year, a provision of Rs.20.00 lakh has been provided which will be released to ICCW for spill-over liabilities.

Creches/da centres for children of working/ailing mothers

In the huge subcontinent which is India, it is estimated that there are around 91 million working women; of these, approximately 90% are in the unorganised sector. These women toil hard and long, invariably outside their homes. Most of these women are mothers. Sadly, their children are either taken by their mothers to the work place or left in the care of elder siblings at home. Everyone is familiar with the sight of a small child crying while the mother works nearby. As familiar is the sight of an elder sibling, invariably a girl trying desperately to take care of her younger brothers and sisters. In either case the children involved have lost out on their precious childhood, the heritage which is rightfully theirs. In the latter instance, the enforced care of the little ones frustrates attempts to educate young girls who have to play out an adult role, a role for which they are unequipped.

It is in this scenario that the provision of day care services for children becomes an absolutely crucial service. By helping to look after these children, day care services play an invaluable role in ensuring that children remain in a stable safe environment instead of near any adult work place, and also gives them a semblance at least of a childhood. Equally important is the removal of the burden of child rearing from the fragile shoulders of young girls who become free to go to school.

It was for the purpose of achieving these ends that two schemes were set up, the Creche Scheme in 1975 and the National Creche Fund in 1994. Children in the vulnerable age group of 0-5 and whose parent's total monthly income is not more than Rs. 1800/- p.m. are given essential day care services under these schemes. The parents of these children are usually migrant, agricultural, construction and casual labourers. Children of those women who are sick or incapacitated on account of some sickness or suffering from communicable diseases are also covered. These two Schemes meet the overwhelming requirement in many families of day care services and the facilities provided at these creches include supplementary nutrition, immunisation, medical and health care. While the Creche Scheme is being implemented by three major organisations, the Central Social Welfare Board, the Indian Council for Child Welfare and Bhartiya Adimiati Sevak Sangh, the National Creche Fund provides assistance to registered voluntary organisations and Mahila Mandals throughout the country to run creches. In addition to this, the National Creche Fund Scheme also has a component for converting existing Anganwadis into Anganwadi-cum Creche Centres to be run by the same agencies which run the ICDS Scheme which in most cases is the State Government. All the agencies are given a grant of Rs. 18,.480/ per creche per annum towards recurring expenditure, this includes the honorarium for two creche workers, and a one time grant of Rs. 4,000/- for meeting the initial cost of establishing a creche. Any agency which would like to convert an Anganwadi into an Anganwadi-cum-Creche Centre will be sanctioned a grant of Rs. 8,100/- per creche per annum. The basic idea behind this conversion is that an Anganwadi in a ICDS Centre normally runs for only 4 hours. This time is insufficient to meet the requirements of children whose mothers/parents work longer hours and it is therefore desirable that these Anganwadis are converted into creche centres which run for 8 hours.

A It is estimated that India today requires 8 lakh creches for its children. Against this, we have been able to set up only 14,925 creches under these two schemes, leaving an enormous gap which should be filled at the earliest. To achieve this, concerted efforts are being made to increase the corpus of the National Creche Fund since the Creche Scheme is a non expanding one.

The Second 'Children of India Concert' was organised by the National Creche Fund on 14th November, 1998 to commemorate Children's Day. The internationally renowned violin maestro Dr. L. Subramaniarn regaled the audience, as did an electrifying performance by a musical troupe from Nigeria.

Physical and financial achievements of the National Creche Fund

The Early Childhood Education (ECE) Scheme was started in 1982 as a distinct strategy to reduce the drop out rate and to improve the rate of retention of children of the age group of 3-6 years in primary schools.

The Scheme is being implemented in nine educationally backward states viz. Andhra Pradesh, Assam, Bihar, Jammu and Kashmir, Madhya Pradesh, Orissa, Rajasthan, Uttar Pradesh and West Bengal. Under the Scheme, financial assistance amount of Rs. 7,980/- per centre per annum is given to voluntary organisations for running the ECE Centres. The Scheme is a non-expanding one and is being continued only in the areas not covered by the ICDS Scheme. During 1997-98, grant to the tune of Rs. 233 lakhs was released to run 2613 ECE Centres in non-ICDS areas in the above states.

Balwadi nutrition programme

The Balwadi Nutrition Programme is being implemented since 1970-71 through the Central Social Welfare Board and four national level voluntary organisations, Bharatiya Adimiati Sevak Sangh, Indian Council for Child Welfare, Kasturba Gandhi National Memorial Trust and Harijan Sevak Sangh, who extend assistance to local voluntary agencies to implement the programme. The Balwadi Nutrition Programme aspires to meet the very basic nutritional requirement of a child in the age group of 3-5 years by ensuring that she/he is provided with 300 calories and 12-15 gms of protein every day. Apart from nutrition supplement, the Balwadis offer a healthy environment, looking after the social and emotional needs of the children. Under the Scheme, a grant of Rs. 17,220/- is given per Balwadi Centre per annum. This scheme is a non-expanding one, and is being continued only in the areas not covered by the ICDS centres. During 1997-98, a total grant to the tune of Rs. 115.0 lakhs was released to Voluntary Organisations for running 710 Balwadis in non-ICDS areas.

National children's board

The National Policy for Children 1974 envisages a National Children's Board under the chairmanship of the

Prime Minister to function as a forum for planning, review and proper coordination of the multiplicity of services aimed at meeting the needs of the children. The National Children's Board was initially set up in December, 1974 with the Prime Minister as its Chairman. The Board is now under consideration for reconstitution.

State recognition for voluntary action

Rajiv Gandhi Manav Seva Award for Service to Children

In pursuance of its policy to support and to encourage voluntary action and in memory of the late Prime Minister Shri Rajiv Gandhi, the Department of Women and Child Development instituted in 1994 the Rajiv Gandhi Manav Seva Award for Service to Children to honour an individual who makes an outstanding contribution in service to children, including care of children with various kinds of disabilities. The award carries a cash prize of Rs. 1 lakh and a citation. Shri Anantrai K. Shah from Bhavnagar, Gujarat has been selected for Rajiv Gandhi Manav Seva Award for Service to children for the year 1998. The Award will be conferred by HRM.

National Awards for Child Welfare

The National Awards for Child Welfare were instituted in 1979 in the International Year of the Child as a state recognition of voluntary action for the cause of the Child. The Scheme envisages awards to 5 institutions and A individuals in a year for the best work done in the field of child welfare.

The National Selection Committee selected the following five institutions and three individuals for the National Awards for Child Welfare, 1998

Institutions:

1. Donyi-Polo Mission School for the Hearing Impaired, Chimpu, Itanagar, Arunachal Pradesh.

2. Seva Niketan Dairy Farm, Junglighat, Port Blair, Andaman & Nicobar islands
3. St. Mary's Convent, Laitumkhrah, Shillong, Meghalaya
4. SOS Children's Village, Aluva, Edathala North, Ernakulam, Kerala.
5. Calcutta Muslim Orphanage, Calcutta, West Bengal.

Individuals :

1. Smt. Shila Barun, President, Kasturba Gandhi National Memorial Trust, Bakthavarpur, Delhi.
2. Smt. Brijabala Nirbheek, General Secretary, Madhu Smriti Sansthan, Ranghbadi, Kota, Rajasthan.
3. Smt. Champa Bahin, Satya Sadha Ashram, Village Pathriya, Sagar, Madhya Pradesh.

The National Awards for Child Welfare 1998 will be conferred on the above mentioned five institutions and three individuals by the President of India.

National Child Awards for Exceptional Achievement

The Government of India instituted an award in 1996 to give recognition to children with exceptional abilities and who have achieved outstanding status in various fields suck as academics, culture, art, sports, music, etc. Children in the age group of 4-15 years are eligible for this award. One gold medal and 6 silver medals are to be given annually.

The Scheme has been revised to increase the number of awards from the existing 7 to 33. In each State/UT, one child with exceptional achievement will now be conferred an award.

The Union Minister for Human Resource Development will confer the National Child Awards for Exceptional Achievement, 1998.

National Bravery Award

The Scheme of National Bravery Award to children for bravery, gallantry and meritorius service was started in 1957. Every year selected children are given National Bravery Award. The National Bravery Award function is organised by the Indian Council for Child Welfare, New Delhi, which is a voluntary organisation of national repute. Since inception of the Scheme, as many as 5,40 children have been awarded. The Department of Women and Child Development supports the Indian Council for Child Welfare financially. A list of National Bravery Award 1998 winners is given at Annexure X.

United nations children's fund

Department of Women & Child Development is the nodal department for UNICEF, which has been associated with India since 19,49 and is now in its fifth decade of cooperation in assisting disadvantaged children and their mothers. UNICEF has its largest programmes in the world, in India.

The Government of India-UNICEF programmes of cooperation is governed and regulated by the Basic Agreement signed in 1949 and executed through the Master Plan of Operations which is normally a five year cycle. Presently, the programme of cooperation between GOI and UNICEF is being executed through a Bridging Programme since 1996-97 which has been extended by another year upto 1998, to enable future preparation for the next MPO cycle 1999-2002. An amount of $ 81.8 million has been committed for the Bridge Programme, 1998 (December).

Traditionally, UNICEF has been supporting India in a number of programmes focusing on Child Development and Women's Development. Preparation for finalisation of the new Master Plan of Operations 19992002 is underway based on the India Country

Strategy note considered by the UNICEF Executive Board on January 20, 1997. The major thrust areas would be to assist the government to fulfil its obligations for universalising child rights and achieving the World Summit goals; improving the position of girls and women in society; and strengthening capacities of communities through the agreed strategies of community convergent action; central focus on resolving gender disparities; decentralisation of responsibilities/ authorities and resources to local levels; and forging new partnerships to involve key partners and leverage UNICEF resources.

The last MPO was completed in December, 1995. UNICEF committed an amount of US $ 486 million for the 1991-95 MPO out of which an expenditure of US $ 308.7 million under GR, SF & Administrative Budget was made (85.1%).

UNICEF Executive Board in its Second Regular Session held in September, 1998 considered the India Country Programme (MPO 1999-2002) and approved the same. A total of US $ 120 million under General Resources and US $ 180 million under Supplementary Funds was committed for MPO 1999-2002.

An amount of Rs. 310 lakhs has been released for India's contribution to UNICEF General Resources for 1998-99.

National plan for action for children

India is a signatory to the 27 survival and development goals laid down by the World Summit on Children, 1990. In order to implement these goals, the Department of Women and Child Development has formulated a National Plan of Action for Children. Each of the concerned Central Ministries / Departments, State Governments UTs and Voluntary Organisations dealing with women and children have been asked to take up appropriate measures to implement the Action Plan. These goals have been integrated into National Development Plans. A Monitoring Committee under., the Chairpersonship of Secretary (Women and Child Development) reviews the achievement of goals set in the National Plan of Action. All concerned Central Ministries

Departments are represented on the Committee. Sixth meeting of the IMCC was held under the chairpersonship of Secretary (WCD) on 25 March 1998 at New Delhi.

The Department addressed the Chief Secretaries of states to prepare State Plans of Action on the lines of NPA, specifying their targets for the mid decade goals as well as for 2000 AD and spelling out strategies for holistic child development. So far 17 State Governments have prepared SPACs. They are Andhra Pradesh, Arunachal Pradesh, Bihar, Goa, Gujarat, Haryana, Karnataka, Kerala, Madhya Pradesh, Manipur, Orissa, Punjab, Rajasthan, Tamil Nadu, Uttar Pradesh, West Bengal, National Capital Territory of Delhi. Other States/ UT are in the process of preparing their respective Plans of Action including constitution of a coordination committee to monitor their implementation.

Universal children's day

India observes Universal Children's Day on 14th November every year, the birthday of India's first Prime Minister Pandit Jawaharlal Nehru, who was an ardent lover of children. The Universal Children's Day is observed on different dates in different countries in accordance with the UN General Assembly Resolution of 14th November, 1954. In commemoration of the day, a theme highlighting a specific issue related to children is selected every year. The theme for the year 1998 was "Empowered Girl -Empowered Society". The booklet on the girl child highlights the persisting gender inequalities and existing cultural beliefs and values prevalent in society, and suggests practical strategies that can restore to the girl child her rights and enable her to emerge as an empowered woman of tomorrow.

His Excellency the Vice President of India released a Special Commemorative Postal Stamp and brochure on the theme at a special function organised by the Department on 14 November, 1998 at New Delhi.

UN convention on the rights of the child

India ratified the UN Convention on the Rights of the Child on 2nd December, 1992 and it represents a commitment to provide to Indian children a "'First Call"' on national resources. India's first periodic report, as a State Party to the Convention has been deposited with the United Nations Committee of Experts on the Rights of the Child, Geneva on 18th March, 1997.

All State Governments / UT administrations have been requested to take necessary action for the implementation of various Articles and clauses of the UN Convention and submit reports on the progress made to meet the obligations chartered in the various articles.

SAARC activity

An Inter-Ministerial Meeting under the chairpersonship of Joint Secretary (WCD) was held on 8th August, 1997 to initiate follow-up on the Ninth South Asian Association for Regional Cooperation (SAARC) Summit of the Heads of State/Government held at Male during 12th to 14th May, 1997. The meeting considered the proposal for a SAARC initiative on nutrition, water and sanitation.

National commission for children (NCC)

A proposal to set up a National Commission for Children is under the consideration of the Government. The objective would be to monitor and evaluate the status of safeguards provided to children constitutionally, legally and otherwise and advice the Government from time to time on steps and measures to be taken. The proposal has been discussed in the Parliamentary Consultative Committee attached to the Ministry of Human Resource Development in its meetings on 26 October 1998 and 23 November 1998 under the chairmanship of the Minister for Human Resource Development. Further action is in progress. Comments of concerned Ministries / Departments and States/UTs have been sought on the revised proposal.

Infant milk substitutes act, 1992

In 1981, the World Health Assembly adopted an International Code on the Marketing of Breast Milk Substitutes. The Government of India recognised this Code and adopted the Indian National Code for Protection and Promotion of Breast-feeding in, December, 1983. To give effect to the provisions of this Code, the Infant Milk Substitutes, Feeding Bottles and Infant Foods (Regulation of Production, Supply and Distribution) Act, 1992 was enacted which came into force w.e.f. I August 1993. The Act provides for the regulation of production, supply and distribution of infant milk substitutes, feeding bottles and infant foods with a view to the protection and promotion of breast-feeding and ensuring the proper use of infant foods and for matters connected therewith or incidental thereto. The Rules framed under the Act also came into force w.e.f. 1 August 1993. In addition to food inspectors appointed under PFA Act, the Central Government has authorised the following four voluntary organisations engaged in the field of child welfare and development and child nutrition to make a complaint in writing against violations of the Act.

Central Social Welfare Board, Samaj Kalyan Bhawan, B-12, Tara Crescent Institutional Area, South of IIT, New Delhi 110 016.

Indian Council for Child Welfare, 4, Deen Dayal Upadhyaya Marg, New Delhi 110 002.

Association for Consumer Action of Safety and Health (ACASH), Room No. 21, Lawyer's Chambers, R.S. Sapra Marg, Mumbai 400 002.

Breast-feeding Promotion, Network of India (BPNI), BP-33, Pitampura, Delhi 110 034.

The efforts made in this direction have placed India as one of the leading countries in the world having legislation to protect; promote and support breast-feeding. As per UNICEF's 1997 report on the "Progress of Nations", India is one of only 16 countries in the world to have enacted legislation to implement the International Code of Marketing of Breast Milk Substitutes in entirety.

For imaginative and effective implementation of the World Health Organisation's International Code of Marketing of Breast-milk Substitutes ' the Government of India has been awarded with the UK Food Group "Hopeful Baby Award" this year, i.e. 1998. This is, indeed, a recognition of the efforts made by the Government of India. In order to check the marketing malpractices in the promotion and sale of infant foods, efforts are underway to further strengthen the Act.

4

Child Labour

The economic exploitation of children in India has always been an area of concern. While official sources estimate the number of child workers to be 17.36 million, others have placed the figure at the much higher level of 44 million. High as they are, even these figures do not reflect the real tragedy of the working child in India. Most children work in highly exploitative conditions and all are deprived of even the most minimal educational facilities.

In rural areas it is fact that the child who does not attend a formal school is a working child. Collection of water, fuel, household chores and taking care of younger siblings all constitute important elements of a child's life. While many of these activities cannot be defined as hazardous work, in as much as they interfere with the normal development of the child and in the child's ability to reach his/her true potential they violate the convention on the Rights of the Child. In the typical environment in which Indian children grow up the concept of a non-working, non-social going child simply does not exist. Any effort to deal with the issue of child labour therefor has to address the question of education.

In this chapter we identify schooling as the single most important means of preventing child labour. To this extent we also view the promotion of education and the elimination of child labour as being mutually supportive processes. Consequently, we believe that the relevance of primary education lies in its potential to eliminate child labour. It is in the context of eliminating child labour that we examine the scope of appropriate legislation governing compulsory primary education.

Elementary education in India is characterised by fictitious enrollment, high drop-out rates and a constantly mounting number of illiterate children. Figures show that although the number and percentage of children attending school is increasing and the number of schools has grown, India's share in the world's illiterates has also risen. In absolute terms, the number of illiterates in the country is increasing as a result of the high drop-out rate among children in the first five years of school. At the same time, corresponding trends are reflected in the statistics of child labour flourishes with more and more children entering the workforce each year.

It is against this background that the Government of India through its plans and strategies has been grappling with the problem of bringing children to school. From the beginning, the question to which academicians and policy makers have addressed themselves is, "How does a poor country like India design an education policy and strategy which will include the children of the poor as well as the better off?" In the process of answering this question policy makes and educationists have uniformly justified the existence of child labour and accepted the inevitability of children's contributions to family income through work. The basic argument which is accepted is that the family needs the wage of the child to supplement its income; it is in fact this income which keeps the family going. it would therefore not be justified to deprive the family of its source of income by forcing a child to go to school. Two major policies which arose out of this conviction were the Child Labour (Prohibition and Regulation) Act, 1986 and the National Policy on Education, 1986. We shall in this paper restrict ourselves to the latter policy although the former is also of some relevance to the issue.

Recognising the "need" for giving access to elementary education to those sections of the population who "cannot" be enrolled into local schools, the National Policy on Education, 1986 announced the continuance of non-formal education (NFE) for working boys and girls as a major thrust area. This constituted an expression of helplessness in the matter of confronting the issue of child labour and additionally gave legitimacy to the employment of children. It also foreclosed any further discussion on the issue of the abolition of child labour and the provision of compulsory education for some time to come. The only apology offered with respect to child labour was to accept its existence as a "harsh reality". The exploitation of children's labour was thus not addressed and instead more and more ambitious and sophisticated policies of non-formal education were designed to reach working children. A closer look at the details of the NFE programme will serve to highlight these observations. The "clientele" for NFE was identified as "children in habitations without schools, school dropouts, working children and girls who cannot attend school." In the first two years these children, through the NEF centres, were to attain primary school level and in the following three years they were to complete the upper primary level. All instruction was to be by local youth who would work as teachers with a remuneration of Rs. 100 to Rs. 200 per month "with the provision of an annual increment of RS. 50 after the completion of two years of satisfactory service till remuneration reaches Rs. 500 per month." Apart from the Government, the work of running NFE centres would be done through voluntary agencies and panchayat Raj institutions. The NFE programme, in design therefore, has all the elements which in the opinion of the policy makers constitute a "good" programme. It does not interfere with the child's work schedule and at the same time is extremely cost-effective. But design apart, can NFE really achieve what it has set out to do?

In actual fact the NFE Programme is a low-cost strategy devised more out of financial compulsion than conviction. It envisages the existence of a band of highly creative and imaginative local schoolteachers available in every village, especially in backward districts, who can with ingenuity condense an eight-year course of elementary education of five years. The can accomplish that, too, with only a half-an-hour session every evening or whenever convenient to children, at a salary which is less than one-fourth of what a regular schoolteacher gets. Simultaneously it conjures an image of a working child who is alert and earnestly waiting to attend the evening classes just to lap up all that is taught within half an hour or even one hour, thus catching up with children in the better-off formal schools who attend school for six full hours. Obviously it does not require an expert in education to predict the efficacy of this programme. While the NFE programme is not the only programme under the New Education Policy, we have focused attention on this system of universalising education mainly because it serves to dramatically illustrate the consequences of the assumptions that have shaped government policy. To what extent are these assumptions valid? In order to examine this we would like to briefly touch upon the experience of the M.V. Foundation (WVF). The MVF has over the last eight years been working in the field of education, especially among working children and bonded labourers. The initial thrust of the programme was almost entirely on the abolition of bonded child labour. The focus over the years has shifted to cover elimination of all forms of child labour through universalising primary education Each year, the organization has been conducting mobilisation camps for working children in order to withdraw them from work and admit them at the appropriate levels in schools.

The methodology adopted has been to rise the conscience of men and women in rural areas, particularly parents of working children. Parent and Teacher Committees have been formed and awareness-building training conducted to sensitise all those involved to the issue of child labour. Children's camps have incorporated, apart from teaching activities, a programme of development of leadership qualities among children. Street plays and campaigns by children themselves to motivate other working children to got to school have also been devised. The MVF programme also involves a strong component of follow-up measures to prevent dropouts among those who have gone through the camp. In the eight years that the programme has been in operation, over 1,000 children have attended these camps and 3,500 have additionally been motivated to go to school. The latest phase of the programme covers 6,000 children spread over 36 villages.

The camps have been a revelation and have provided rich material on the attitudes of children, parents and government officials towards the problems of child labour and illiteracy. The have also provided pointers to the basic elements that must be incorporated in any scheme dealing with these problems. In the main, the camps have shown that

1) Abolition of child labour and universalisation of school education are practically synonymous.
2) Parents of working children are willing to make adjustments to enable their children to go to school.

3) The income of a working child is not the motivating factor, in most cases, for the parents to sent their children to work.

4) There is no alternative to using government institutions in order to bring about universalisation of education as NGOs cannot provide the infrastructure on the necessary scale.

5) There is considerable scope for involving the village community in universalising elementary education.

It is instructive to examine the implications of the MVF experience in the context to the Government approach to universalising primary education. The first significant outcome has been that a large number of children have been motivated to join schools. In fact, even children engaged in the most exploitative from of work, bonded labour, have been withdrawn from work and admitted to schools. Time and again, the annual camps of the MVF have demonstrated that children who are normally assigned the status of victims of the "harsh reality" of child labour are willing to go to school. Importantly, parents are willing to make such sacrifices as are necessary to ensure that children continue in school.

While it would be difficult for the MVTF to claim that these results would hold in any situation, the fact remains that over a period of eight years positive results have been observed with respect to 5,000 children. Obviously the argument of the harsh reality of child labour has been overemphasized.

The second aspect which the MVF experience emphasizes is the existence of a demand for educations in rural areas even among parents belonging to the economically weaker sections of the society. Field experience shows that parents have not only disposed of assets such as cattle to enable their children to continue in school but have also stood up to the employers of the children when they attempted to enforce contractual obligations against loans advanced. In the extremely feudal and backward setup that prevails in the villages of the Rangareddy district of Andhra Pradesh where MVF activities are concentrated, this is no small sacrifice.

It is against this experience that we assert that the failure of the NFE programme lies not in its faulty execution. In fact, its greatest failure is in its assumption that labourers cannot be withdrawn from work and therefore have to be given the benefits of education outside working hours. The fact that there is an unfulfilled demand for formal education even among the poor in rural areas has been totally denied in this attempt to expand primary education. There is a singular lack of faith in the fact that people, even poor people, value education and learning and are prepared to make extraordinary sacrifices to educate their children.

The issue of compulsory education has always been something of a nenigma. At the theoretical level very few disagree that all children should receive education, at least upto the primary stage, or with the fact that children should not work. In fact, the State has committed itself not only to the universalisation of primary education but also to the abolition of child labour through various pronouncements, not the least of which are the Directive Principles of State Policy enshrined in the Constitution of India. This-commitment has been further strengthened by the fact that India is one of over 150 countries to have ratified the Convention on the Rights of the Child, which articulates a series of children's rights including the right to compulsory and free primary education. In spite of all this, the general attitude of policy makers has been that the country cannot afford the distraction of a compulsory education norm. A number of reasons are given for this, but two major objections are worth noting. The first questions the role of the State in determining the manner in which the children are to be education. The second stresses the inability to implement such legislation which would relegate it to legislation on paper only.

As far as the first objection is concerned, in a society where the State has always played a significant role in shaping the social behavior of citizens through legislative means, it is difficult to question the desirability of the State's intervention with respect to education. Today, in our country there is legislation on issues ranging from minimum age of marriage to protection of civil rights and abolition of the category of untouchables. For the State to legislate on an issue concerning a child's right to development, would not be something out of the ordinary.

The second objection, however, merits a more detailed examination. It has been observed that in this country a large number of laws governing social issues have been passed but have never really been implemented. Although these laws have been developed to control undesirable social practices, the State has not been able to guarantee effective enforcement. Any number of examples ranging from the SITA (Suppression of Immoral Traffic Act) to BLSA (Bonded Labour System Abolition) can be cited to illustrate this. Legislation to provide compulsory education, therefore, is likely to meet a similar fate. Further, it is argued that legislation governing compulsory education may be sued as an instrument of harassment against the parents.

These arguments view the issue from one side only, namely that of administration. Social activities have, how-ever, long viewed legislation of this nature as a means to compel the State to take action. The BLSA, for instance, has proved to be an extremely powerful weapon for NGOs to deal with the problem of child bonded labour in situations where the State has not been prepared to take *suo motu* action.

Thus, even though appropriate legislation may not necessarily mean that the objectives of the legislation will be achieved, its very existence creates an enabling provision where by the State can be compelled to take action. At the very least such legislation reflects the commitment of the State to promote an ideal and progressive value system. More importantly, such legislation provides others working in the field with a legitimacy which otherwise wouldn't exist. The importance of this aspect can be appreciated with respect to all those activists who have utilized the BLSA to release bonded child labourers. Thus, while administrators and academicians may lament the inability to implement social legislation, the fact remains that the BLSA has lent enormous strength to many of the activists working in the area of bonded labour.

Legislation to provide for compulsory education, therefore, would be of immense value in situations where the efforts of the State are constrained in responding to the requirements of the people. We have already seen that the government response to the problem of illiteracy and child labour has been quite equivocal. On the other hand, our experience in the field has shown that there exists an enormous unrecognized demand for formal education and that parents are willing to make sacrifices to utilize educational opportunities. As long as the existing infrastructure can meet the demand there is no crisis but the fact is that, more often than not, the infrastructure is inadequate.

For instance in the limited area wherein our organization alone is functioning, we would require educational facilities for over 6,000 more students. Taking the existing facilities into account this would mean at least 60 more classrooms and teachers. Under the present circumstances there is absolutely no way in which we can compel the State is absolutely no way in which we can compel the State to provide these facilities. We, thus, have a situation where the same parents and children who have been written off as victims of the harsh reality of socio-economic circumstances are demanding educational facilities and the State itself is either unable or unwilling to respond. It is in this context that we feel there is a need for suitable legislation binding the State to provide compulsory education.

Child slavery in India

Democracy and its three pillars—liberty, equality and fraternity— enshrined in the Constitution of India are relatively meaningless in view of the fact that 120 to 140 million children are working in this country. Of these, 55 million children between the ages of six and 14 are languishing in servitude.

They are employed mostly in agriculture and industries such as carpet weaving, brassware manufacture, glass—and bangle-making, leather, gem cutting and polishing, matches and fireworks, stone quarries, brick kilns and handloom.

Socio-cultural factors, including the abominable caste system and ethnic and gender discrimination, are responsible for the perpetuation of the scourge of child labour. These factors exercise a significant negative influence, worse even than socio-economic factors such as grinding poverty, unemployment and illiteracy. Little wonder that 90 per cent of bonded child labourers belong to untouchable castes and tribes.

In India, the phenomenon of child bondage was exposed in 1984, only after the sordid plight of 32 bonded children was brought to public notice by the Bonded

Labour Liberation Front (BLLF) through a writ petition in the Supreme Court of India. These ill-fated children, aged six to 12 years, were kidnapped from Chhichori village in Palamau district of Bihar and were bonded to a loom owner of Belwaria village in Mirzapur district of Uttar Pradesh. The hapless children were beaten with bamboo sticks, hung upside down from a jackfruit tree and branded with red-hot iron rods.

We found that this was not an isolated instance. The entire carpet belt, the Mirzapur and Bhadohi area, benefits from the labour of bonded children. So the BLLF entrenched itself in this area and took up the challenging and difficult tasks of redeeming children from slavery, restoring them to their native places and rehabilitating them. It was observed that there was a continuous inflow of children to the carpet industry from bihar and that there was an organized cartel engaged in procuring children through dubious means, including kidnapping and supplying these children directly to carpet manufacturers. This practice has been continuing uninhibitedly and is a blatant violation of Articles 15 (3), 23, 24, 39 (e), 39 (f) and 45 of the Indian Constitution and prohibitive laws, viz, the Bonded Labour System Abolition Act, 1976, and the Child Labour Regulation Act, 1996.

Currently 300,000 children are engaged in the carpet manufacture sector alone. Through direct measures including persuasion, raids and court injunctions, more than 7,000 children have been released and returned to their homes. Some NGOs are involved in the rehabilitation process being conducted by State Governments.

It is commonly maintained that child servitude is a harsh reality, fostered by socio-economic and historical compulsions. It is believed that four factor, namely poverty, unemployment, population growth and illiteracy, are the main reasons for this malady and that their redress is a prerequisite for eliminating child servitude.

But we argue the other way. Our direct experience and findings from various studies conducted by researchers, corroborates the fact that child servitude is equally, if not solely, responsible for causing and perpetuating unemployment, poverty, population growth and illiteracy.

Today in India we have 55 million children in servitude on the one hand and an equal number of unemployed adults, on the other hand. According to rough estimates, the respective figures of these phenomena have been running parallel since 1947. At that time the number of unemployed adults was roughly equal.

No Government can scale down adult unemployment without curbing child labour. This is so because the maximum job opportunities created every year are preferentially given to children as their physical and mental vulnerability makes them easy to exploit. In addition, children represent the cheapest source of human labour. Our logical apprehension is that if we do not eradicate child servitude today, we will be responsible for perpetuating the poverty, abject misery and ill health of 55 million adults in the country. It should be noted that the growth rate of the population is much higher among those communities in which unemployment is rampant. Obviously, if child labour is not controlled, impoverished parents will continue to succumb to the 'necessity' of enlarging the number of earning members in the family.

Similarly, there exists a correlation between illiteracy and child servitude. In areas where there are more job opportunities for children, the drop-out rate in schools is extremely high. If we do not liberate 55 million children from their jobs today, we will be responsible for keeping them illiterate for their entire lives. Thus, the natural corollary is that the level of illiteracy cannot be reduced without eradicating child servitude.

In India, an aggressive anti-carpet campaign was launched; the premises of manufactures were raided, children were liberated and their rehabilitation started. In addition, the issue has been publicised widely and political will has been generated for the total eradication of this menace. SACCS's partner in Bangladesh has taken up the issue of child employment in heir garment industry. SACCS has launched some credible measures to combat child servitude. It under took a 2000-km marathon march in February 1993. The march aroused a considerable amount of awareness among adults and children.

Another novel measure adopted in 1993 by this organization was to generate political will among contestants for seats in the State legislative Assembly of Uttar Pradesh under the banner of Save Childhood. It was the first time in Parliamentary history that a written commitment was obtained form candidates pledging that they would make efforts to abolish child labour and enact a law for the free and compulsory primary education of children below the age of 14. Those who were averse to this campaign were blacklisted and this names were published in the local newspapers along with an appeal not to vote for them.

It is heartening to report that foreign NGOs, especially those in Germany, Britain, the United States, Sweden and the Netherlands, have taken up the cause of child servitude seriously and created pressure on their governments and parliaments for the enactment of suitable legislation banning the import of products made by children. As a result of this movement, the Tom Harkin Bill has been introduced in the U.S. Senate Seeking a ban on the entry of products made by children. The European parliament is considering a similar resolution. These developments have agitated industrialists and traders of export products, as well as some members of the top echelons of the Government of India. In some cases, frantic efforts have been made to slow down the passage of legislation by using dubious means. In other cases diabolical propaganda against human rights organizations and eminent social activists has been carried out.

For the last several years we have been pressuring the Government of India to appoint a National Commission on bonded Labour, to include children, vested with the power to identify, release and rehabilitate victims of bondage. But all efforts have, so far, been in vain.

We have been unable to accept the attitude of the Government when our demands are in consonance with Constitutional Guarantees and the provisions of the prohibitive laws of the land. Let the conscience of our countrymen also revolt against the abomination of child slavery and force the powers that be to act - now. Let children in the workforce be replaced by adults and let children be granted free and compulsory schooling with all necessary incentives.

Sale of Children

The phenomenon of the sale of children is universal. The tragic circumstances leading to the abuse and exploitation of children cuts across the barriers between the developing and developed world. The issue confronts most societies, although he typology and degree vary from country to country. Children are not only sold or exploited at the national level, but they are also trafficked across frontiers far and wide.

Concerning the notion of "sale," different interpretations appear in the two major legal systems—common law and civil law systems. The concept of the sale of children has many forms:

— a sale involves a child sold by one person (the seller) to another (the buyer);

— a child transferred to another in exchange for a sum of money or other considerations which do not constitute the price of the child but which nevertheless represent unjustified profits, for instance, bribes;

— a child is rented to another person, for example, for the purpose of sexual exploitation or exploitation of her/his labour when the sum paid is completely unrelated to the work the child has to do;

— a child is held until the parent or guardians in a position to meet a financial obligation.

In order to secure a consensus interpretation, one may use the definition dived from the 1956 Supplementary Convention on the Abolition of Slavery, the Slave Trade and Institutions and Practices Similar to Slavery as follows:

"The transfer of a child from one party (including biological parents, guardians and institutions) to another, for what ever purpose, in exchange for financial or the reward or compensation."

It is not a simple matter to define who is a child. This is because age criteria can vary across different systems or different cultures. In addition, there is an admixture of other terms, for example "juvenile", "minor", "adolescent" and "youth".

Nevertheless, as we are all aware it was not until 1990 that the convention on the Rights of the Child gave in Article 1 the standard concerning the definition of a "child".

"...a child means every human being below the age of 18 unless, under the law applicable to the child, majority is attained earlier."

Again, as in the notion of "sale" and "children," different approaches can be seen in regard to the 'sale of children". For instance, one UN document limits the notion to sale for adoption, sale for forced labour and sale for prostitution. On the other hand, one non-government organization's report includes the sale of children as their sale for

— adoption and marriage
— prostitution and sexual exploitation
— pornography
— cheap bonded labour
— begging, stealing and other criminal actions
— organ transplants.

In addition, as child labour entails the sale of a child, the following concepts of sale could also be considered: armed conflict; adult criminal activities: forced labour or abducted children; debt bondage; labour in the unorganized sector; labour in the organized sector; child prostitution; pornography and sexual exploitation; forced marriage; disabled children in the labour force; domestic labour; apprenticeship and family-supervised labour.

It is recognised that the exploitation of child labour is a from of sale of children. Generally speaking when one considers the notion "child labour" per se, it is not necessarily detrimental to children. However, when it gives rise to exploitation, usually be another party who has power over the child, it may result in negative consequences for children, both with regard to their rights and their development. it also constitutes sale because the child becomes the object of a transaction in cash or in kind. it appears that, in many parts of the world, children are sold into several types of employment, either by their parents, guardians or other intermediaries.

Recently, the International Labour Organisation (ILO) estimated that there were some 88 million working children between ten and 14 years of age. Instances of exploitation are to be found in all regions of the world but Asia and South America figure high in the number of children in difficult circumstances. It is noted that the worst forms of child labour exploitation often take place in the informal sector and small-scale industries.

Causes of exploitation

Generally, the exploitation of child labour may arise from a variety of root causes, including poverty, migration, gender discrimination and criminality.

Poverty: Much of the exploitation appears to be a consequence of the pervasive poverty in developing countries. Like wise, economic needs push children to undertake exploitative working developed countries. As children are cheaper and easier to employ, adults are kept out of the labour market.

Migration: According to the notion of "globalisation," at present, it appears that people have become more mobile, travelling easily to other countries. This mobility is also reflected in their search for jobs. As a result, it leads to the emergence of migrant labourers and immigrants shedding new light on the old problem of child labour.

Gender Discrimination: In many societies the preference for boys, coupled with a chauvinistic attitude towards the development of women, often places girls at a disadvantage. Viewed by many countries as having lower priority, the girl child is usually denied access to educational and occupational opportunities which could protect her from labour exploitation.

Socio-cultural Disparities: With respect to the sale of children for exploitative child labour, socio-cultural disparities may also contribute to the sale of children. Many societies display historical injustices and traditional taboos. The phenomenon has racial and social origins, interwoven with issues of class and caste and the remnants of slavery. It is obvious that children used for labour exploitation are lured from particular racial or social groups, rather than from the well endowed groups in power.

Criminality: As one commentator has noted, the sale of children is the product of crime. Although child labour has been with us from time immemorial, criminal syndicates and individuals are manipulating children to sell drugs, to steal and to commit other offences is probably an apt example of this situation. Much of it is linked to corruption within national systems and some law enforcement authorities colliding with criminal elements. This is compounded by the fact that although various countries have laws to protect children, there is a huge gap between the norms and existing practices; many countries suffer from poor law enforcement. The exploitation of child labour is often the product of such deficiencies and related vested interests.

At the international level, various instruments provide an umbrella of protection for child labourers. Under the auspices of the ILO, a series of conventions and recommendations on the exploitation of child labour has been developed. One key convention is Convention Number 138 which establishes 15 as the basic minimum age of employment, although reduction to 14 may be possible in developing countries. The ILO conventions and recommendations have been strengthened by the advent of the Convention on the Rights of the Child. The CRC emphasises anew the issue of sale linked with child, labour. Article 32 states that "children should be protected from economic exploitation and from performing any work that is likely to be hazardous or to interfere with the child's education, or to be harmful to the child's health or physical, mental, spiritual, moral or social development." The Convention calls for the stipulation of pluridisciplinary measures, for example, legislative, administrative, social and educational measures to:

(a) Provide a minimum age or minimum ages for admission to employment;
(b) Provide for appropriate regulations of the hours and conditions of employment;
(c) Provide for appropriate penalties or other sanctions to ensure the effective enforcement of the present article.

In the case of migrant workers, the International Convention on the Protection of the Rights of All Migrant Workers and Members of their Families, 1990 also protects those in irregular situations, for instance, those employed without proper documents in another country; they retain their rights vis-a-vis their employers, even in such a context. Although various legal frameworks have been established, the issues of implementation and programme planning to realise specific targets remain.

Implementation: The 1990 World Declaration on the Survival, Development and Protection of Children, highlighted the need for specific programmes of action at the national level. In addition, the UN Commission on Human Rights adopted the Programme of Action for the

Elimination of the Exploitation of Child Labour in 1993. This Programme of Action advocates a number of measures which should be implemented, particularly at the national and local levels. These include the following:

- Information campaigns to raise awareness of the problem;
- Educational and vocational training to prevent child labour exploitation;
- Social action to help families and their children;
- Development aid;
- Stipulation and application of labour standards;

The adoption by States of appropriate policies and programmes, for example, provision of primary education for all;

Moreover, in terms of programming, in Islamabad in November 1992, the International Labour Office, within its interdepartmental project on the Elimination of Child Labour, helped to organise the Asian regional seminar on Children in Bondage, which developed and adopted a Programme of Action Against child Bondage. The Programme of Action advocates the following measures:

Review the adequacy of existing legislation. In particular, the following aspects should be covered:

- Definition (the various forms of bondage)
- Objective (its total abolition)
- Specification of sanctions
- Compensation of victims
- Liquidation of debts and other obligations
- Enforcement machinery, for example measures for speedy trial
- Enabling provisions for the establishment of special courts

— Adverse publicity for violators
— Establishment of rehabilitation schemes

Enforcement:

Establish mechanisms to promote and monitor enforcement, e.g. vigilance committees, task forces

— Strengthen the judiciary
— Provide appropriate penalties to deter violations
— Publicise violations
— Complement legal machinery with public awareness campaigns and the dissemination of information
— Provide information and training for targeted groups, e.g. officials of implementing authorities, the judiciary, trade unions, religious groups
— Conduct research and studies

Concerning laws prohibiting or regulating child labour, it appears that these vary in aspects such as the age of employment and the type of work allowed. The enforcement of such legislation of often weak, and tends to cover only the formal sector. In 1993, instances of rampant child labour exploitation were found in both developing and developed countries, though the extent varied according to the region.

In South Asia, the issue of child marriage was raised several times in 1993, particularly concerning customers buying young brides. The plight of child domestic workers and transactional trafficking of children emerged throughout the year. There is also a demand factor regarding South Asian children, both local and transactional, particularly with customers from the Middle East countries. In addition, numerous concerns were expressed in relation to children trafficked for camel racing in the Gulf countries. In this respect, however, there has been a positive initiative: the United Arab

Emirates recently banned the use of child jockeys and ordered that they be returned home.

In East Asia, the sale and trafficking of children for labour exploitation is still rampant both locally and across borders. The issue is closely linked with the sex market.

In Africa, the exploitation of child labour in the informal sector was reported in various countries in 1993. In particular, the girl child is a victim of exploitative domestic service. At times, there is a link with the remnants of slavery, such as the sale of children for forced labour, particularly from certain ethnic groups.

In Central and South America, the number of children at work is large, especially as there is a vast population of street children. There were disturbing incidents of killings of street children during the past year. In this region, too, the problems of child domestic workers and the use of children in the informal sector are rampant. At the other extreme, children are at times employed to sell drugs.

In Europe, the problem of child labour exploitation poses a challenge to many countries. This includes a specific linkage with children used as instruments of crime and as domestic workers.

The general observation gained is that while there are national and international laws, including various Plans and Programmes of Action which cover most of the situations, law enforcement leaves much to be desired. In addition, the existing laws tend to be remedial rather than preventive. In relation to the sale of children for child labour exploitation, the following recommendations are offered:

General: States, national and international organisations are invited to bear in mind strategies of prevention, protection and rehabilitation in curbing the exploitation of child labour. All strategies involve short-and long-term planning, implementation and evaluation. Realisable goals depend upon close coordination, adequate budgetary allocations and willingness to cooperate between the national and local levels, including federal and state links.

Prevention: A key priority for action in the short-term, with long-term implications, is in the area of prevention. States along with national and international organisations should promote anti-poverty strategies, improved flow of information, universal primary education, community consciousness raising, mobilisation, the satisfaction of basic needs, occupational opportunities and alternative forms of employment for families.

Protection: Protection of children from child labour exploitation depends upon a adequate and effective laws and policies together with their implementation at the national and local levels. All countries already have laws which can be used to protect children, for instance, the criminal law. These should be implemented in a more committed manner. The quality of the law enforcement authorities, namely police force, immigration authorities, judges, inspectors and others, needs also to be improved. In relation to transnational child labour exploitation, improved links between INTERPOL and national police are required to identify transnational networks. Moreover, extradition arrangements should be expanded so as to facilitate the transfer of alleged criminals to face charges in the country where the abuse has taken place.

Rehabilitation: States and national and international organisations should take remedial action to help children who are exploited. This may include juridical remedies, such as prosecution of abusers, and the provision of legal aid and assistance, and/or socio-medical remedies such as the provision of hospices, counselling and other support facilities. On another front, appropriate spiritual remedies, for example, religion, should also be considered as a tool to counter problems.

Facilities should be provided to help those with health problems, including HIV/AIDS. These may include medical and community facilities to help children and their families, as well as measures to protect them against discrimination and other harm. Emphasis should be placed upon family-based and community-based rehabilitation rather than State institutionalisation. Particular attention should be paid to child trafficking. This entails proper safeguards, including independent monitoring and follow-up, for children to be returned to their country of origin. Pending their return to the country of origin, they should not be treated as illegal immigrants by the receiving countries but dealt with humanely as special cases of humanitarian concern. Upon the children's return, the countries of origin should treat them with respect in accordance with international human rights principles.

In relation to child labour, the whole range of measures advocated by the UN Commission on Human Rights' Programme of Action for the Elimination of the Exploitation of Child Labour, 1993 should be implemented. There should be stricter law enforcement in the case of child labour, with more incentives for exemplary law enforcement personnel. All vestiges of bondage should be eradicated, and attention should be paid to the plight of the girl child. The Programme of Action against Child Bondage, 1992 should also be placed as a priority for all parties concerned.

More emphasis should be placed on the plight of domestic labour, particularly in regard to children; laws may be required to prevent abuse in this field. Again, their basic human rights should be protected. Illegal, or undocumented child labourers should get greater protection. They should be deported to their country of origin only if their safety and basic human rights are guaranteed. This should be seen in the context of the International Convention on the Protection of the Rights of All Migrant Workers and Members of Their Families, 1990.

The world, you feel, must surely have banished such obscenities to the distant past. But the quote is from a report on the matchstick-making industry of modern-day Sivakasi, in India. And similar descriptions of children at work in hazardous conditions can be gathered from countries across the world. In Malaysia, children may work up to 17-hour days on rubber plantations, exposed to insect and snake bites. In Portugal, children as young as 12 are subject to the heavy labour and myriad dangers of the construction industry. In Morocco, they hunch at looms for long hours and little pay, knotting the strands of luxury carpets for export. In the United States, children are exploited in garment industry sweatshops. In the Philippines, young boys dive in dangerous conditions to help set nets for deep-sea fishing.

The world should, indeed, have outgrown the many forms of abuse labouring children endure. But it hasn't, although not for lack of effort. Child labour was one of the first and most important issues addressed by the international community, resulting in the International Labour Organization's (ILO) 1919 Minimum Age Convention.

Early efforts were hobbled, in part, because campaigners struggling to end child labour appealed to morality and ethics, values easily sidelined by the drive for profit and the hard realities of commercial life. Child labourers were objects of charity of humanitarian concern but they had no legal rights.

Today's world is different at least in this respect. Children have rights established in international laws, not least in the Convention on the Rights of the Child, which has now been ratified by all but a few countries. Ratification specifically obligates governments—in article 32 — to protect children "from economic exploitation and from performing any work that is likely to be hazardous or to interfere with the child's education, or to be harmful to the child's health or physical, mental, spiritual, moral or social development."

But beyond that article, children's exploitation in work contravenes many more of the rights enshrined in the Convention, among them children's rights to care by their parents, to compulsory and free primary education, to the highest attainable standard of health, to social security, and to provisions for rest and recreation. The rights of those children whose primary activity is work are, without question, in jeopardy.

Looking at children's work through the lens of children's rights and the Convention on the Rights of the Child, as this State of the World's Children report seeks to do, offers not only new ways of understanding the problem of child labour but also provides new impetus and direction to the movement against it. As we will see, child labour is often a complex issue. Powerful forces sustain it, including many employers, vested interest groups and economists proposing that the market must be free at all costs, and traditionalists believing the caste or class or certain children denudes them of rights.

Our lodestar must always be the best interests of the child. It can never be in the best interests of a child to be exploited or to perform heavy and dangerous forms of work. No child should labour in hazardous and exploitative conditions, just as no child should die of preventable illness.

On this point there can be no doubt. Work that endangers children's physical, mental, spiritual, moral or social development must end. Hazardous child labour is a betrayal of every child's rights as a human being and is an offence against our civilization.

The recent surge of interest in child labour has too often been founded upon—and contributed to—four myths about child labour that it is vital to confront. The first is that child labour is uniquely a problem of the developing world. The second is that child labour emerges inevitably and naturally out of poverty and thus will always be with us. The third is that most child labourers are at work in sweatshops producing cheap goods for export to the stores of the rich world. And the fourth is that there is a simple solution to the child labour problem—a 'trade sanction' or 'boycott'—that will end it once and for all.

Child labour only happens in the poor world—While the vast majority of working children are found in developing countries, children routinely work in all countries. In every country, rich and poor, it is the nature of the work children do that determines whether or not they are harmed by it—not the plain fact of their working. Few people in the industrialized world, for example, would look upon the employment of a child to deliver newspapers for an hour or two before school as an exploitative form of child labour, despite the fact that the child will certainly be paid less than normal adult rates for the job. Often such a job will be encouraged in the interest of the child's gaining experience of the 'real world' of work and commerce.

This is also how children's work is regarded by many families in the developing world—with the difference that these families are often in dire need of the income or help their children can provide, whereas children in industrialized countries are often working for pocket money.

When all forms of work are considered, the percentage of children working in industrialized countries can be surprisingly high. In the United Kingdom, for example, the most reliable estimates available show that between 15 and 26 per cent of 11-year-olds and between 36 and 66 per cent of 15-year-olds are working.

Most of these child workers in industrialized countries also attend school. But there is a naivety in the assumption that the only kind of work undertaken by children in the West is on the 'pocket money' model. Industrialized nations tend to see themselves as having completely eradicated the harsher forms of child labour and thus preach that poorer countries should follow their example.

Yet hazardous forms of child labour can be found in most rich countries. Usually, the exploited children come from ethnic minorities or immigrant groups, as with the Gypsy and Albanian communities in Greece. In the US, for example the majority of child workers are employed in agriculture, and high proportion of them are from immigrant or ethnicminority families. A study by the US General Accounting Office showed a 250 per cent increase in child labour violations between 1983 and 1990. In a three-day sting operation in 1990, the US Department of Labour discovered more than 11,000 children working illegally. The same year, a survey of Mexican-American children working on New York state farms showed that almost half had worked in fields still wet with pesticides and more than a third had themselves been sprayed, either directly or indirectly.

Child labour will never be eliminated until poverty disappears — It is true that the poorest, most disadvantaged sectors of society supply the vast majority of child labourers. The conclusion often drawn from this is that child labour and poverty are inseparable and that calls for an immediate end to hazardous child labour are unrealistic. We are told we must tolerate the intolerable until world poverty is ended.

This is very convenient for all those who benefit from the status quo. But it is also untrue. The fact remains that when a child is engaged in hazardous labour, someone—an employer, a customer or a parent—benefits from that labour. It is this element of exploitation that is overlooked by those who see child labour as inseparable from poverty. However poor their families may be, children would not be harmed by work if there were not people prepared and able to exploit them. And child labour, in fact, can actually perpetuate poverty, as a working child grows into an adult trapped in unskilled and badly paid jobs.

Of course, poverty must be reduced. Its reduction by economic growth, by employment generation and by investment, by better distribution of income, by changes in the global economy, as well as by better allocation of government budgets and better targeting of aid flows will reduce the potential pool of child labourers. But hazardous child labour can and must be eliminated independently of wider measures aimed at poverty reduction.

At the highest level, governments have begun to move on the issue, to make good the commitments they assumed in ratifying the Convention on the Rights of the Child. In New Delhi in 1996, for example, labour ministers of the Non-Aligned Movement agreed that "exploitative child labour wherever it is practised is a moral outrage and an affront to human dignity." They resolved to give "immediate priority for total and de facto elimination of child labour in hazardous employments." At the local level, activists' groups and non-governmental organizations (NGOs) are exploring ways to remove children from dangerous work situations and provide alternatives for them. And in August 1996, the third South Asian Association for Regional Cooperation (SAARC) Ministerial Conference on the Children of South Asia committed member States to ending bonded labour by the year 2000 and to "eliminate the evil of child labour" by 2010.

The end of hazardous child labour dose not have to—and must not—wait for the end of poverty. World poverty cannot be eliminated by the end of the decade. But hazardous child labour— and the grave violation of the rights of the children involved—can be.

Child labour Primarily occurs in export industries—Export industries are the most visible sector in which children work. Soccer balls made by children in Pakistan for use by children in industrialized countries may be a compelling symbol. But we must not lose sight of the tens of millions of children all around the world who work in non-export areas, often in hazardous or exploitative conditions. In fact, only a very small percentage of all child workers are employed in export-sector industries—probably less than per cent.

A 1995 study in Bangladesh, for example, revealed that children were active in more than 300 different kinds of jobs outside the export sector. These ranged from household work to brick-making, from stone-breaking to selling in shops and on streets, fro bike-repairing to garbage-collecting and rag-picking. What is more, this assessment took into account only jobs done in cities. Most children work on farms and plantations or houses, far from the reach of labour inspectors and from media scrutiny.

If we allow the notion that the most exploited child workers are all in the industrial export sector to tale hold, we would do a grave disservice to that great majority of children who labour in virtual invisibility. The only way to make headway against child labour is for consumers and governments to apply pressure through sanctions and boycotts—This is incorrect on two counts. First, it implies that all the momentum for action of child labour is generated by Western pressure—and that people, NGOs, the media and governments in developing countries have been ignoring or condoning the problem. In fact, activists and organizations, both local and international, have been diligently at work in developing countries for years, exposing child labour abuses, developing local and national programmes and promoting consumer awareness in their own

The ILO International Programme on the Elimination of Child Labour is one important example. Launched in 1991 to help children in six countries, it now works with NGO and government partners in 19 countries. To cite just two others, in a UNICEF-assisted programme in the Philippines, teams composed of government inspectors, social workers, police, NGOs, prosecutors and the media regularly investigate working children's conditions, removing those in danger. And in Bangladesh, where primary education is a high priority, a joint NGO/government non-formal education programme for 1.4 million poor urban children was designed in late 1995.

Second, this myth implies that there is one clear highway, usually involving trade sanctions and consumer boycotts, speeding a newly impassioned global society all the way to the resolution of the problem.

International commitment and pressure are undoubtedly important. But sanctions affect only export industries, which, as we have seen, exploit a relatively small percentage of child labourers. And sanctions are also blunt instruments with long-term consequences that may not be foreseen, with the result that they harm, instead of help, children.

The Harkin Bill, which was introduced into the US Congress in 1992 with the laudable aim of prohibiting the import of products made by children under 15, is a case in point. As of September 1996, the Bill had yet to find its way onto the statute books. But the mere threat of such a measure panicked the garment industry of Bangladesh, 60 per cent of whose products—some $900 million in value—were exported to the US in 1994.

Child workers, most of them girls, were summarily dismissed from the garment factories. A study sponsored by international organizations took the unusual step of tracing some of these children to see what happened to them after their dismissal. Some were found working in more hazardous situations, in unsafe workshops where they were paid less, or in prostitution.

This, then, was a classic case of good motives gone wrong. However, not all was lost. A ground-breaking agreement was reached to protect the affected children. A clear lesson can be learned in all of this. Because of their potential to do harm, in any situation where sanctions are contemplated, a child-impact assessment would need to be made at the point of application, and constant monitoring would be needed thereafter to gauge the long-term effects on children.

The phrase 'child labour' conjures up a particular image: we see children chained to looms in dark mills and sweatshops, as if in a long and nightmarish line running from Lancashire in the 1830s right through to the South Asia of the 1990s.

In reality, children do a variety of work in widely divergent conditions. This work takes place along a continuum. At one end of the continuum, the work is beneficial, promoting or enhancing a child's physical, mental, spiritual, moral or social development without interfering with schooling, recreation and rest. At the other end, it is palpably destructive or exploitative. There are vast areas of activity between these two poles, including work that need not impact negatively on the child's development.

At the most destructive end, no one would publicly argue that exploiting children as prostitutes is acceptable in any circumstances. The same can be said labour 'bonded child labour', the term widely used for the virtual enslavement of children to repay debts incurred by their parents or grandparents. This also applies to industries notorious for the dire health and safety hazards they present: for example, the charcoal furnaces in the Brazilian state of Mato Grosso do Sul, or the glass-bangle factories of Firozabad in India. Hazardous work is simply intolerable for all children.

But to treat all work by children as equally unacceptable is to confuse and trivialize the issue and to make it more difficult to end the abuses. This is why it is important to distinguish between beneficial and intolerable work and to recognize that much child labour falls into a grey area between these two extremes.

The physical harm is, of course, the easiest to see. Carrying heavy loads or sitting for long periods in unnatural positions can permanently disable growing bodies. Hard physical labour over a period of years can stunt children's physical stature by up to 30 per cent of their biological potential, as they expend stores of stamina that should last into adulthood.

Children are also vulnerable psychologically: they can suffer devastating psychological damage from being in an environment in which they are demeaned or oppressed. Self-esteem is as important for children as it is for adults. Education is one of the keys that will unlock the prison cell of hazardous labour in which so many children are confined. It is almost impossible to overemphasize this point.

Education helps a child develop cognitively, emotionally and socially, and it is an area often gravely jeopardized by child labour. Work can interfere with education in the following ways:

— it frequently absorbs so much time that school attendance is impossible;

— it often leaves children so exhausted that they lack the energy to attend school or cannot study effectively when in class;

— some occupations, especially seasonal agricultural work, cause children to miss too many days of class even though they are enrolled in school;

— the social environment of work sometimes undermines the value children place on education, something to which street children are particularly vulnerable;

— children mistreated in the workplace may be so traumatized that they cannot concentrate on school work or are rejected by teachers as disruptive.

All cultures share the view that the younger the children, the more vulnerable they are physically and psychologically and the less they are able to fend for themselves. Age limits are a formal reflection of society's judgement about the evolution of children's capacities and responsibilities.

Almost everywhere, age limits formally regulate children's activities: when they can leave school; when they can marry; when they can vote; when they can be treated as adults by the criminal-justice system; when they can join the armed forces — and when they can work.

But age limits differ from activity to activity and from country to country. The legal minimum age for all work in Egypt, for example, is 12, in the Philippines 14, in Hong Kong 15. Peru adopts a variety of standards: the minimum age is 14 in agriculture; 15 in industry; 16 in deep-sea fishing; and 18 for work in ports and seafaring.

Many countries make a distinction between light and hazardous work, with the minimum age for the former generally being 12, for the latter usually varying between 16 and 18. The ILO Minimum Age Convention also broadly adopts this approach, allowing light work at age 12 or 13, but hazardous work not before 18.

Nevertheless, ILO also establishes a general minimum age of 15 years—provided 15 is not less than the age of completion of compulsory schooling. This is the most widely used yardstick when establishing how many children are currently working around the world.

Nobody knows for sure. ILO, one authority on the subject, considers the existing statistics vastly inadequate and unreliable and the process of data collection fraught with complications. A recent ILO limited survey, which indicated that 73 million of the world's children are employed—equivalent to 13 per cent of those aged 10 to 14—helps illustrate some of the problems.

The survey was limited for many reasons. Many national governments did not respond. It did not include children at work in industrialized nations. It did not count the millions of child workers believed to be under

10 years of age, nor those employed in the informal sector, or attending school who might also be working. Nor did it include the biggest group of invisible workers: all those children—mainly girls—who are engaged in domestic labour, whether for their own families or as servants.

The collection of solid and reliable data regarding child labour is limited also by the fact that, in certain instances, it is presumed officially not to exit and therefore is not included in surveys or covered by official statistics. Further uncounted child labourers can be discovered if we surmise that children currently not enrolled in or attending school are working in some form or another. In India alone that would add some 90 million children, most of them girls, to the total. So, while it is impossible to cite a single authoritative figure, it is clear that the number of child workers worldwide runs into hundreds of millions.

ILO, to better quantify the problem, recently launched experimental surveys in Ghana, India, Indonesia and Senegal, which employed local statisticians to study a sample of about 4,000 households and 200 businesses in each country. The results showed that the average percentage of economically active children aged between 5 and 14 was 25 per cent, and in Senegal it was as high as 40 per cent.

Worldwide, the big picture looks something like this: the vast majority of all child labourers live in Asia, Africa and Latin America. Half of them can be found in Asia alone, although their proportion may be declining in South-East Asia as per capita income increases, basic education spreads and family size decreases. Africa has an average of one in three children working. In Latin America, one child in five works. These proportions have increased partly due to the economic crisis of the 1980s and, in Africa, because of the lack of public investment in education as well as because of armed conflict. In both Africa and Latin America, only a tiny proportion of child workers are involved in the formal sector. The vast majority work for their families, in homes, in the fields and on the streets.

Child labour has increased substantially in Central and Eastern European countries as a result of the abrupt switch from centrally planned to market economies. In industrialized countries, such as the UK and the US, meanwhile, the growth of the service sector and the quest for a more flexible workforce have contributed to an expansion of child labour. Political unrest and HIV/AIDS in African countries have resulted in increased reliance on child labour.

To see behind this big picture, the need for reliable measurements of the prevalence of child labour, according to internationally agreed definitions, is paramount. Governments, NGOs and international institutions need to work together on this massive task.

Above all, we need to know how many children are involved in detrimental work, at the worst end of the continuum. This is the group of children that policies and programmes need to reach most urgently.

Without this clearer information, the true scale of the problem will remain unknown. What has long hidden in the shadows will only emerge into the light, fully and finally, when we can measure it, and thus systematically move to eradicate it.

Most children who work do not have the power of free choice. They are not choosing between career options with varying advantages, drawbacks and levels of pay. A fortunate minority have sufficient material means behind them to be pulled towards work as an attractive option offering them even more economic advantages. But the vast majority are pushed into work that is often damaging to their development by three key factors: the exploitation of poverty; the absence of education; and the restrictions of tradition.

The most powerful force driving children into hazardous, debilitating labour is the exploitation of poverty. Where society is characterized by poverty and inequity, the incidence of child labour is likely to increase, as does the risk that it is exploitative.

For poor families, the small contribution of a child's income or assistance at home that allows the parents to work can make the difference between hunger and a bare sufficiency. Survey after survey makes this clear. A high proportion of child employees give their entire wages to their parents. Children's work is considered essential to maintaining the economic level of the household. A review of nine Latin American countries has shown that without the income of working children aged 13-17, the incidence of poverty would rise by between 10 and 20 per cent.

If employers were not prepared to exploit children there would be no child labour. The parents of child labourers are often unemployed or underemployed, desperate for secure employment and income. Yet it is not they but their children who are offered the jobs. Why? Because children can be paid less, of course. (In Latin America, for example, children aged 13-17 earn on average half the pay of a wage earning adult with 7 years of education.) Because children are more malleable: they will do what they will do what they are told without questioning authority. Because children are more powerless: they are less likely to organize against oppression and can be physically abused without striking back.

Put simply, children are employed because they are easier to exploit. Many employers, if challenged, will plead their own relative poverty and their need to pay the lowest wages in order to compete and survive. Others are more unashamed about their role, seeing the exploitation of children's work as a natural and necessary part of the existing social order. Owners of bonded labourers quoted by an Indian researcher, for example, believed that low-caste children should work rather than go to school. " Once they are allowed to come up to an equal level, nobody will go to the fields. Fields will be left uncultivated everywhere. We have to keep them under our strong thumb in order to get work done."

Exploitation of the poor and the powerless not only means that adults are denied jobs that could better have sustained their families. It not only means that children are required to work in arduous, dangerous conditions. It also means a life of unskilled work and ignorance not only for the child but often for the children of generations to come. Any small, short-term financial gain for the family is at the cost of an incalculable long-term loss. Poverty begets child labour begets lack of education begets child labour begets lack of education begets poverty. Yet, poverty is not an eternal verity. It is sustained or diminished by political and economic policies and opportunities. Unfortunately, both national and international economic developments in recent decades have served to increase inequality and poverty.

The 1980s marked a serious downturn in the fortunes of many developing countries, as government indebtedness, unwise internal economic polices and recession resulted in economic crisis. The World Bank and the International Monetary Fund (IMF) responded by imposing on indebted nations, in return for loan guarantees, a package of policy prescriptions known as structural adjustment programmes. These sweeping economic reforms aimed to orient countries towards the needs of the global economy, promoting export crops and offering incentives to foreign investors while at the same time slashing government expenditure. All too often, the cuts in expenditure fell on health and education, on food subsidies and on social services, all needed most by the poor.

Firsthand experience in most countries shows that the real cost of adjustment is being paid disproportionately by the poor and by their children. It is also being paid by increasing numbers of child labourers. In Zimbabwe, for example, both government and ILO reports have linked the explosion of child labour directly to the impact of the country's structural adjustment programme.

Gradually, structural adjustment programmes have been modified in an attempt to mitigate their effects on the vulnerable. In new agreements being concluded between governments and the international financial institutions, public expenditure on primary education and other basic social services is increasingly being protected from budget cuts. But most developing countries are still living with the policies of the recent past: unmodified adjustment packages still impact heavily on their poorest citizens. And it is in this state that they must now face the implications of the worldwide scramble for competitiveness associated with 'globalization'.

And many still concentrate scarce resources on military rather than social priorities. Sub-Saharan Africa now spends around $8 billion annually on the military, despite the fact that 216 million people in the region live in poverty. Similarly, South Asia—with 562 million in poverty—spent $14 billion on the military in 1994.

A serious attack on poverty will reduce the number of children vulnerable to exploitation at work. Social safety nets are essential for the poor, as are access to credit and income generating schemes, technology, education and basic health services. Budgetary priorities need to be reexamined and redirected in this light.

Tackling the exploitation itself does not have to wait until some future day when world poverty has been brought to an end. Hazardous child labour provides the most powerful of arguments for equality and social justice. It can and must be abolished here and now. Cuts in social spending have hit education—the most important single step in ending child labour—particularly hard.

In all regions, spending per student for higher education fell during the 1980s, and in Africa and Latin America, spending per pupil also fell for primary education.

A pilot survey, sponsored by the United Nations Educational, Scientific and Cultural Organization (UNESCO) and UNICEF and carried out in 1994 in 14 of the world's least developed countries, reinforced concerns about the actual conditions of primary schools. In half of these countries, classrooms for grade 1 have sitting places for only 4 in 10 pupils. Half the pupils have no textbooks and half the classrooms have no chalkboards. Teachers commonly have to attempt to handle huge classes—and average of 67 pupils per teacher in Bangladesh and nearly 90 per teacher in Equatorial Guinea. In 10 of the 14 countries, most children are taught in a language not spoken at home. And most homes, of course, have no books or magazines in any language.

Education is clearly underfunded, but the school system as it stands in most developing countries is blighted by more than just a lack of resources. It is too often rigid and uninspiring in approach, promoting a curriculum that is irrelevant to and remote from children's lives.

The quality of teaching is frequently abysmal and the discipline violent, as 11-year-old Sudhir from Kone in India can testify: "In school, teachers would not teach well. If we ask them to teach us alphabets, they would beat us. They would sleep in the class. If we asked them about a small doubt, they would beat us and send us out. Even if we did not understand, they would not teach us. So I dropped out of school."

Sudhir's decision to drop out of school is hardly surprising. And that decision—often made by parents—is mirrored worldwide. Overall, 30 per cent of children in developing countries who enrol in primary school do not complete it. The figure rises to 60 per cent in some countries. In Latin America, enrolment in school is comparatively high, yet only half those who enter school finish it, broadly the same proportion as in Africa with its much lower levels of enrolment. Even Brazil, one of the richest countries in the region, has a primary school completion rate of only 40 per cent.

Education has become part of the problem. It has to be reborn as part of the solution.

Traditional expectations

The economic forces that propel children into hazardous work may be the most powerful of all. But traditions and entrenched social patterns play a part, too. In industrialized countries, it is now almost universally accepted that id children are to develop normally and healthily, then they must not perform disabling work. In theory at least, education, play and leisure, friends, good health and proper rest must all have an important place in their lives.

This idea emerged only relatively recently. In the early decades of industrialization, work was thought to be the most effective way of teaching children about life and the world. Some residue of this notion remains in the widespread expectation that teenage children should take on casual jobs alongside school, both to gain an understanding of the way the world functions and to earn spending money of their own.

There is a darker side to the expectations about children's work. The harder and more they are likely to be considered traditionally the province of the poor and disadvantaged, the lower classes and ethnic minorities. In India, for example, the view has been that some people are born to rule and to work with their minds while others, the vast majority, are born to work with their bodies. Many traditionalists have been unperturbed about lower caste children failing to enrol in or dropping out of school. And if those children end up doing hazardous labour, it is likely to be seen as their lot in life.

The rigidity of the caste system in India only dramatizes what is true in most of the world, including the West. The dominant cultural group may not wish its own children to do hazardous labour, but it will not be so concerned if young people from racial, ethnic or economic minorities do it. In northern Europe, for example, child labourers are likely to be African or Turkish. In the US, they are Asian or Latin American; in Canada, they are Asian. In Brazil, they tend to be the descendants of slaves or the children of indigenous people with no political clout. In Argentina, many are Bolivian and Paraguayan. In Thailand's fishing industry, many are from Myanmar. And as traditional forces push children into work in many parts of the world, the situation is worsened by the growing culture of consumerism.

Understanding all the various cultural factors that lead children into work is essential. But deference to tradition is often cited as a reason for not acting against intolerable forms of child labour. Children have an absolute, unnegotiable right to freedom from hazardous child labour—a right now established in international law and accepted by every country that has ratified the Convention on the Rights of the Child. Respect for diverse cultures should not deflect us from using all the means at our disposal to make every society, every economy, every corporation, regard the exploitation of children as unthinkable.

The shapes of child labour

The many manifestations of child labour can be broken down into seven main types, none of which are unique to any one region of the world. These are domestic service, forced and bonded labour, commercial sexual exploitation, industrial and plantation work, street work, work for the family and girls' work.

Child domestic workers are the world's most forgotten children, which is why it is worth considering their plight before that of other, more familiar groups of child workers. Although domestic service need not be hazardous, most of the time it is just that. Children in domestic servitude may well be the most vulnerable and exploited children of all, as well as the most difficult to protect. They are often extremely poorly paid or not paid at all; their terms and conditions are very often entirely at the whim of the employers and take no account of their legal rights; they are deprived of schooling, play and social activity, and of emotional support from family and friends. They are vulnerable to physical and sexual abuse. What more miserable situation could there be for a child—sometimes as young as age five — than to experience such conditions among often hostile strangers?

Consider, for example, a day in the life of seven-year-old Marie, from Haiti. She is a restavek—Creole for rester avec—the local term for a type of child domestic found all over the world, one who has been handed over by a poor rural family to live with and provide domestic 'help' for a usually urban, wealthier family. She gets up at five in the morning and begins her day by fetching water from a nearby well, balancing the heavy jug on her head as she returns. She prepares breakfast and serves it to the members of the household. Then she walks the family's five-year-old son to school; later, at noon, she brings him home and helps him change clothes.

Next, she helps prepare and serve the family's lunch before returning the boy to school. In between meal times she must buy food in the market and urn errands, tend the charcoal fire, sweep the yard, wash clothes and dishes, clean the kitchen and—at least once a day—wash her female boss's feet. She is not allowed to bathe in the water she brings to the household. She is regularly beaten with a leather strap if she is slow to respond to a request or is considered disrespectful. Needless to say, she is not allowed to attend school.

The very nature of domestic work means that those doing it are shut away from the eyes of the world, unprotected from abuse. As we have seen, this isolation also makes it difficult to establish reliable estimates of the number of children involved. Some idea of the scale of the problem can, however, be gleaned from local surveys.

A survey of middle-income households in Colombo (Sri Lanka) showed that one in three had a child under 14 years of age as a domestic worker. A study of a lower-middle-class residential area in Nairobi (Kenya) found that 20 per cent of households employed children in 1982, though by 1991 this had dropped to 12 per cent, perhaps due to falling living standards. A survey of domestic workers in Uruguay found that 34 per cent had begun working before they were 14. A survey in India, noting that 17 per cent of domestic workers were under 15 years old, reported that girls aged 12 to 15 were the preferred choice of 90 per cent of employing households. Children are often preferred to adults precisely because they can be dominated more easily and, of course, paid less.

The impact of a life like Marie's on a child's development is profound. An obvious negative is poor nutrition, since it is rare that child domestics share equally in the family meals. A Peruvian girl says: "They would give us two rolls to eat with tea. After that I used to go to bed. Meanwhile they were eating buttered toast, coffee with milk, steak, and on top of that, grapes, pears, apples and peaches." The evidence is not just anecdotal: a study of 15-year-old restaveks in Haiti compared them with other local children and found them on average 4 centimetres shorter and 18 kilograms lighter.

Sexual abuse is often regarded by the employer as part of the employment terms. Jeanne, a 15-year-old working in Cotonou (Benin), has the normal heavy workload, is unpaid and is beaten when her employers are dissatisfied with her work. But her greatest problem is the family's 23-year-old son, who rapes her regularly. If she resists, he creates situations that lead to her being beaten.

Even when not sexually abused, child domestics can suffer severe damage in terms of their psychological and social development. They are very often cut off from the community, denied rest and play. In Lima (Peru), a survey estimated that nearly a third of domestic workers never leave the home where they work. Haitian psychologists who have worked with restaveks describe conditions of depression, passivity, sleep and eating disorders, as well as chronic fear and anxiety. Among the most common adjectives used to describe child domestic workers are 'timid' and 'listless'. Childhood has been stolen from these children.

Research in this field is still in its infancy. But to promote it, early in 1996 Anti-Slavery International organized a seminar at Charney Manor, Oxfordshire (UK) for NGOs and institutes that have investigated the situation of children in domestic service. Supported financially by ILO-IPEC and by UNICEF, participants came from Bangladesh and Nepal in South Asia, Indonesia and the Philippines in South-East Asia, Kenya in East Africa, Senegal and Togo in West Africa, Haiti in the Caribbean and Guatemala in Central America—eloquent testimony to the extent of the problem. Several major common themes emerged:

"There is no problem." In virtually all countries where children carry the burdens of household work, society does not regard it as a reprehensible practice. Even some of the activists at the seminar were not convinced that the practice itself—as opposed to its most exploitative forms—was damaging. Access to children working in homes is very difficult. Several researchers reported obstruction from employers. Even where access was obtained, it was difficult to conduct meaningful interviews with children when employers insisted on remaining present.

The need for accurate estimates of the numbers of child domestics and the conditions under which they work was emphasized. Information about how many suffer physical or emotional damage, and to what degree, is even more hidden behind closed doors.

Accurate information can be put to good use. In Kenya, for example, evidence of psychological and emotional damage has helped convince parents and society at large that the problem must be tackled. Both there and in Senegal, community drama projects have raised awareness, particularly in the rural areas likely to be the source of future domestic workers. A different approach has been taken in Sri Lanka, where the Government has targeted employers with large newspaper advertisements stressing that employing child domestics is illegal.

Many of the forms of child labour practised around the would are 'forced' in the sense that children are taught to accept the conditions of their lives and not to challenge them. But the situation of some children goes far beyond the acceptance of poor conditions. They find themselves in effective slavery. In South Asia, this has taken on a quasi-institutional form known as 'bonded' child labour. Under this system, children, often only eight or nine years old, are pledged by their parents to factory owners or their agents in exchange for small loans. Their lifelong servitude never succeeds in even reducing the debt.

In India, this type of transaction is widespread in agriculture, as well as in industries such as cigarette-rolling, carpet-making, matchstick-making, slate and silk. The most notorious of these is the carpet industry of Mirzapur-Bhadohi-Varanasi in Uttar Pradesh. According to a recent study, the thousands of children in the carpet industry are "kidnapped or lured away or pledged by their parents for paltry sums of money. Most of them are kept in captivity, tortured and made to work for 20 hours a day without a break. Little children are made to crouch on their toes, from dawn to dusk every day, severely stunting their growth during formative years. Social activists in the area find it hard to work because of the strong mafia-like control that the carpet loom owners have on the area."

Of course, most worst-exploited children belong to

the most marginalized segments of society. As in other countries, these ethnic minorities and disadvantaged groups are routinely seen as having no rights whatsoever. Often they themselves have come to believe that they deserve no rights.

This kind of virtual child slavery is usually associated only with India, Nepal and Pakistan. But it exists in other parts of the world, too. In Brazil, for example, forced labour is found from the charcoal-burning projects of Minas Gerais and Bahia to the sugarcane estates of Espiritu Santo and the norh-east. While most such labour is performed by adults, children are inevitably involved also. In 1993, a British Member of Parliament reported having seen children working to cool down charcoal kilns with mud in Acailandia. Also in 1993, children as young as four were said to be at work in the cotton harvest in Parana. In Mauritania, thousands of children are still born each year into effective slavery. A tradition for generations, servitude was officially outlawed in 1980, but 400,000 black Africans serve as slaves, either formally or informally, to their Berber masters. Another example is in Myanmar, where hundreds of thousands of people, including children, work on construction projects aimed at fostering tourism and economic expansion, often in appalling conditions.

Governments of countries where forced child labour exists must redouble their efforts to stamp out the practice and challenge the vested interests that so immorally maintain and benefit from it.

The underground nature of the multi-billion-dollar illegal industry in the commercial sexual exploitation of children makes it difficult to gather reliable data. But NGOs in the field estimate that each year at least 1 million girls worldwide are lured or forced into this form of hazardous labour, which can verge on slavery,. Boys are also often exploited.

When scandals about child prostitution in developing countries break in the international media, it is usually a story about the phenomenon called sex tourism in which holiday-makers from the rich world, mainly, though not exclusively, men, travel to locations such as Brazil, the Dominican Republic, Thailand and elsewhere in search of sex with children.

But we should not lose sight of the fact that many thousands of young girls in numerous countries serve the sexual appetites of local men from all social and economic backgrounds. And widespread child prostitution exists in industrialized countries. In the US alone, at least 100,000 children are believed to be involved.

Direct links between the commercial sexual exploitation of children and other forms of exploitative labour are numerous. Notorious in their own right for appalling working conditions, Nepalese carpet factories, where 50 per cent of the workers are estimated to be children, are common sites of sexual exploitation by employers as well as recruitment centres for Indian brothels. Children are especially powerless to refuse abuse by employers, either as perpetrators or intermediaries.

Village loan-sharks often act as procurers for city brothels, lending money to the family that the daughter's work must pay off. However it happens, almost all such children are betrayed by those they trust and may end up trafficked long distances and across borders. Rescue and rehabilitation is complicated for children. They often end up being prosecuted by the very legal system that should be protecting them. Even if they make it home, perhaps having been deported as illegal immigrants, they may face stigma and rejection by their families and communities. Shunned, ignored and invisible, they often have little choice but to return to the brothel or the streets.

The physical and psychosocial damage inflicted by commercial sexual exploitation kames it one of the most hazardous forms of child labour. No matter how high the wages or how few the hours, the children involved have to confront serious health risks every day, including respiratory diseases, HIV and sexually transmitted diseases, unwanted pregnancies and drug addiction. But they are also plunged into a distorted reality in which violence and distrust, shame and rejection are the norms. "We have the same place that bums do in society," said a 15-year-old Senegalese girl exploited through prostitution. "No one wants to know us or be seen with us."

It is crucial that the international public should understand the layers of complicity that envelop this area of child exploitation. Although it is always easier and more comfortable to blame the exploiting 'pimps' or 'perverts' or even the victims themselves, no social sector can escape responsibility for the commercial sexual exploitation of children. Families—entrusted with the care, nurture and development of children—may be complicit in allowing the child's sexual exploitation. Research has consistently indicated that child abuse and incest are common precursors of the commercial sexual exploitation of children. Then, in addition to the people who actually buy sex, there are the traffickers, agents and intermediaries who profit from the sale of children. There are the professional criminals and syndicates that run brothels. There are the entrepreneurs who organize sex tours or who produce tourist brochures encouraging the notion that young girls or boys are sexually available. And there are all the people, including corrupt or apathetic officials, who look the other way.

Beyond even these actors are more elusive and impersonal influences that contribute to the child sex trade, such as a deeply rooted gender discrimination that blunts the perception of violence committed against girls. Global market forces have also contributed to the problem by widening the gap between rich and poor—encouraging migration, destabilizing families, destroying support systems and safety nets. Conflicts and wars, dozens of which are occurring around the world, also create conditions in which children are sexually exploited.

The problem is out in the open now, after decades of what has amounted to a cross-cultural conspiracy of silence. The World Congress against Commercial Sexual Exploitation of Children, held in Sweden in August 1996, put the issue on the world's agenda for the first time. The Agenda for Action agreed upon by participants will guide governments in developing programmes to address the problem.

Industrial and plantation work

"Children work on all types of jobs, such as carrying molten loams of glass stuck on the tips of iron rods, which are just two feet away from their bodies; drawing molten glass from tank furnaces in which the temperature is between 1,500 and 1,800 degrees centigrade and the arm is almost touching the furnace because the arm of a child is so small; joining and annealing the glass bangles where the work is done over a small kerosene flame in a room with little or no ventilation because a whiff of air can blow out the flame. The whole factory floor is strewn with broken glass and the children run to and fro carrying this burning hot glass with no shoes to protect their feet. Naked electric wires are to be seen dangling everywhere because the factory owners could not be bothered to install insulated internal wiring." This is a description of the glass-bangle industry in Firozabad (India), in which one quarter of the workforce—around 50,000—are children under 14.

All over the world, children work in hazardous conditions. The industries are manifold, from leather-working in the Naples region of Italy to the pre-industrial brick-making of Colombia and Peru, which can involve children as young eight.

Children are sometimes exploited in mining operations that would be considered too risky for adults in the industrialized world—for example, in the diamond and gold mines of Cote d'Ivoire and South Africa, and in Colombian coal mines. Typically, the children work with the barest minimum of safety equipment and constantly breathe in coal dust.

The respiratory problems faced by child miners are also common in other industries. Many suffer from tuberculosis, bronchitis and asthma. Children working in earthenware and porcelain factories, for example, are often unprotected from the silica dust. In the lock industry, they inhale noxious fumes given off by dangerous chemicals. In the brassware industry, children work at high-temperature furnaces and inhale the dust produced in polishing. The numbers of children exploited by plantation agriculture across the world may be just as great — and the dangers associated with much of their work are no less appalling. In Brazil's sugar plantations, for example, children cut cane with machetes, a punishing task putting them at constant risk of mutilation. They make up a third of the workforce in some areas and are involved in over 40 per cent of the work-related accidents. Brazilian children are also exposed to snakebites and insect stings on tobacco plantations, and carry loads for beyond their capacities, In Colombia, young people who work on flower-export farms are exposed to pesticides banned in industrialized countries.

In Africa, meanwhile, children work on the plantations that grow the export crops on which the continent's economies rely— from the cocoa and coffee and sisal plantations of Tanzania. In Zimbabwe, children work a 60-hour week picking cotton or coffee for about $1. An ILO study on child labour in Zimbabwe found that the most significant exploiters of child labour seemed to be the large scale commercial farmers who have used children in their fields for decades, especially during planting and harvesting. These commercial farmers campaigned against the Government's draft child labour regulations in 1995, on the grounds that they would interfere with children's right to work. The same year, farmers asked a District Education Officer to close down the schools to allow children to help bring in the tea and coffee crops. The request, which was reported in the local press, was turned down.

In Indonesia, children—most of them girls—work on tobacco plantations for $0.60 a day, well below the legal minimum wage. In Nepal, children work on tea estates for wages so low that they often need to work 14 hours a day. Children are also employed on the tea plantations of Bangladesh, India and Sri Lanka, while child labourers in the sugarcane and rubber plantations of Thailand are at constant risk of injury from dangerous equipment.

While much of this industrial and plantation work is carried out by national subcontractors, some of it is overseen by transactional corporations whose products find their way into the ordinary stores and homes of the West. The maquiladoras (assembly plants) of Central America and Mexico are a case in point. Large corporations based in rich countries have transferred their assembly functions to poorer countries to take advantage of their lower wage and benefit costs. In a much publicized case in Honduras, for example, 12- and 13-year-old girls working for a US-based transnational were locked inside a textile factory. Hours were long, wages pitiable, the temperature hit 100 degrees Fahrenheit and there was no safe drinking water.

Such cases have led activists both in the home and the host countries of these transnationals to pressure them to establish codes of conduct not only for their operations but also for those of the subcontractors they use. All corporations should adopt such codes of conduct as an essential step towards eliminating hazardous child labour.

But most child labour in the formal economy cannot be tied so directly to the operation of transnationals. This is why national as well as transnational companies need to adopt codes of conduct that bar hazardous child labour.

Street work

In contrast with child domestic workers, some children work in the most visible places possible—on the streets of developing world cities and towns. They are everywhere: hawking in markets and darting in and out of traffic jams, plying their trade at bus and train stations, in front of hotels and shopping malls. They share the streets with millions of adults, many of whom regard them as nuisances, if not as dangerous minicriminals. What most of these children actually do on the streets is, of course, work.

The street is a cruel and hazardous workplace, often jeopardizing even children's lives. They can be murdered by organize crime, by other young people or even by the police. The world reacted in horror in 1993 when Rio de Janeiro police officers massacred six street children. In

1996, a Rio police officer confessed and became the first-ever police officer to be convicted of the murder of street children. But the killings of street youth had already started in Rio by 1990. A report from the state juvenile court stated that, on average, three street children are killed every day in Rio, many by police at the request of merchants who consider the begging, thieving and glue-sniffing a major nuisance.

Many children do pursue these activities. But many more struggle at legitimate work on the street for their own or their family's survival. Children who work on the streets often come from slums and squatter settlements, where poverty and pre-carious family situations are common, where schools are overcrowded and poor, and where safe places to play simply do not exist. Their numbers have increased in places experiencing armed conflict, like Freetown (Sierra Leone) and Monrovia (Liberia), as caretakers have been killed, the economy disrupted and family and community ties severed.

Street child labour, virtually unheard of prior to the transition to a market economy, is now a growing problem in the Russian Federation. In Kyrgyzstan, in Central Asia, the numbers of children working on the streets, selling food and other products, have increased dramatically over the last three years. Many have dropped out of school or never attended classes. On the streets, they shine shoes, wash and guard cars, carry luggage, hawk flowers and trinkets, collect recyclables and find a myriad other ingenious ways to make money. The amount they earn may be small but is sometimes more than they would receive from formal-sector work.

The large majority of these children return home each night. They are children on the streets, not of them. Still, life is often precarious and violent, unhealthy and unfair. Some are able to combine some schooling with their street work, bit nevertheless many are exploited and cheated by adults and peers and must spend many hours earning their survival. Many suffer from malnutrition and from illnesses including tuberculoses. Self-esteem is often low, despite the superficial air of exaggerated self-confidence they may assume to appear street-smart.

For about 1 in 10, the street does become home. Inevitably these children become more prone to engage in marginal and illegal work, such as begging and petty thieving. Many are led into the illicit, thrilling and dangerous world of crime syndicates that run rings for pickpocketing, burglary, drug trafficking and prostitution. The subculture that envelops the lives of these children is marked by aggression and abuse, exposing them to extreme hazards.

Scavenging is one example of the extreme risks children face in street work. In cities across the developing world, young children spend their days picking up used paper, plastics, rags, bottles, tin and metal pieces from the street, garbage dumps and waste bins, and selling them to retailers for recycling. "The nature of their work is... most unhygienic, dangerous, demeaning... They develop several kinds of skin disease like ulcers, scabies, etc. While collecting rusted iron pieces, they usually receive cuts on their hands and become susceptible to tetanus. The broken glass lying hidden in the garbage may injure their bare feet, which may develop into festering wounds. Many other sicknesses arise from exposure to extreme weather conditions, like cases of sunstroke, pneumonia, influenza and malaria. Carrying heavy loads under the arms or on their back adversely affects the height, weight, strength and stamina. Added to these hazards is the lure of eating thrown away or leftover food... [leading] to digestive disorders and food poisoning."

Attempts are being made in many countries to wean children off the streets and to protect them while they are on the streets. One inspiring example of action is in Brazil, long a country identified with the 'problem' of street children. The National Children's Movement—a partnership between the children and voluntary 'educators', themselves from poor backgrounds—was established in 1985, and its first meeting in 1986 caused a national sensation, helping to enshrine child rights in the fledgling democracy. Each of its national congresses—the fourth was held in 1995—has heralded a new advance in thinking about children's problems. Just as important, the Movement bases its organization on small groups (nucleos de base) of working children who meet to discuss common problems and to take joint action. This model of organization seeds to empower children. "What would I do if there was no nucleo de base?" and 11-year-old delegate to a reporter. "I would go right out and start one."

Work for the family

Of all the work children do, the most common is agricultural or domestic work within their own families. Most families around the world expect their children to help in the household, whether preparing food, fetching water or groceries, herding animals, caring for younger siblings or more arduous work in the fields. This kind of work can be beneficial. Children learn from a reasonable level of participation in household chores, subsistence food-growing and income generating activities. They also derive a sense of self-worth from their work within their families.

But it is by no means always beneficial. On the contrary, work for the family many demand too much of children, requiring them to labour long hours that keep them from school and take too great a toll on their developing bodies. Such work can prevent children from exercising their rights and developing to their full potential.

One powerful testimony to the rigours of work in the rural home comes from a group of Nepalese children now working in a Kathmandu carpet factory. They were attracted by stories of the excitement of the city and by the idea of earning wages both for themselves and to send back to their parents. But most of all, they said, they had come to the factory because life at home was so difficult: climbing up seep slopes to get fodder, risking leeches; having to labour endlessly to feed the family. To avoid these lives, they had ended up in carpet-making, an industry notorious for its exploitation. In rural Africa and in South Asia, children begin helping with domestic chores well before school age. Girls must fetch the household's water and fuelwood. Children of both sexes help with farm work, looking after animals and performing all tasks to do with water, jobs often physically taxing in the extreme. They also work in the informal sector of the rural economy, including traditional crafts and small trades essential to village life, especially shopkeeping.

Similar patterns of early labour are reported in a survey of five Latin American countries. In rural Colombia, for instance, one in four children aged 6 to 9 and one in three aged 10 and 11 work, either in the home, tending the family vegetable garden, caring for animals, or helping in a grocery store or small business. In the country's large cities, one in six of 10-and 11-year-old children and one in ten of 6- to 9-year-olds participate in the labour market in some way.

Much of this work, particularly by girls within their homes, is invisible to the statistician aiming to measure the scale of child labour. It is also excluded from child labour legislation, partly because of the difficulty of policing child labour within the family. Yet to accept that such work cannot be regulated is to accept that hundreds of millions of children can have no legal protection.

Legislation must be made more inclusive, but this will not of itself protect these children. The difficulties of enforcement will remain. But at the very least it will spread the message that there are strict limits as to what can be expected of a child's labour in the home. It may also make affirmative action more possible, and open social discussions involving parents and community members on what is considered to be good for a child.

"Nearly all our girls work as sweepers," says a mother from India, herself a sweeper or latrine-cleaner. "Why should I waste my time and money on sending my daughter to school where she will learn nothing of use?... So why not put my girl to work so that she will learn something about our profession? My elder girl who is 15 years old will be married soon. Her mother-in-law well put her to cleaning latrines somewhere. Too much schooling will only give girls big ideas, and then they will be beaten up by their husbands or abused by their in-laws."

Most of the hazards faced by boy labourers are faced by girls, too. Yet girls have extra problems of their own: from the sexual pressures of employers to exclusion from the sexual pressures of employers to exclusion from education. No strategy to combat child labour can begin to be successful unless these special dangers facing girls are systematically taken into account.

In virtually every area of life and in every country, as these annual State of the World's Children reports have long noted, girls and women routinely bear burdens and endure treatment that reflect their unequal status. So it is with child labour. Working girls are often invisible, treated as if they did not exist.

According to ILO, 56 per cent of the 10- to 14-year-olds currently estimated to be working in the developing world are boys. Yet, if we were able to measure the numbers of girls doing unregistered work as domestic help, or working at home to enable other family members to take up paid employment, the figures would show more female child labourers than male. Girls also work longer hours on average than boys, carrying a double workload — a job outside the home and domestic duties on their return.

In Guatemala, working girls spend an average of 21 hours a week on household duties on top of a 40-hour working week outside. And in five Latin American countries surveyed, domestic work by girls in their own home was widespread, with many failing to attend school.

All over the world, more girls than boys are denied their fundamental right to primary schooling. In some regions, including the Middle East and North Africa, sub-Saharan Africa and especially South Asia, the gender gap is still enormous. Educational equality between the sexes is being approached in East Asia and Latin America and the Caribbean, nut elsewhere little progress has been recorded.

Gender bias is not simply a question of attitudes—it is enshrined in all the main institutions of society. Nepal illustrates the point only too well. Women's socio-economic status is often deplorable. And while the proportion of men who can read and write—37 per cent—is extremely low, the 11 per cent figure for female literacy is appalling. The overwhelming majority of girls either have never gone to school or have dropped out to work. Discrimination soon becomes exploitation. Lack of education, early arranged marriages, stark poverty and lack of power make girls enormously vulnerable. Long before they are physically prepared for it, many are forced to work, most of them ending up, if not in domestic service then in the carpet industry, on tea estates or in brick-making.

The gender gap becomes a vicious circle for girls all over the developing world. Unable to attend school because of their low social status or their domestic responsibilities, they are denied the extra power and wider horizons that education would bring. If they seek work outside the home, their opportunities are limited to the most menial tasks. Their low status is reinforced and passed on to the next generation.

Both the individual and the society suffer. It is well established that the more schooling a girl has, the fewer children she will bear. The more children a poor family has, the more child workers there will be.

5

Food and Nutrition

The Food and Nutrition Board (FNB) established in 1964 in the Department of Food in the then Ministry of Agriculture, was transferred to the Department of Women and Child Development on Ist April, 1993 in pursuance of the National Nutrition Policy adopted by the Government. The infrastructure of FNB is comprised of a technical wing at the Centre, four Regional Offices at Delhi, Mumbai, Calcutta and Chennai and 43 Community Food and Nutrition Extension Units (CFNEUs) located in 27 States/Union Territories.

The programmes of FNB aim at creating nutritional awareness and promoting nutrition of the people through various projects in the field of nutrition and food technology. The programmes have been reoriented from time to time to meet the challenge of changing nutritional scenario. Some of the regular programmes and new initiatives taken by FNB are as under :

Regular programmes

— Nutrition education and orientation

— Training in home-scale preservation of fruits and vegetables

— Development of educational and training material

- Mass awareness campaigns
- Development and promotion of nutritious foods
- Monitoring of supplementary feeding at Anganwadis
- Fortification of foods
- Food analysis and standardisation
- Research and development

New initiatives

- Implementation of National Nutrition Policy, National Plan of Action on Nutrition
- Micronutrient Malnutrition Control Activities District Nutrition Profiles
- Nutrition Surveillance System
- Strategy for Reducing Child Malnutrition
- Creation of nutritional awareness at various levels

Nutrition Education and Orientation

Creating nutritional awareness at all levels is one of the prime pre-requisites for nutrition promotion in the present age.

Nutrition education of the community in rural, urban and tribal areas through the field infrastructure of FNB comprising 43 CFNEUs is one of the primary activities of FNB. Each CFNEU is equipped with a mobile van, audiovisual equipments and aids, and manned by technically trained personnel. It organises live demonstrations supported by lecture-cum-discussion, film/slide/video shows and exhibitions on various aspects of food, nutrition and health. The demonstration programmes are planned in advance in collaboration with the concerned agencies of the State Government, educational institutions and non -governmental organisations.

During the period April to December, 1998 CFNEUs organised 10,068 Nutrition Demonstration Programmes, 7,821 of which were in rural areas and 4,347 for SC/ST community. About 3.5,4 lakh people, comprising mainly of women, benefited from these programmes, 47.53 percentage (1.68 lakhs) of which belonged to SC/ST community.

CFNEUs also provided nutrition education support to concerned sectors of the Government implementing developmental programmes. Nutrition orientation of grass root level functionaries and their supervisors is undertaken by organising Integrated Nutrition

Education Camps (INECs) and Orientation Training Courses (OTCs) with a view to utilise the existing infrastructure of the Government for imparting basic nutrition messages to the community. Five day INECs are organised by CFNEUs for grass root level workers namely Anganwadi Workers, multipurpose health workers, ANMs, health educators, adult education supervisors, mahila mandal adhyakshas (NGOs), gram sevikas etc., in the field. Five day OTCs for training supervisors and trainers of grass root level functionaries namely CDPOs, ACDPOs, supervisors, instructors, health trainers, adult education instructors, trainers from voluntary organisations etc., are organised at the state level training institutes, home science colleges etc. Intensive practical education on various aspects of food, nutrition, health and hygiene is provided through these programmes. An exhibition with the help of panels, posters and live display is also organised in each of these programmes to highlight the nutritional needs of infants, pre-school children and other vulnerable groups. 72 INECs/OTCs have been organised during the year upto December, 1998.

Networking with NGOs for nutrition education

activities initiated in 1992-93 with a view to expand the coverage under nutrition education activities has been temporarily discontinued with effect from 1st April, 1998 for want of its formal inclusion in the scheme of Integrated Nutrition Education. 30 NGOs were provided modest financial and technical support for organising nutrition demonstration programmes and exhibitions upto 1997-98.

Training in Home Scale Preservation of Fruits and Vegetables

The CFNEUs impart education and training in home-scale preservation of fruits and vegetables to housewives and adolescent girls with a view to promote preservation and consumption of fruits and vegetables which provide much needed micronutrients, as well as to provide necessary skills which could be useful for income generation purposes. Two training courses of two week duration are organised per month by 33 CFNEUs, out of 43, having processing facilities. 24 such courses are organised exclusively for tribal-adolescent girls and women by four CFNEUs every year. Processing facilities for fruits and vegetables are offered to the community on payment of nominal charges. Nutrition component is also added in these training courses and preparation of nutritious recipes including instant infant foods from roasted cereals, pulses and oil seeds suitable for infants and young children are also taught during the training.

638 training courses benefiting 18,762 women / adolescent girls have been organised upto December, 1998, the number of SC/ST trainees being 4,052. 17 courses have been organised for tribal adolescent girls and women benefiting 503 trainees. The community prepared 208MTs of fruit and vegetable products at the units for their domestic consumption during the period April to December, 1998.

Development of Educational/Training Material

Development of educational and training material including both the print and the electronic software is an important activity of the board. Folders, posters and booklets developed and produced by FNB are distributed to the concerned field agencies and public during the nutrition education programmes. Video films and spots developed and produced in regional languages are provided to Regional Kendras of Doordarshan for telecast and are also shown by the CFNEUs during nutrition education programmes. Considering the vast outreach of radio, this medium of communication has also been well utilised by FNB for creating mass awareness in nutrition.

Two Video Films of about 10-15, minutes duration titled 'Poshan Bagiya' (Nutrition Garden) and 'Turant Shishu Ahaar' (Instant Infant Food) and two video spots on 'Value of Colostrum' and 'Improving Iron Intake' produced during last year in four languages were dubbed in eight more languages for use by CFNEUs during their field programmes. Three radio spots of 30 seconds duration on Nutrition, Health and Sanitation produced in Hindi and broadcast during the National Nutrition Week, 1997 were translated in regional languages and broadcast during the year.

A Radio Sponsored programme on 'Poshan Aur Swasthya' (Nutrition and Health) comprising 28 episodes on various aspects of nutrition broadcast during the years 1997 and 1998 through 30 CBS Stations in 12 regional languages evoked a very good response from the public. Encouraged by this response and recognising the importance of disseminating nutrition messages to the public, the radio sponsored programme with 30 episodes on various aspects of food, nutrition and health is being taken up in a new format during the current year.

A bilingual Desk Calendar on Nutritional Anaemia for the period April, 1998 to March, 1999 was produced and widely distributed to Centre and State Governments, CGHS Dispensaries, health centres, schools etc. for creating mass awareness.

A Wall Calendar with messages on nutrition for promoting healthy eating practices has been developed for the period April 1999 to March 2000.

A Wall Hanger titled 'Pregnant Women Need More Nutrition and Care' and a chart titled 'Guidelines on Infant Feeding' were produced in Hindi, English and regional languages and distributed to Directorates of ICDS, MLTCs, AWTCs, NIPCCD and its regional units, exhibition units of DAVP, FNB infrastructure, NGOs, field units of Directorate of Field Publicity and Department of Family Welfare during the year for preventing onset of malnutrition.

Two Posters titled 'Nursing Mothers Need to Eat More' and 'Give Foods from Family Pot to the Infants' have been developed for production in Hindi and English for promoting nutrition of lactating mothers and sound complementary feeding practices.

Mass awareness campaigns

Nation-wide celebration of important events like National Nutrition Week, involving all like minded agencies ' Doordarshan, AIR, leading newspapers, participating in prestigious melas/exhibitions and organising exhibitions, film and slide shows during nutrition education programmes, giving programmes on T.V. and AIR and arranging press coverage of integrated nutrition education programmes for wider coverage are some of the important strategies adopted for creating nutritional awareness among the masses.

National nutrition week

The XVII National Nutrition Week was celebrated throughout the country from 1-7 September, 1998 on the theme of 'Nutrition Promotion : Role of Family and Community" enlisting support from Department of Rural Development, State Governments ' educational institutes and NGOs. The Chief Secretaries of all the states, State Secretaries in-charge of Women and Child Development and Secretaries of 13 concerned sectors of the Government were provided background material on the theme with the request to disseminate the same through their field programmes A half page supplement in prominent newspapers in Hindi, English and regional languages was brought out on the occasion which carried a message from the Hon'ble Minister for Human Resource Development, an article from Secretary (WCD) on 'Nutrition and Family' and some useful messages on Nutrition under 'Do You Know. A message from HRM was telecast on the eve of National Nutrition Week on the national network of Doordarshan at prime time. T.V., radio and press covered various programmes organised by CFNEUs during the week.

The special feature of this year's National Nutrition Week was a workshop on 'Nutrition Promotion : Role of Family and Community' at national level which was organised on 2-3 September, 1998 at Vigyan Bhavan, New Delhi. The programme of the workshop covered vital issues for promoting the nutrition of the people, such as Role of State Government, Need for Nutrition Surveillance, Role of Panchayati Raj Institutions, Communicating Nutrition through programmes of Education Sector, Home Science Institutions, Role of Youth Organisations, Community Mobilisation, Gender equity in family nutrition needs, Food Security, Nutrition Hygiene and Sanitation, and a panel discussion on Role of Family and Community in Women and Child

Development. The workshop was attended by Secretaries /senior officers of concerned sectors, State Secretaries in-charge of Women and Child Development, technical experts from concerned sectors and national institutes, eminent nutrition scientists like the Chancellors of Avinashilingam Deemed University, Coimbatore, and M.S. University, Baroda, representatives of NGOs and international organisations, and media personnel.

Programmes organised by the field units of FNB during the nation-wide celebration of National Nutrition Week included 5 State level workshops, 789 live demonstrations, 182 films and video shows, 90 group discussions, 77 healthy baby shows, 129 competitions and 25 fruit and vegetable preservation training programmes, World Breast Feeding Week

World Breast Feeding Week from 1st to 7th August, 1998 was celebrated on the global theme of Breast Feeding—The Best Investment' throughout the country. Background information and necessary guidance was given to all the field units with a view to facilitate effective organisation of a variety of programmes during the week in collaboration with Breast Feeding Promotion Network of India, State Governments, NGOs and Home Science Colleges. 841 demonstrations, 204 exhibitions, 227 film and slide shows and a number of rallies were organised by the field infrastructure of FNB.

World food day

FNB collaborated actively with the Ministry of Agriculture in organising World Food Day on the theme 'Women Feed the World' on 16th October, 1998. The field units of FNB organised special programmes like seminars, workshops, exhibitions, etc., throughout the country on this specific theme. FNB printed 2 million postcards carrying the message of the World Food Day for creating awareness among people.

Global Iodine Deficiency Disorder (IDD) Day

The Global IDD Day was celebrated on 21st October, 1998 for eliminating iodine deficiency disorders. The field infrastructure of FNB organised special nutrition education programmes on prevention of Iodine Deficiency Disorders on 21st October, 1998, and celebrated this day in collaboration with State Health Departments.

FNB participated in important exhibitions/melas namely Social Development Fair and Perfect Health Mela during the year to reach the message of nutrition to the masses. Live demonstrations, displays and nutrition exhibitions were organised in these melas/fairs. FNB's participation in Perfect Health Mela from 18-27 November 1998 received the best Central Government participation award.

Development and promotion of nutritious foods

FNB has been promoting setting up of nutritious food units through State Governments. Three Ready-to-Eat Extruded Food Units functioning at Hyderabad, Jaipur and Gangtok and four Energy Food Units at Belgaum, Chitradurga, Dodaballapur and Raichur in Karnataka were set up through respective state government agencies. Three units at Bhubaneswar, Gurgaon and Pondicherry are in different stages of establishment.

FNB also set up 12 Community Based Nutritious Food Units during 1992-97 through NGOs with financial assistance from UNICEF. One time grant of Rs.5.00 lakhs was extended to each NGO for establishing a self -sustainable unit for production of low cost nutritious foods at the community level.

Monitoring of supplementary feeding at Anganwadis

FNB, through its field infrastructure of 43 CFNEUs has been assessing the quality and regularity of supplementary feeding at anganwadis since 1993. Each CFNEU inspects about 15 Anganwadis per month in its area of operation with regard to type of food received, its storage at Anganwadi, food preparations made and given to beneficiaries along with amount and acceptability, safe drinking water and hygienic conditions. Based on the assessment, suggestions are provided to the field staff as well as State Governments for improving the quality of supplementary feeding at ICDS. During the period April to December 1998, CFNEUs have inspected 5,472 Anganwadis for monitoring of supplementary feeding component.

Fortification of food

Fortification of milk with vitamin A

The scheme introduced in 1980 is implemented through cooperative dairies of the states. The objective is to replace the amount of vitamin A lost during the toning process in the milk so as to prevent the deficiency of an important micronutrient, viz ' vitamin A in the urban population including slum dwellers. The present scheme involves reimbursing the cost of fortification to the dairies for an initial period of 3 years and thereafter, the dairies bear the cost of fortification on their own. 32 dairies are fortifying milk with vitamin A at present. About 25 lakh litres of fortified milk is produced daily.

The Report of the Task Force &on Micronutrients of the Department has recommended fortification of all toned and double toned milk with vitamin A in the country.

The matter is being pursued with the Department of Animal Husbandry in the Ministry of Agriculture.

Fortification of common foods with limiting nutrients has been one of the instruments of the National Nutrition Policy. The Department of Sugar and Edible

Oils in the Ministry of Food has constituted a task force to explore the possibility of fortification of sugar with vitamin A. Similarly, the Ministry of Food Processing Industries has constituted working groups for fortification of wheat flour, rice and ready-to-eat extruded foods with iron and other micronutrients. FNB is extending technical expertise to this task force and working groups. Studies on double fortification of salt with iron and iodine are also being supported through UNICEF.

Food analysis and standardisation

FNB is entrusted with the analysis of fruit and vegetable products under the regulation of quality control of these products for domestic consumption as well as for export. The four Quality Control Laboratories (QCLs) at Delhi, Mumbai, Calcutta and Chennai also analyse supplementary foods used under feeding programmes, milk fortified with vitamin A besides fruit and vegetable products. ' During the year 1998-99, the four QCLs analysed 12,936 samples.

FNB renders technical expertise in various committees for food quality and food standardization. FNB is represented in the National Codex Committee and shadow-committees, Labelling Committee etc., of Department of Health; various committees of Bureau of Indian Standards (BIS); Technical Standardisation Committee (Food Stuffs), and Food and Agriculture Research Development Panel of Ministry of Defence. During the year, FNB participated in Codex Committee on Nutrition and Food for Special Dietary Uses held at Berlin (Germany) from 21-25 September, 1998.

The Regional Officers meeting of FNB was held on 11th November, 1998 under the chairpersonship of Secretary, WCD. The working of the Regional Offices and

CFNEUs was reviewed and the changing role of Food and Nutrition Board and its infrastructure in the current nutrition scenario emphasised. The recommendations of the National Workshop on Nutrition Promotion : Role of Family and Community organised at Delhi on 2-3 September, 1998, and summary report of the Nutrition Surveillance Project undertaken through National Institute of Nutrition, Hyderabad were shared with the field officers with a view to sensitise them towards the current challenges in the field of nutrition, need for creating mass awareness on nutrition and promoting inter-sectoral coordination.

Research and development

6.5. A Research and Development activities are essential for improving the existing interventions and for undertaking innovative approaches for control of malnutrition. Some of the important R&D projects completed during the year include Development of India Nutrition Profile, Nutrition Surveillance Model & Food Based Dietary Guidelines.

New initiatives

Implementation of National Nutrition Policy, National Plan of Action on Nutrition

A number of initiatives have been taken up since 1993 as a follow up of National Nutrition Policy. A National Plan of Action on Nutrition formulated and approved by the Inter-ministerial Coordination Committee and printed and released in 1995, serves as a framework for operationalising multi-sectoral strategy for nutrition promotion. It highlights the role of 14 concerned sectors for nutrition improvement. Progress in sectoral activities is obtained from concerned sectors periodically.

Integration of nutritional concerns in various development policies and programmes is considered important for maximising the positive nutritional outcomes of various sectoral programmes. In order to achieve this objective, the existing Interministerial Coordination Committee on Nutrition Policy and the Food and Nutrition Board Advisory Committee were amalgamated and reconstituted into the Food and Nutrition Council under the chairmanship of Hon'ble Minister for Human Resource Development through a Gazette Notification in November, 1997. It is envisaged that the Food and Nutrition Council will provide a forum which will facilitate nutrition orientation of development policies and thus help in attaining the national nutrition goals set up by the Nutrition Policy.

The first meeting of the Food and Nutrition Council was held on 23rd December, 1997. The meeting highlighted the need for controlling malnutrition in a mission mode approach. As recommended by the Council, the new scheme on Implementation of National Nutrition Policy was reformulated in the form of a 'Nutrition Mission' for implementation during the IX Plan, which is under consideration. The Council also recommended promoting complementary feeding of infants, and nutrition of adolescent girls and pregnant women by creating nutritional awareness at all levels. Requisite educational material were developed for preventing onset of malnutrition among 0-2 year old children.

State level actions on the National Nutrition Policy were pursued during the year. The nutritional concerns for women and children were discussed in the meeting of State Ministers and Secretaries in-charge of Women and Child Development held at Vigyan Bhavan on 22-23 July, 1998. A note on activities of FNB was also shared with them with a view to promote better collaboration in the field. The National Nutrition Policy, National Plan of

Action on Nutrition, the Report of the Task Force on Micronutrients, Food Based Dietary Guidelines and other nutrition documents were shared with the State Secretaries during the meeting.

States of Andhra Pradesh, Assam, Arunachal Pradesh, Gujarat, Goa, Himachal Pradesh Kerala, Karnataka, Meghalaya ' Pondicherry, Punjab, Rajasthan, Sikkim, Tamil Nadu and West Bengal have taken action for constituting inter-departmental coordination mechanism for operationalising the multi-sectoral strategy of Nutrition Policy.

Micronutrient malnutrition control activities

A Task Force on Micronutrients (vitamin A and iron) was constituted in the Department with a view to accelerate the progress in prevention and control of these two micronutrient deficiencies. The report of the Task Force duly approved by HRM has been shared with the Secretaries of concerned sectors, national institutes and state governments with a view to incorporating recommendations in existing and future interventions. FNB also collaborated actively in the National Consultation Meet on Anaemia organised by the Department of Family Welfare during 16-17 October, 1997.

FNB participated actively in the meetings of the core group constituted by the National Human Rights Commission (NHRC) on the problem of nutritional anaemia and iodine deficiency disorders. A pilot project on Development of a Comprehensive Model for Controlling Nutritional Anaemia was also prepared and shared with the NHRC.

The issue of undertaking estimation of haemoglobin of the sample population during the 2nd National Family Health Survey was also-taken up with the Department of

Family Welfare. Advocacy and sensitisation for micronutrient malnutrition control was also taken up through the field infrastructure of FNB during their nutrition education programmes.

The District Nutrition Profiles of 187 districts from 18 States/UTs prepared through three national level research organisations were critically analysed and consolidated into a comprehensive document titled India Nutrition Profile. The document provides a detailed data base highlighting food consumption patterns, nutrient intake of different age groups, gender-wise nutritional status in terms of weight deficit and nutritional deficiency signs, as well as vital information on breast feeding and complementary feeding practices prevalent in different parts of the country. The special Feature of the document is the district-wise mapping of under-nutrition among pre-school children and the extent of chronic energy deficiency among adult population in 18 states. The document was released by the Hon'ble Minister for Human Resource Development on 22nd July, 1998 in the meeting of the State Ministers and Secretaries in-charge of Women and Child Development at Vigyan Bhavan, New Delhi.

Development of District Nutrition Profiles of the three states of Uttar Pradesh, West Bengal and Orissa sponsored to NIN, Hyderabad was followed up during the year.

Nutrition surveillance system

Nutrition surveillance has been recognised as an important enabling mechanism to reduce malnutrition. Establishing a National Nutrition Surveillance System in the country has also been the mandate of the Nutrition Policy. Recognising the importance of nutrition surveillance, a project was undertaken in collaboration with National Institute of Nutrition, Hyderabad and the government of Andhra Pradesh. The project has been successfully completed and has demonstrated that nutrition surveillance can be undertaken utilising the existing infrastructure of ICDS with improved training, monitoring and supervision. It has also brought out that the levels of malnutrition were brought down in different districts of Andhra Pradesh through the Nutrition Surveillance Project. The Nutrition Surveillance Model thus developed was discussed in the National Workshop held at Delhi on 2-3 September, 1998 and the need for establishing surveillance system in the states has been incorporated in the recommendations of the workshop.

The World Food Summit held in 1996 advocated setting up Food Insecurity Vulnerability Information and Mapping System (FIVIMS) at national levels. FNB participated in regional expert consultation on FIVIMs for Asia-Pacific region organised by FAO at Bangkok during 20-23 October, 1998. An Interministerial Coordination Committee has been set up in the Ministry of Food, the focal point for FIVIMS in India with active representation of FNB.

Strategies for Reducing Child Malnutrition

The project on Development of National Strategies for Reducing Child Malnutrition was coordinated by FNB under the Regional Technical Assistance Programme of Asian Development Bank and UNICEF. The final report on National Strategies for Reducing Child Malnutrition submitted by the Administrative Staff College of India, Hyderabad has been shared with the concerned Secretaries of the Government, members of the Steering Committee and National Institutions. An abridged version of the report is being prepared to serve as an advocacy document to make malnutrition a public policy issue and promote action for control of malnutrition from various quarters.

Creation of Nutritional Awareness at Various Levels

Efforts for creation of nutritional awareness at different levels have been intensified in recent years. Food Based Dietary Guidelines for Indians developed in collaboration with the Nutrition Syndicate was released by the Hon'ble Minister for Human Resource Development on 22nd July, 1998 in the meeting of State Ministers and Secretaries in-charge of Women and Child Development. This illustrated booklet provides simple guidelines for general masses and grass root level workers on food needs of various age groups, nutritional significance of various foods for different age groups, prevention of diet related chronic disorders like *diabetes mellitus*, hypertension, cardio-vascular diseases etc. The booklet is being translated in Hindi and other regional languages and is also being printed by Department of Family Welfare for providing to the grass root level functionaries of the health infrastructure.

6

Health and Sustainable Regional Development

Housing is a state subject but the Union Government is responsible for the formulation of policy with regard to programmes and approaches for effective implementation of the social housing schemes, particularly those pertaining to weaker sections of the society. The National Housing Policy is enunciated in the Five Year Plan and the state goverments implement the schemes in accordance with the plan priorities and local requirements.

In tune with the policy of the Government, a National Housing Policy (NHP), taking into account the developments on national and international scene on Shelter Sector after 1988 and also in the light of comments received from state governments and different sections of the community has been evolved. Special emphasis has been given in the policy paper on the specific needs of rural housing. The policy document outlining the strategy under the Eighth Plan has since been endorsed by Parliament in 1994.

The long term goal of the NHP is to eradicate houselessness, to improve the housing conditions of the inadequately housed and to provide a minimum level of basic services and amenities to all. It recognises that the magnitude of housing task calls for involvement of various agencies including government at different levels, cooperatives, the community and the private sector.

The policy envisages a major shift in Government's role to act more as a facilitator than as provider. The needs of vulnerable sections of society will continue to be atended to by the Government. It envisages to facilitate housing activity of the lower and middle income groups and to encourage within the framework of housing policy and local planning, the voluntary agencies in efforts to upgrade shelter, extend basic services, augment incomes and promote environmental conservation. The policy has been incorporated in the Housing Chapter on the Eighth Plan.

During the Eighth Plan, emphasis will be on social housing schemes including Minimum Needs Programme projects in rural areas, strengthened role of HUDCO, shelter for the homeless, technology transfer, housing information system and housing for Central Government employees. All the state governments have been requested to formulate detailed action plans for implementation of the policy.

Although housing is basically a State level activity, the Central Government is responsible for the formulation of broad policy framework of this sector and overseeing the effective implementation of the social housing scheme, particularly for the weaker sections of the Society.

The Central Government strives to create a conducive environment for generating housing activity so as to meet its growing demand. The Delhi Rent Bill, 1994 has been passed by both the Houses of Parliament and it recieved the assent of the President on 23.8.1995. Soon after the Delhi Rent Act, 1995 was passed by the Parliament, representations were received from a section of traders-tenants demanding changes in some of the provisions of the Act. On the other hand, some forums representing house owners are pressing for an early notification of the Act and enforcement thereon. All these issues are under the consideration of the Government.

The Indira Awas Yojana (IAY), meant for the poorest of the poor belonging to scheduled castes and scheduled tribes and free bonded labour in the rural areas, had been further extended to cover non-SC/ST poor families, subject to certain conditions. Houses, under IAY scheme are built in clusters so that common facilities can be provided easily. Under IAY, 2,81,754 houses were built during 1996-97 (upto October, 96) as against 8,63,889 in 1995-96.

The Urban Basic Services for the Poor (UBSP) scheme was launched with a total outlay of Rs. 100 crore for the Eighth Plan period. The aim of the scheme is to improve the quality of life of the urban poor specially the most vulnerable sections of the population such as women, children, youth, Scheduled Castes/Scheduled Tribes and minorities.

As on 30th November, 1996, more than 8000 Neighbourhood Development Committees comprising primarily of urban poor women have been set up in 318 towns for the provision of basic services. 3877 mini plans have already been prepared and 574 community organisers are in the field working as catalysts for enriching community participation.

In its efforts to enchance the flow of funds particularly in rural areas and its easy accessibility to the needy rural populaltion, the National Housing Bank

(NHB) till the end of April 1996, has subscribed to the "Special Rural Housing Debentures" (SRHDs) of State Level Cooperative Land Development Banks (SLDBs) to the tune of Rs.180.91 crore to the cooperative sector institutions, the share of SLDBs works out to 51.1 per cent.

Recognising the importance of providing housing to women, particularly those belonging to the vulnerable sections, NHB has announced a "Direct Financing Scheme for Housing for Women". Under the scheme, NHB will directly finance the projects of public agencies and local bodies for the benefit of women belonging tot he Economically Weaker Sections (EWS) and Lower Income Group (LIG) categories.

Water supply and sanitation are important basic needs for the improvement of quality of life and enchancement of productive efficiency of the citizens. Although State Governments are responsible for supply of drinking water in villages, Central assistance is being provided under the Accelerated Rural Water Supply Programme (ARWSP) with 100 per cent grants—in—aid subject to a matching provision (except for DDP areas where matching provision is regular) being made by State Governments under Minimun Needs Programme (MNP). The National Drinking Water Mission (NDWM) renamed as the Rajiv Gandhi National Drinking Water Mission (RGNDWM) is looking into the need for providing sustainable safe drinking water to entire rural population over the next few years.

The coverage of rural population with drinking water supply and sanitation facilities in rural and urban areas increased rapidly. An outlay of Rs.1170.86 crore has been provided in 1996-97 budget for the Rural Water Supply and Sanitation Schemes.

The scheme of rural sanitation is aimed at supplementing the efforts made under different Central and State sector programmes for improving sanitry facilities in the rural areas. It includes, inter alia, construction of sanitary latrines for individual households below the poverty line, village-complexes for women, drains and other sanitation facilities.

A total number of 1,66,353 and 37,422 sanitary latrines were constructed for Scheduled Castes and Scheduled Tribes respectively during 1995-96.

The Government has reaffirmed the crucial role of public investment in social sectors like health. It has also been recognised that alongwith the States, the Centre also bears the responsibility to ensure that primary health care is provided to every citizen.

Providing access to good primary health care has been included in the minimum needs programme.

Specific plans will be drawn up during the Ninty Plan to ensure that new primary health care entre is established for a population of 5,000 people and is efficiently managed. The primary health care centre provide basic health and family welfare services to the rural population.

The Chief Ministers' Conference held in July 1996 has recommended that all out efforts will be made to attain 100 per cent coverage ofprimary health service facilities in rural and urban areas by 2000 A.D. The Panchayati Raj System will be activised in association with voluntary organisations in extending family planning and primary health care services.

The Central assistance for building the infrastructure for delivery of primary health care will be stepped up and the norms for this purpose will be relaxed further in areas inhabited by SC/ST/primitive/tribal groups and hill and desert areas. Indigenous systems of medicine like Ayurveda, Unani and Siddha and Homeopathy will be given adequate coverage indelivery of primary health care service.

The Government will work to achieve tangible results in promoting the small family norms so that the gains from development reach everybody.

Family Welfare programme has been given an over—riding national priority. Totally reoriented towards clients' needs and quality care, the programme now plans to provide services through an integrated Reproductive and Child Health Package.

The essential components of RCH services have been classified under four braod heads viz. Prevention and Management of Unwanted Pregnancy, Maternal care including ante—natal, delivery and post—partum services, Child survival services fro new born and infants and, Management of Reproductive tract infections/ Sexually transmitted diseases.

From April 1996, the Family Welfare Programme has become target free in its quest for improved performance. While changing from provider driven approach to a demand driven approach, decentralised, participatory planning has been introduced to create a sense of belongin among the people at grassroots level. Planning is now being encouraged through involvement of more private rural medical practitioners, anganwadi workers and non—government organisations.

To enhance community participation in the Programme, a scheme has been introduced on watershed development for small farmers, integrating Family Welfare issues with provision for community mobilisation and participation. A comunity award scheme has also been introduced for the best performing village in the district.

The campaign mode approach adopted in he Pulse Polio Immunisation (PPI) programme has led to record social mobilisation and immunisation of 8.7 crore children on December 9, 1995 and 9.3 crore children on January 20, 1996. PPI is being repeated this winter on December 7 & 18 January. Through the same campaign mode of approach, a special health check—up programme was arranged for all primary school children all over the country during this summer. This programme is also likely to be repeated next year. A register of births and deaths will be maintained by every village panchayat.

A National Illness Assistance Fund is being set up for the poor who ae below poverty line. This will assist them for specialised treatment for life threatening illness and treatment for injuries in hospitals where the treatment cost exceeds Rs. 1.50 lakh. Budget provision for 1996—97 of Rs. 5 crore for the Centre and Rs. 2.50 crore for the States has been made. States have also been asked to set up similar funds for this purpose. Fund will be supported by donations which will be given 100 per cent income tax exemption.

The State Health System project, which was earlier in operation in Andhra Pradesh will now be extended to Punjab Karnataka and West Bengal. The objective is to put in place a first referral health system which would provide vital support and lend credibility to primary helath care services. This will help in the development of a cohesive, efficient and sustainable health system.

Step are being taken to eliminate donation of blood by professional donors; all blood banks will be licensed within two years. These steps will ensure that blood transfused is free from infections.

Nearly half of the budget provision 1996—97 for medical and public health has been provided for National

Programmes for Control of Communicable and Other Diseases.

The Central Government has recently announced a scheme to encourage non-residents of Indian nationality/ origin to ivest in the urban development and housing sector. The scheme has three components:

Under the first component, existing or new companies, both private and public limited, engaged or proposing to engage in the urban development and housing including roads and bridges, manufacturing of building materials and application, to issue equity shares/convertible debentures to non-residents of Indian nationality/origin upto 100 per cent of the new issue with repatriation benefits. The repatriation of original investment will be allowed after a lock-in period of three years from the date of issue of equity shares/convertible debentures with prior permission of the reserve Bank of India;

The second component of the scheme relates to the acquisition of immovable properties by individual NRIs. It makes three provisions in this respect. Firstly, foreign citizens of Indian origin and non-residents holding Indian passports are to be allowed, against application to repatriate the original investment in equivalent foreign exchange in residential properties upto a maximum of two houses. Secondly, general permission has been granted to foreign citizens of Indian origin, whether residents in India or not, and to non-residents holding Indian passports to acquire by way of purchase or inheritance and transfer or dispose of by sale, commercial immovable properties situated in India. Repatriation of original investment in equivalent foreign exchange will be allowed by the Reserve Bank of India on receipt of an application. Finally, general permission has been granted to foreign citizens of Indian origin, whether resisdents in

India or not, to acquire, transfer or dispose of residential properties upto two houses situated in India by way of gift from or to a relative who may be an Indian citizen or a person of Indian origin, whether resident in Indian or not, subject to the condition that gift tax, if any, shall be paid. Apart from repatriation of the original investment in equivalent foreign exhange, the rental income and the proceeds of any investment out of such income will be allowed to be repatriated in a phased manner over a period of three years as per the RBI's Circular No. 18 dated 19 August 1994 and

Under the third component of the scheme, overseas corporate bodies predominantly owned by non-residents of Indian nationality/persons of Indian origin, understood to include overseas companies, partnership firms, societies and other corporate bodies which are owned directly or indirectly to the extent of at least 60 per cent by individuals of Indian nationality/origin resident outside India and overseas trusts in which at least 60 per cent of the beneficial interest is irrevocably held by such persons, are allowed to:

(a) invest in the development of serviced plots, construction of built-up residential premises, construction of residendtial and commercial premises, development of townships, development of infrastructure facilities, manufacture of building materials and participatory ventures in these areas and in housing finance institutions;

(b) repartriate the principal investment in foreign exchange and in net profits upto 16 per cent earned after the first three years of investment; and

(c) repatriate divided on equity/interest on shares/ convertible debentures subject to the payment of applicable taxes without any lock-in period.

The above scheme has opened the way for substantial investment by non-residents of Indian nationality/origin in the urban development and housing sector.

National Building Organisation

National Building Organisation (NBO) was established in 1954 as an attached office of Ministry of Urban Development primarily to take up research in low cost building designs, improvement of the building and housing conditions along with the socio-economic aspects. NBO also functions as the regional centre for housing for ESCAP. In the past NBO has been taking up public supporting research works in building designs, building materials and other socio-economic aspects. Publications hae been brought out covering all these aspects and also housing statistics. A number of experimental housing projects to suit different geo-climatic regions of the country have been taken up in the past through 15 regional housing development centres. NBO has been restructured during the year 1992 to take up mainly the socio-economic, management information system and creation of data bank functions. Besides, the computer facilities in the Organisation have been strengthened. The functions relating to building materials and designs have been taken out of the purview of the NBO and given to Building Material and Technology Promotion Council, an autonomous body within the Ministry. A standing committee has been set up to examine matters relating to housing including periodic review of the NHP, and its implementation as per indicators decided by it.

Housing for Central Government Employees

With a view to providing housing facilities to the Central Government employees, Central Government Employees Welfare Housing Organisation (CGEWHO) has been set up as a registered society under the aegis of the Ministry of Urban Development. Housing schemes in Bombay (New Bombay and Kharghar), Calcutta, Madras, NOIDA (UP) and Panchkula have been announced. Gurgaon Scheme has also been announced on 17 July 1995. The organisation has go allotment of land in Gurgaon, Lucknow and Chandigarh. It is pursuing with other state governments for land allotment. CGEWHO is also pursuing a proposal for a turnkey project at Bangalore.

In spite of 'Housing' being considered as a priority sector activity, investment in housing as a percentage of the total investment in the country, has declined from 34 per cent in the First Plan to 10 per cent in the Seventh Plan. Public Sector outlay for housing in Central and Stae sector during Eighth Plan is Rs. 6,377 crore. The following initiatives have been taken during the last five years as part of the National Housing Policy :

- The National Housing Bank (NHB) set up in 1988 as a subsidiary of RBI is functioning under administrative control of the Banking Division/ Department of Economic Affairs. It has launched the under mentioned schemes:
- Home Loan Account Scheme–a contractual deposit scheme linked to guaranted loan. More than seven lakh accounts have been opened in various commercial banks and housing finance institutions and an amount of Rs. 394.14 crore mobilized as deposits at the end of June 1994;
- The cumulative refinance assistance provided by NHB upto 31 March 1995 is Rs. 2,254.04 crore; and
- Land Development and Shelter Programmes of public/private agencies operated through Housing and Urban Development Corporation (HUDCO) and commercial banks to increase the supply of service land and houses–Rs. 218.28 crore advanced till March 1995;

— During 1994-95, Rs. 723.78 crore have been allocated as banking finance, as 1.5 per cent of incremental deposists with the commercial banks for housing loans, out of which 30 per cent will be channeled to individual/household sector. Compared to total allocation of Rs. 567.27 crore for 1993-94, the total disbursement made by scheduled commercial banks was about Rs. 425.25 crore. For 1994-95 loans allocated to states by LIC and GIC are Rs. 218.34 crore and Rs. 76.67 crore respectively;

— Now about 20 housing finance institutions both in the public and private sector recognised by the National Housing Bank are operating;

— During 1994-95, HUDCO sanctioned loan worth Rs. 1,763 crore. The actual loans released by HUDCO upto 28 February 1995, were Rs. 617 crore. About 90 per cent dwelling units financed by HUDCO are for economically weaker sections and low income groups. As on 30 April 1995 over 57.3 lakh units have been sanctioned under various housing schemes of the HUDCO of which about 28.5 lakh units are in rural areas. In addition over 3.9 lakh developed plots and 28 lakh basic sanitation Integrated Low Cost Sanitation (ILCS) untis have been sanctioned till 30 April 1995;

— Under the nehru Rozgar yojana (NRY) scheme for upgradation of the housing stock of the poor, a front-end subsidy of Rs. 1,000 per household is provided by Central and state governments along with Rs. 3,000 loan from HUDCO. This is implemented in collaboration with municipal bodies; and

— As an Action Plan item, Footpath Dwellers Night Shelter Scheme is being implemented as a Centrally–sponsored scheme in the metropolitan and other major urban centres. Since April 1991 and as on 30 April 1995, 60 schemes benefiting more than 20,000 footpath dwellers have been sanctioned by HUDCO in various parts of the country.

The Working Group set up by the Planning Commission for formulation of Eighth five Year Plan has estimated that public sector investment in housing will be of the order of Rs. 25,000 crore during the Plan period and Rs. 97,530 crore will be needed to meet the new and incremental demands for housing and upgradation of unserviceable houses totalling 21.77 million units at 1991-92 prices.

Technology application in Housing is very crucial to mitigate the problem. Building materials account for 65 to 75 per cent of the total cost of construction. The demand for building materials has been continuously rising with the increasing need for housing both in rural and urban areas.

Inadequate technology extension facilities, lack of coordination and promotion programmes at the Central and state government levels to support production ventures have been largely responsible for very limited application of these emerging technologies. In the rural areas the problem is more severe due to decreasing access to traditional materials such as timber, bamboo, thatch which mostly form part of bio-mass.

Commercial exploitation by various industries has aggravated the situation. A change in policy is, therefore, essential to give due priority to shelter construction through better availability of alternate materials at affordable prices and by minimising commercial exploitation of bio-mass.

In this context, the following initiatives have been taken:

- As part of the Eighth Plan exercise, the demand and likely shortage of some of the major building materials have been estimated along with the potential for production of alternative building materials. Some more fiscal concessions for innovative and cost effective building materials have been granted in the 1995-96 budget;
- The Building Materials and Technology Promotion Council has been functioning as a registered society under the aegis of the Ministry of Urban Affairs and Employment to provide for an appropriate platform for technology transfer, application in the shelter sector and large-scale commercial productionof innovative builiding materials. Minister of Urban Affairs and Employment is the Chairman of the Council. The Council will complement the extension and dissemination activities of National Building Organisation. The Council has taken a lot of initiatives in utilisation of flyash and other wastes, introduction of new specifications by CPWD and BIS and to increase the entrepreneurs interface with the financial institutions and research * are being set up;
- Some of the technologies and new materials and components already tested, manufactured on a pilot scale have been identified for large scale extension;
- A network of building centres has been set up as a Centrally–sponsored scheme through HUDCO to train artisans and others for transfer of appropriate technology to rural and urban areas. So far, 422 building centres have been identified, out of which 204 have become functional upto 30 April 1995 and
- Non-governmental organisations (NGOs)/voluntary organisations are increasingly being supported to supplement governmental efforts.

Land is a critical input in housing and there is acute

shortage of serviced land, particularly in urban areas which is responsible for inadequate housing activity. For every million additional units at least 6,000 hectare of developed land is required. To tackle this problem, concerted steps are proposed for:

- increased supply of serviced land through land acquisition, negotiated purchase and land readjustment, suitable amendments to LA Act;
- modification of development plans and regulations for cheaper legal shelter and intensive land use; and
- A separate division has been set up in the HUDCO to finance city level urban infrastructure development schemes and National Housing Bank in order to stimulate housing activity in refinancing land development schemes.

Another important aspect of the life of the weaker tribes which has not received adequate attention is health. Medicinal plants and herbs grew plentifully in the tribal areas but no systematic efforts seemed to have been made to procure them or acquire their knowledge.

The tribals did not get any encouragement in procurement of these herbs. There was also a fund of medical knowledge extant in the minds of tribal medicine-men. Generations of tribals had sought medical relief through this knowledge. Special research institutions should be established at the Centre and State to identify, consolidate and document this knowledge so that it was not lost for ever.

The Lepchas of Sikkim are good botanists. They have special knowledge of every specific plant, tree and herb of the region. In fact, they have their own botanical names of each of these. It is said that a Lepcha would not die of 'snake and mad dog bite' because of the relief they get through their expert knowledge of herbal medicine.

There is also need for great emphasis on development of tribal skills and technology. Programmes for the development of women and children in rural areas (DWCRA) launched by the government as subscheme of Integrated Rural Development Programme should be specially launched in the areas of the weaker tribes to help improve the quality of life of women and children of these groups.

Voluntary organizations like the various associations of these tribals, could be of greate help in furthering tribal development programmes such as establishment of creches, Balwadis, tailoring and craft centre, adult education centre, medical care centre, centre for nutritional programmes and midday meals. These tribal organizations might be financed through donations, grants from institutions, government, etc. to undertake various activities for bettlement of their own live.

Development of communication drinking water facility, posts and telegraph facilities and electrification also need to be provided to them.

In India for centuries, the dais have attended at the births of nearly all babies and even today in villages, they attend more than three fourths of all deliveries and there does not seem to be any apparent sign of their disappearence from the health scene in the foreseeable future. Doctors and trained mid-wives are still few and it is the usual custom to call 'dais' for deliveries.

'Dais' provide client-centred services. They conduct deliveries at the homes of their clients, whom they provide a culturally accepted package of services, both during pre-natal and post-natal stages. Incidentally, the package of services provided by them also include treatment of common maladies of mothers and children and measures for family planning.

'Dai' is a non-government honorary worker, but her role is extremely important in conducting deliveries. They are a dependable source for information about pregnancies and births occuring in the village and also problems of pregnant women and nursing mothers. They perform multiplicity of roles, and, therefore, they are for villagers their lay gynaecologists, herbalists, nutritionists and psychiatrists.

They provide services in an atmosphere of cordiality, mutual trust and interdependence in contrast to the strange impersonal atmosphere of the hospital. They provide maximum care and attention to women's physical and mental state of health, right from the time of confirmation of pregnancy till 40 days after days the child birth.

Though the 'dais' are experienced, they know nothing about germs and the need for clean hands for hygeine. All over India many mothers use to die of infection, and babies suffer due to tetanus. Even today in back ward areas, these avoidable deaths occur. They have been performing the deliveries mostly through primitive methods like cutting the umbilical cord with trowel, sickle, knife and scissors, etc. mainly because of poor infrastructure.

But their role in the village health system cannot be undermined. W.H.O. has recognized the early involvement of T.B.A.S. also known as 'Granny Midwife', 'Dakun' etc., in family planning programmes.

Such a recommendation was given in view of the fact that traditional birth attendants constitute a substantial source for assistance in meeting maternal and child-care needs in Africa, Asia and Latin America, where one finds them in almost every village. Countries like India, Pakistan, Indonesia, Malaysia, Thailand,

Sudan, Ghana and the Philippines have already made some attempts to involve the TBAs into their health care delivery system. But no regional survey have been undertaken to iedentify such functionaries.

Especially in India, with more emphasis on privatisation of health services and subsequent doctors being covered under Consumer Protection Act (COPRA), the health services are becoming very costly making majority of the population to depend on traditional birth attendants. The long queues in government hospitals; unhygienic conditions, travelling long distances, non-availability of accommodation, medicines, etc., force villagers to get the pregnancy done within the village and that too from 'dais' because of non-availability of other health services.

This indicate the quite obvious and understandable reasons for their continuing role in the village health system. From the social administrative point of view and given the present social setting, the TBAs may be declared useless, irrelevant and obsolete and their practices banned by legislation but they play an important role in organising efforts to improve the health of the community and fill in the void in some pockets where facilities for modern treatment are easily available.

What can be done is giving them training, making them a part of health system, thus ensuring safety of the new baby and reducing maternal mortality rate. Recently, 'mid-wifery' has been legalised in Canada for those who register with local health authorities. A step in this direction can also be taken in India. Although government has taken steps in this direction, but the results are yet far from satisfaction. By making them a part of the health system, it is certain that we can move a step forward to achieve the target of providing health for all by 2000 A.D.

There are over 6.5 lakh of practitioners the Indian Systems of Medicine in the country. They largely work in remote rural as well as urban slum areas and thus, could play an important role in improving the quality and outreach of health care. During the Eighth Plan the DEptt. of ISM & H has been formed to provide a new thrust and focus to the ongoing programmes. The focus will be to ensure quality and relevance of the undergraduate training, a period of internship with possible multi-professional inter-action and periodic qcourses to update the knowledge and skills of the practitioners.

Lack of close supervision and monitoring at the peripheral level and the inadequate community awareness and participation have come in the way efficient and effective implementation of the Health programmes. With the seventy third and seventy fourth Constitutional amendments, the Nagar Palikas and Panchayati Raj Instutitions will play increasing role in ensuring planning, implemntation and monitoring of health services at the local level.

They will also ensure effective coordination of programmes at the local level between related sectors such as sanitation, safe drinking water and women and child development, so that optimal benefit and the vulnerable segments receive the attention that they need.

At the time of Independence communicable disease had been the major cause of morbidity and mortality in the country. Though health is a state subject, several centrally sponsored programmes for control of communicable diseases were initiated over the last four decades.

National Malaria Eradication Programme was the oldest of all these. It was launched in 1953 and had achieved spectacular success in rapidly reducing the morbidity and mortality due to malaria from estimated 75 million cases and 0.8 million deaths at the time of Independence to 0.1 million cases and no death in 1965. Unfortunately since then there has been a resurgence of malaria in several parts of the country. Increasing prevalence of Falciparum malaria, resistance of mosquitoes to insecticides and malarial parasite to commonly used antimalarial drugs have been the source of concern.

The Modified Plan of Operation is being implemented; special attention is being paid to the vulnerable North-Eastern States by providing 100 per cent Plan assistance for this programme. Other vector borne diseases also have been receiving due attention. Re-emergence of diseases like Kala Azar has been a cause of concern.

Deteriorating urban and rural sanitation, poor water and solid waste management and ever increasing overcrowding result in communicable disease which continue to be the major cause of morbidity and mortality in the country. Emergence of new infections like HIV add to the existing disease burden due to communicable diseases. The emergence of drug resistance in many bacteria and resistance to insecticides among vectors have added to the existing problems of disease control.

Other major National Programmes that have received attention of the Eighth Plan aim to combat tuberculosis, leprosy and HIV infection.

The performance in many of these national programmes has been suboptimal due to lack of critical manpower at the primary health care level. Efforts are underway to identify the gaps in infrastructure and manpower, and fill them as expenditiously as possible so that the programmes become fully operational. In addition efforts are being made to improve the operational efficiency, the quqality of services, make services more responsive to client needs, ensure that health care providers have the necessary skills and support including referral facilities and supplies they need.

Simultaneously through health education efforts will have to be made to improve the client and the community awareness of the existing services and how to utilise them optimally, so that available services are effectively utilised and community participation in the programme optimised.

At the time when many of the disease control programmes were initiated sufficient health infrastructure and manpower were not available for managment of major health problems; so a vertical programme infrastructure was created to operationalise these programmes in the absence of primary health care infrastructure. By the end of the Eighth Plan the primary health care infrastructure is well estiablished and so efforts are being made to ensure that existing vertical programmes are horizontally integrated at district level so that the primary health care institution truly becomes the nodal agency for channelising comprehensive Health Services to the population.

In order to assist the primary health centre/CHCs officers to carry out horizontal integration, it is envisaged that the middle level public health programme managers who are currently heading the vertical programme at district level will be given the additional task of ensuring coordination and implementation of integrated Health Programme at Primary Health Care institutions in defined blocks.

Provision of appropriate drugs of good quality at affordable cost is essential for success of disease control programmes. Equally important is to restrict, and if possible, eliminate, the use of irrational drug formulation and fixed dose drug combination. Recognising this, provisions for strengthning the food and drug control organizations in the States and Centre were made in the Eighth Plan. However, implementation of the scheme has been patchy and tardy. This will be taken up on priority basis during the next few years.

Any health programme is as good as the personnel who constitute the health system. Both in the State and in the Central Sector over 75 per cent of the budget goes to meet the salary of the employees. Unlike health service planning, the health manpower planning in India did not receive adequate attention. There is gross inadequacy of the number of para—professionals and over production of doctors and specialists in the country. There are regional disparities both in quantity and quality of the health care professionals. These have come in the way of effective implementation of the health programmes. It is imperative that health manpower appropriate in quality and adequate in quantity is available for catering to the health care needs of the populaltion. In addition to the existing institutional mechanisms, the open university system and the vocational courses will assist the States in production of adequate number of the para-professionals of appropriate categories and ensure that the quality of preservice training is optimal.

It is essential to establish an institutional mechanism for health manpower planning at district, State and Central level so that the task of health manpower planning, based on the data on availability and needs at the district, State and the national level, and the function of health manpower production proceed in tandem. This will ensure that appropriate mix of the health personnel of requisite quality are produced to meet the existing and changing health care needs of the population in the public, private and voluntary sectors.

In the rapidly changing health care scenario it is essential that all professionals and para-professionasl undergo periodic retraining so that their knowledge and skills are updated. Continuing multi-professionals education enables the professionals and para-professionals to function effectively as a team for effective and efficiently delivery of health care.

In addition to the existing inservice training courses in various institutions, the Open universities will play an increasingly important role in this direction.

The Indian Council of Medical Research has been the nodal agency forbio-medical research in the country. Bio-medical and health systems research is carried out by research institutions, universities, medical colleges and non-governmental organisations and are currently funded by several agencies including ICMR, DST, DBT, CSIR and concerned Ministries. Basic, clinical, applied and operational research studies relevent to major health and population problems in the country have been the focus of research programmes.

It is noteworthy that most of the National Health Programmes in the country are based on applied and operational research studies carried out by ICMR.

Efforts are underway to achieve koptimal coordination of the research activities by networking and if needed by multi-agency funding of important projects.

Development, testing and quality control of drugs in the modern system of medicine and ISM & H, development of immunodiagnostic tests for common communicable diseases which could be used at the primary health care institutions, development and testing of alternative strategies for control of communicable and non-communicable diseases and operational research for efficient implementation of the RCH (reproductive and child health) package through PHC planning are some of the major research areas which have been initiated in the recent years.

Given the existing conditions of poor environmental sanitation and the weakness of the public health system it may not be possible to completely prevent out breaks of communicable diseases in the near future.

Nevertheless, early detection and prompt response could result in rapid containment and control of the outbreak, reduction in morbidity and mortality. The building up of the disease surveillance and response mechanisms have received considerable attention during the Eighth Plan period. It is felt disease surveillance and response must be based at district level ensure prompt response. This system needs to be given the necessary back up laboratory support and epidemiological expertise so that containment measures are based on suond data and are logical.

This back up system should be evolved through strengthening and optimal utilisation of the facilities and expertise available in the National Institutions/medical colleges.

Increasing incidence of hospital acquired infections and accidental infection in health care providers and waste disposers renders it imperative that efforts are made to improve infection control and waste management through utilisaton of appropriate affordable technology at all levels of health care. Planning Commission and the Ministry of Health and Family Welfare Programme have initiated steps to take up specific pilot projects.

Increasing longevity, demographic transition resulting in rapidly rising numbers of aged population, urbanisation, increasing pollution, a change over from traditional diets, sedentary life style and increase in the stress of day to day living have led to the increase in life style related disorders and noncommunicable diseases.

Noncommunicable diseases such as cardio-and cerebro-vascular diseases resulting in heart attacks and strokes, diabetes and common malignancies are emerging as major public health problems in the country. Pilot projects for district based integrated noncummunicable disease control programmes carried out through the existing primary and secondary level facilities, using diabetes as a model, have been initiated in the Eighth Plan.

The experience gained will be used to expand such programmes.

Rapidly growing population, urbanisation, changing agricultural, industrial and water resource management, increasing use of pesticides and fossil fuels have all resulted in perceptible deterioration in the quality of environment and attendant adverse health consequences.

Pilot projects exploring the dimensions of the problem and aimed at seeking realistic solutions were initiated during the Eighth Plan period. Efforts are also under way to document extent of the problem of environmental pollution and its impact on health status of the population. Prevention and management of health consequences of environmental deterioration will receive increasing attention.

Over the last two decades occupational health has received considerable attention. Continuous monitoring of safety of work environment and workers' health status, both in the organised and unorganised sector with emphasis on gender specific and child labour related issues, documenting the magnitude and types of the occupational health problems, initiating appropriate preventive and remedial measures will be developed into a structured health programme are being taken up wherever possible.

Several major development activities in any field such as Agriculture, Industries, Urban and Rural Development have resulted in environment changes; some of these could have health implications. In order to minimise these it has been suggested that all large development projects should have Health Impact assesment and then necessary provision for health care of people involved in development activities and prevention and management of health consequences of developmental activities on the population living in the vicinity of the project should be incorporated and costed as part of the project. These suggestions are being considered by appropriate implementing agencies.

The past fifty years have witnessed the development of a vast health care infrastructure and manpower aimed at providing health care to the population. National Programmes have been evolved and implemented to control major public health problems.

The investment in Public health has shown considerable increase over the plan periods. However there has not been any increase in the proportion of the Plan outlay allocated to health sector. There is an increase in the disease burden due to communicable and non-communicable disease caused by the growing population, newer diseases and changing life styles.

There are evolving technologies for health care and increasing expectations of the population for health care. All these have resulted in the ever widening gap between what is possible and what is affordable. It is imperative that in the coming decades this gap is bridged and at the same time equity and excellence are ensured in health care services.

The market for biopesticides is also growing rapidly. Bio—pesticides contain micro—organisms which prevent insect larvae from developing into adults. Biopesticides may include 'beneficial' predatory insects which eat pests, and pheromones which anc confuse insects and disrupt mating. Adopting a similar technique, Australia has been able to control the growing population of rabbits. Likewise, Japan has been able to successfully eradicate the melon fly on serveral islands through the release of strile insects.

In India, the menace of rats and mosquitoes, frequently spreading epidemics like plague, lamaria, dengue fever, etc. can be effectively controlled by indigenous development of such techniques to suit local conditions.

Biopesticides generally pose lower risks to human health and the environment than their chemical counterparts. Thus developing new biopesticides through specific research would help in limiting the growing use of herbicides, insecticides, etc. and providing an eco–friendly solution to most agricultural problems.

After proving its worth in medical sciences and agriculture, biotechnology is now begning to have a significantly impact on the environmental sciences. In fact, biotechnology has quite a large potential to contribute to the detection, prevention and remediation of environmental pollution and degradation.

Even though modern bioitechnology is not new to environmental sciences, it has taken long to have a noticeable impact in this field. One of the earliest and most widespread applications of biotechnology was waste water treatment plants.

These plants work by degradation of organic waste with the help of micro—organisms. Developed during the nineteenth century, such plants have seen only minor changes during all these years. One of the main reasons for the slow progress of modern bio—technology in environmental science has been the lack of adequate concern for the environment. On the other hand, medical and agricultural applications have attracted more attention by virtue of more tangible outcome in these cases.

But as the concern for the environment increased in the eighties and nineties, environmental biotechnology is now fast gaining prominance.

In US, $ 83.3 million was spent in 1993 on R & D in environmental bioitechnology, which was 2.1% of total biotechnology R & D in the country. Germany and the Netherlands have so far taken a lead in manufacturing and exporting biological technologies for treating waste water and air. Japan is also making efforts to develop export—oriented environmental biotechnology industry. However, the progress in India is lack–lusture as not much attention is being given.

Biotechnology is certainly not the technology to keep the environment clean. But biological clean—up methods are much more sustainable than chemical or physical methods for waste treatment. The simplest procedure adopted for disposal of waste is production of methane by anaerobic digestion. Bio—gas production is one such application.

Environmental biotechnologies utilise micro—organisms and their parts or products. Earthworms, which are among the most widespread natural clean—up agents, are also used in environmental biotechnology to purify soil. In the cleaning—up of air pollution, biotechnological methods such as biofilters are the most effective. Biotechnology is also used to clean—up oil spills.

Global warming can be reduced with the help of biotechnology by improving the photosynthetic ability of plants to fix carbon dioixide. Biotechnology can also help reduce desertification. Bio—polymer molecules help enhance water retention in the soil. Plants resistant to salt and drought can also be developed.

The impact of biotechnology is pervasive. Biiotechnology being a multi—faceted activity can produce many products and achieve many worthwhile claims. Biotechnology needs to be developed to suit local conditions e.g. for a country like India, new varieties using low inputs of water, fertilisers and pesticides to suit local soil conditions need to be developed. Similarly, tackling of plague, malaria, dengue fever, etc. will have to take into account local factors.

Thus the scope of biotechnology is vast and complex, but ill—defined. Only concerted indigenous efforts will help in making use of the full potential of this useful technology.

The immediate environment of man comprises air on which depends all form of life. It has been estimated that a man can live for 5 weeks without food, for 5 days without water, but for only 5 minutes without air. Normally the air is composed of 78.1 part Nitrogen, 20.93 part oxygen and 0.03 part carbondioxide. The balance is made up of other gases which occur in traces. In addition to these gases air also contain water vapour, and suspended matter such as dust, bacteria, pores and debris.

Therefore, the term air pollution is applied when there is excessive concentration of foreign mater in the outdor atmosphere which is harmful to man or his environment. Pollution of air has resulted in sickness and deaths. More than 100 contaminants have been identified. The important ones are carbonmonoxide, sulphur dioxide, Nitrogen dioixide, Ozone, Lead, etc. Air pollution is a growing menace to health through out the world.

Most of the pollutants are associated with fossil fuel consumption. Two main categories of outdoor air pollutants are recognised. Industrial smog predominate in large industrial areas. It is a combination of smoke and fog and results from combustion of fuel and consists primarily of sulfur dioxides and particulate complexes. Combustion of coal, oil and other fuel is another source of smoke, dust and sulphur dioxide. Photochemical smog occurs in areas shich a high density of motor vehicles. Motor vehicles, truck, trains, aircraft and other forms of transport emit hydrocarbons, carbonmonoxide, lead, nitrogen dioxide and particulate matter.

In strong sunlight certain of these hydrocarbons and oxide of nitrogen may be converted into photochemical pollutant of oxidising nature. Burning of refuse, agricultural activities e.g. crop spraying, pest control and nuclear energy programmes also contribute to air pollution.

Sulfur dioxide is a major atmospheric pollutant in many urban and industrial areas, produced by the burning of sulfur content of coal and crude oil. The major source of environmental pollution are poer plants, oil refineries, and industries such as smelters, paper pulp mills and wineries. The sulfur dioxide released in the atmosphere is oxidized to sulfur trioxide in the presence of sunlight and high humidity which immediately combines with water to form sulfuric acid. Sulfur trioxide and sulfuric acid are much more irritant than sulfur dioxide.

Nitrogen dioxide is a pollutant generated in the outdoor environment mainly from automobile exhaust. In the presence of flame temperature oxygen combines nitrogen to form nitric oxide, a gas of litlle significance as an air pollutant. However when nitric oxide is vented into the air and cools rapidly, a fraction is converted into nitrogen dioxide. At home wood burning, fireplaces, kerosene heater and improperly vented gas stoves give rise to nitrogen dioxide pollution.

Ozone is a gas which is a key component of a complex mixutre of photochemical oxidant and fine particles called "Smog". It is formed by a series of sunlight driven reactions of nitrogen oxides and volatile organic compounds arising from combustion sources. Indoor sources of ozone include air "purifiers" and ion generators and office equipment with electric motors or ultraviolet lights, such as photocopy machines. In indoor environment (e.g. home, work, school) concentration of ozone are generally lower than outdoor.

Carbon monoxide (CO) duduced in ambient air comes mainly from vehicular exhaust with a bimodal peak corresponding to the morning and evening rush hours. Catalytic converters on motor vehicle decreases CO in exhaust. Indoor air can be contaminated by cigarette smoking and outdoor air that enters building from the street traffic. High exposures are relatively rare and are primarily associated with certain occupations (e.g. fire fighting) and from exposure to the product of combustion in an enclosed space from improperly vented combustion appliances and of charcoal briquettes for barbecuing and space heating. Combustion from fires, stoves, and motor vehicles generates CO at concentrations of 1% to 6% (10,000 to 60,000 ppm).

Lead: The leaded gasolines/petrol is the main source of wide spread dispersion of this metal throughout the biosphere. A marked reduction in the ambient levels of airborne lead resulted since 1970s with the use of unleaded gasoline. In countries where leaded gasolilne is still used airborne lead from automotive emissons continues to accumulate in the environment.

Premature infants, newborn, and elderly and people with chronic disease of the lungs or heart are at higher risk. Pre-school and school children appear to be sensitive to air pollution health effects. The traffic policeman, the automobile mechanics, the drivers may have unusually high risk from exposure to community air pollution due to substantial exposures in association with their occupations.

Cigarette smoking is the predominant risk factor in producing respiratory diseases and lung cancer. Air pollution have a more than additive effect. This means that cigarette smokers are at unusual higher risks if they live in areas with substantial air pollution and that the effects of air pollution on chronic disabling pulmonary diseases are more likely to occur in cigarette smokers. During periods of low winds and still weather dissipation of domestic pollution due to heating and cooking will be impaired. In such condition if smoking or cooking occurs indoors, exposures to carbonmonoxide and nitrogen oxides may be quite high.

The problem of air pollution was first brought to a sharp focus when air pollution epidemics took place in the middle of 20th century. In 1952 London Fog epidemic, many people became ill and some 4000 deaths occurred.

Since these episodes evaluation of exposed populaltions, have been performed in urban areas around the world to examine the impact of air pollution on human helath. Overall, these studies show a consistent pattern of association between increased sulfur dioxide and particulate concentrations and mortality. The acute bronchonstrictor effects of sulfur dioxide have been well established for more than 20 years. Patients with asthma represent a susceptible subgroup responsive to the effect of SO_2 and H_2SO4 at a concentration that have no effect on normal subjects.

Sulfur dioxide is highly soluble in water, nearly all the inspired gas is absorbed in the nasal mucosa and very little reaches to the lungs undernormal resting conditions. Oral breathing reduces the uptake of sulfur dioxide in the nose, but increases pollutant delivery to the lungs. In some patients of asthma oral breathing predominates because of associated nasal obstruction.

Ozone is a powerful oxidant. The respiratory system is the primary target of the ozone toxicity. Inhalation of ozone can result in damage to almost all parts of the respiratory tract, depending upon concentration.

Studies on animals have documented the inflammation of the respiratory tract, damage to epithelial cells and marked increase in susceptibility to bacterial infection following acute ozone exposure. Redness and swelling of the airways has been observed after ozone exposure the cytotoxicity of ozone may be largely due to its interaction with unsaturated lipids which generate damaging free radicals.

Moreover, long lived radicals could enter the blood stream and exert effects on body temperature of blood pressure or remote organs such as the liver.

The evidence that ozone is determental to health is increasing. The concentration that sometimes occur in urban areas cause modest reductions of lung function both in children and exercising normal adults. There is a wide variation of susceptibility to these effects. Increased symptoms and lung function decrement usually occur in the same subjects.

The major mechanism of ozone induced reduction in lung function is the inability of the exposed individual to inspire fully. Ozone exposure potentiate the allergic response and is harmful to asthmatics.

Nitrogen dioxide is less potent than ozone as an oxidant. According to intensity and duration of exposure, respiratory illness ranges from slight irrigation, burning an pain in the throat and chest to violent cough and shortness of breath. Acute Nitrogen dioxide poisoning leading to pulmonary odema and deaths has been recognized.

There is a great paucity of information on chronic Nitrogen dioxide exposure because damage develops slowly. Moreover nitrogen dioxide is usually associated with other pollutants, which renders assesment of its action difficult. Indoor sources of combustion add NO_2 to indoor air. The use of gas for cooking might have a small effect on children and asthmatics. Sulfur dioxide has an additive effects on lung functions on healthy individuals.

The exposure to nitrogen dioxide in indoor air might increase the occurrence of respiratory infections because both short and long—term exposures to notrogen dioxide exposures impair the ability to clear inhaled infectious organisms. An increased incidence of respiratory illnesses during childhood predisposes to the development of chronic respiratory diseases in adults.

Nitrogen dioxide is also an ingredient of cigarette smoke. Smokers employed in an environment polluted by automobile exhaust are believed to be particularly vulnerable to harm from nitrogen dioixide.

The toxic properties of CO are attributed to its high affinity for oxygen carrying protein (haemoglobin) to form a chemical complex called carboxyhaemoglobin (COHb). The exposure to CO is expressed as percentage of total haemoglobin bound to CO. In healthy individuals who do not smoke or are not otherwise exposed to CO,

COHb level ranges from 0.3 to 0.7%. Inhaled CO is thought to be responsible for the further elevation of COHb levels to about 1% in non smokers.

A significant proportion of the urban non smokers population has COHb level in excess of 1.5%, suggesting widespread exposure to environmental Co. Cigarettes, cigars and pipe smoking commonlyu commonly result in blood COHb levels of 2-14%. Patients of obstructive airways disease who continue to smoke tend to have higher COHb levels than smokers free of cardiiopulmanary disease.

Acute CO poisoning, with COHb levels over 30 to 50%, results in damage mainly to the heart and brain because less oxygen is carried on haemoglobin secondary to the formation of COHb. Patients with Ischemic heart disease, are particularly sensitive to CO.

Earlier onset of angina and ECG changes indicative of myocardial ischemia have been documented during exercise in such pateints at COHb level in the range of 2 to 6%. The adverse effect of maternal smoking on foetal growth and development are now well accepted. CO a major component of cigarette smoke, interfers with the transport of oxygen to the developing tissues. Similar effects have been postulated for ambient CO exposures.

The route of exposure of lead is through both inhalation and ingestion. Most of the lead deposited on the airways is cleared by mucociliary blanket of the lungs and swallowed. Approximately 10% is absorbed in the gastro intestinal tract and gets deposited in the bones. Women with previous lead exposures may have elevated blood levels during periods of high bone turnover (e.g. pregnancy, lactation, or hyperthyroidism).

Their urborn children may be exposed transplacentally, and newborns through breast milk to high levels of lead. Foetuses, infants and children are considered to be particularly susceptible to the adverse effects. Early childhood lead exposures has neurobehavioral effects such as various learning dosorders, reading disabilities, poor vocabulary and grammatical reasoning.

Inspite of decades of laboratory clinical and epidemiologic research, however the health effects of exposure of humans to pollutants remain incompletely characterized. Finally most environmental exposures involved multiple pollutants. Control of exposures in life is an important component of appropriate preventive action. Escape of toxic substances into the ambient air can be prevented by an variety of engineering methods such as enclosure, ventilation and air cleaning.

A major contribution in this field is the development of arrestors for the removal of contaminants like convertors to reduce automobile exhaust. Use of technology that reduces pollution like use of electricity and natural gas in place of coal. The control of an air pollution is ultimately an engineering problem.

Human rights are a extensive as human life and, whether or not enshrined in national constitutions or bills of right or in international covenants to which nations are signatory, first order rights are inherent and inalienable. As Jefferson said, "the God that gave us life, gave us liberty at the same time".

These rights are not gifted and cannot be taken away except by due process of law. To act otherwise is to violate Human Rights. There are, however, a whole series of rights, other than the basic or fundamental freedoms, which are statutory or derive from subscription to international or regional covenants.

Human Rights may be broadly classified as civil

and political (so-called civil liberties and democratic rights), and social, economic and cultural. The latter include rights to development, the rights of women and children, a whole new family of environmental rights, rights to education and health, and to employment and to enjoy the fruits of labour. Both sets of rights are growing.

Thus, freedom of speech and expression has developed to encompass the right to information. Privacy is now increasingly protected. There will be refinements and new situations will bring forth new rights such as now, in some societies, of pays, and may be for victims of AIDS.

A comparison of South Asian constitutions will probably indicate a broad similarity in the basic rights enunciated. Interpretations and implementation might vary.

Derogations are permitted in emergency situations and these instances have been extensive in all parts of South Asia and have sometimes continued long after the proximate cause, perhaps well justified in some cases, has passed. The Indian Emergency (1975-77) and martial law or emergency regimes in Pakistan, Nepal, Bangladesh and Sri Lanka can also be cited.

Many statutes contain preventive laws (preventive detention in India), and special laws may be invoked in given circumstances such as declaring certain areas to be disturbed and applying therein summary procedures (such as the Armed Forces Special Powers Act in India).

The South Asian nations are members of the United Nations and have variously subscribed to a number of international instruments including the international Covenants on Civil and Political Rights/Economic and Social Rights, the Geneva Conventions, ILO conventions and so forth. However, retification has not always followed speedily or at all. For instance, India took a long time to ratify the Convention on the Rights of the Child and has yet to ratify the Convention Against Torture.

The record of the other South Asian governments would probably reveal similar lags or omissions which need to be overcome. Even where ratifications has taken place it is not certain whether governments have cared to create public awareness about national adherence to these conventions and to explain their implications or to examine whether national laws need to be upgraded, expanded or created to give them an enforceable statutory basis.

This is an exercise national governments should be asked to undertake and could be the subjects of a report of SAARC.

While human rights are proclaimed, newly-independent nations have sometimes been prone to stress sovereign or national rights, the rights of the state, over individual human rights.

This was true worldwide until the second world war and in some ways continue to be so even in the more industrially advanced and politically older or mature societies because of the fears and compulsions of the cold war. With the end of the East-West divide, the West has given more emphasis to human rights and democratic governance and has come to attach trade and aid conditionalities for "good performance". While this may be justified at one level, the question that arises, as it does in the domestic domain, is who will police the policeman?

Also, how far observing is the human rights record of smaller and weaker countries. Such conditionalities are also creeping into the field of environment, the rights of so-called indigenous people, a misnomer when applied to South Asian societies, and so on.

Development, gender, minority, regional and environmental rights, among others, are of great importance to South Asia where poverty, gender inequalities, disparities, illiteracy, bonded labour and child labour are widespread. Poverty robs the individual of dignity and, often, children of their childhood. While, therefore, development rights are vitally important, there are no hierarchy of rights.

All rights, political, civil cultural, social and economic, are indivisible and mutually reinforcing. This is a normative value that South Asia must accept and proclaim so that one right is not used to supersede and thereby deny another.

South Asia has a number of human rights organisations, statutory and voluntary. In India, for scheduled castes and tribes and statutory bodies such as the Press Council, the Minorities Commission, the National Commission for Women, and the Commissioner for Linguistic Minorities.

A statutory Human Rights Commission has been brought into being by ordinance and incorporates many improvements in relation to an earlier Bill. Pakistan has a very active non-governmental Human Rights Commission whose reports merit wider distribution in the region. The Human Rights Organisation of Nepal (HURON) played an important part in securing the change-over from the panchayati system to the vigorous multi-party democracy that was established in 1991.

Bangladesh has a Coordinating Council for Human Rights (CCHRB) which aims to publish annual reports.

All the countries of South Asia are in transition and there is much ferment: violence, terrorism, ethnic discords, the rise of religious fundamentalisms, basic rights, but the exploitation of religion for partisan political ends, can be dangerous as India has discovered. Likewise caste.

With the process of nation-building still underway, individual and state rights tend to clash. A more careful study of events and trends and a sharing of experience could promote clarity and wisdom in dealing with highly complex and volatile situations.

Human rights violations regrettably occur everywhere around the globe in greater or lesser measure. What matters, however, is that violation, aberrant action and derogations are brought to light by the media, the law enforcement agencies and human rights groups or by the community at large and the guilty are brought to book.

While human rights mechanisms need to be strengthened or even created where necessary, human rights problems most often begin where due process and the criminal justice system break down. This then leads to false cases, torture, custodial death, extortion, rape, corruption, et al. The public preception of a breakdown in the local criminal justice system led to the Bhagalpur blindings in Bihar in the 1980s when there was widespread public approval of known criminals being blinded while in detention for fear that they would otherwise be bailed out or released and continue with their depredations.

The restoration of the efficacy, integrity and speed of the criminal justice system (including the working of the police and jails) is perhaps the single most important item that should be on the South Asian human rights agenda. For prevention is better than cure. Political interference with the police, the politicisation of crime and the criminalisation of politics have played havoc.

Dealing with human rights violations then becomes a case of trying to shut the stable door after the horse has bolted. The understaffing of courts, mounting arrears and costs, and dilatory procedures are discrediting the rule of law.

Yet the judiciary has been innovative. In India, for example, public interest litigation has opened new doors, overriding former impediments of locus standi in relations to the cause of action and treating a single case as a class action. Judicial verdicts have also amplified Article 21, the Right to Life, to embrace "rights to livelihood, health, education, shelter, dignity, minimum wage, environment" (Upendra Baxi).

Environmental issues have come to the fore in South Asia with poverty, population and livestock pressures leading to deforestation, erosion of common property resources and environmental degradation generally.

The land can no longer support burgeoning numbers and the region is spawning its share of inadvertent cities and threatens to (and does) explode with crime and violence. Water and energy shortages confront us and industrial, pollution and development blight are increasingly visible, though yet in the early stages. The warning signals are there.

South Asia's environmental problems are largely related to the economics of survival, poverty in a broad sense being the worst polluter. Population control and ensuring an early demographic transition are of the highest importance. Primary education and health and improving the status of women hold the key as Sri Lanka, and Kerala and Goa in India have well demonstrated. The pace of development must be hastened and the fruits of development more equitably shared.

There have to be alternative sources of fodder and fuel, improved land-use patterns, better land and water management and greater emphasis on biofertilisers and integrated pest management so as to avoid incremental toxicity entering the food chain. Rivers are becoming sewers. The Ganga Action Plan, now being extended to the Yamuna, Damodar, Gomati and other rivers, represents the largest river clean-up operation ever undertaken anywhere. Conservation, substainability and maintenance of bio-diversity have become key ideas.

South Asia is setting new pollution standards and seeking to upgrade technology and maintenance systems, but there is a long way to go. Environmental groups are active and environmental awareness is spreading. Indian courts have ordered the closure of polluting industries for failure to ensure minimal emission of effluent standards despite being allowed resonable time, access to credit, and technical assistance to upgrade their technology. Environmental tribunals are contemplated.

Two problems will have to be confronted. One is internal pressure from local groups and communities to adopt alternative strategies of development: decentralised, low-energy, appropriate technology, small-is-beautiful, back-to-nature systems.

While the opposition to ostentatious consumption, crass consumerism and waste is widel'y shared, there will be reservations about nostalgia, romanticising the past, overlooking the tremendous growth of population which is likely to double or triple again before it stabilises in South Asia, and ignoring the demand for minimal life styles and national infra-structure in a globalised setting. There has to be a practical via media. At the other end of the scale, the North would like to globalise tropical forests and bio-diversity and points to population growth as a looming ecological threat, leading to green house warming, a possible sea-rise, and destablising climate changes.

This ignores the unsustainable life styles of the North and its massive contribution to global warming since the industrial revolution, but more particularly, in the past few decades. Global conferencing and the Rio meet have brought about some convergence, but maybe not nearly enough.

South Asia, as a clearly demacrated monsoonal geopolitical entity, should concert action on both the regional and global planes.

The Himalayan-Karakoram barrier constitutes a critical watershed the greening of which should be worth something as a global carbon sink and oxygen bank. Debt-for-nature swaps and debt forgiveness by the North, linked to environmental improvement and technological upgradation in South Asia, should be jointly explored. The natural disaster study undertaken by SAARC (1989-91) marks a beginning towards collective action on environmental issues and optimal harnessing of shared natural resources such as rivers and bio-diversity.

There could be joint studies and research programmes in South Asia to meet the challenge of global warming and sea-rise effects, to fight locusts and study seismicity.

On the human rights plane, it is perhaps not widely known that a South Asian Forum for Human Rights was formally set up in Kathmandu in February, 1993, a spinoff from a suggestion mooted at the World Human Rights Congress in Delhi in 1990. This is a non-governmental body that plans to promote networking and interaction among human rights groups in the region.

All the SAARC nations other than the Maldives are represented. It is still at an embryonic stage but could grow.

The setting up of SAARC observer groups to monitor elections in the region represents another initiative. Perhaps the time has come to moot the establishment of a human rights cell within SAARC or more informally to gather information, liaise and sensitise governments on issues and opportunities that call for concerted action.

Human rights and environmental issues are very much on the national, regional and international agenda today. These concerns have wide linkages and need to be properly understood and fully internalised in national and regional policies and instruments.

In the pre-nationalisation days, large and medium industry and wholesale trade accounted for over 78 per cent of the bank credit. By March 1994, share of these sectors (excluding credit for public food procurement) had declined to about 42.7 per cent. Correspondingly, share of priority sectors, food procurement agencies, etc, has shown significant improvement.

Extension of credit to small borrowers in the hitherto neglected sectors of the economy has been one of the major tasks assigned to the public sector banks in the post-nationalisation period. To achieve this objective, banks have drawn up schemes to extend credit to small borrowers in sectors like agriculture, small scale industry, road and water transport, retail trade and small business which traditionally had very little share in the credit extended by banks.

Taking into account the need to provide resource requirements to weaker sections, for specific needs, consumption credit (with certain limits) has been included in priority sector advances. Number of borrowal accounts with public sector banks for these categories of borrowers increased from 3.28 lakh to 337.38 lakh between June 1969 and March 1994. Amount outstanding during the same period increased from Rs. 441 crore to Rs. 53,875 crore. Public sector banks accounted for 35.3 per cent of the total bank credit by March 1993.

With a view to increase credit flow to small and poor borrowers, commercial banks were advised by the Reserve Bank of India to provide at least 10 per cent of their net bank credit of 25 per cent of their priority sector advances to weaker sections comprising of small and marginal farmers, landless labourers, tenant farmers and share-croppers, artisans, village and cottage industries, Scheme of Urban Micro Enterprises (SUME) and beneficiaries of Inteegrated Rural Development Programme, some scheduled castes and scheduled tribes and beneficiaries of Differential Rate of Interest (DRI) scheme.

As at the end of March 1993, the amount of outstanding advances extended by public sector to weaker sections was Rs. 12,779 crore and accounted for 9.1 per cent of their net bank credit and 24.0 per cent of priority sector advances.

Banks were intially given a target extending 15 per cent of the total advances as direct finance to the agriculture sector to be achieved by March 1985.

This target was subsequently raised to 18 per cent to be achieved by March 1990. in terms of the guidelines issued by Reserve Bank of India in October 1993, both direct and indirect advances for agriculture will be taken together for assessing the target of 18 per cent provided lendings for indirect agriculture should not exceed one fourth of the total agriculture lending target of 18 per cent of the net bank credit. As on March 1994, public sector banks extended 13.1 per cent of the total advances to the agriculture sector.

People belonging to the scheduled castes and scheduled tribes have been recognised as the most vulnerable sections. Bank have been asked to make special efforts to assist them with adequate credit to enable them to undertake self-employment ventures toacquire income generating capital assets so as to improve their stantard of living. At the end of march 1994, the total outstanding amount of loan extended to scheduled castes/scheduled tribes by poublic sector banks was Rs. 4,737 crore involving 97.5 lakh borrowal accounts.

The concern for human poverty and its eradication to improve human environment have been the central focus of our development planning in the country since the inception of the planing era. Various schemes have been formulated and implemented with the sole objective of removing poverty and thereby increasing the quality of life of the people in the lower ranks of population.

The explicit manifestation of the government's concern for poverty alleviation got its expression when the first 20-Point Programme was launched on 1 July 1975 under the connotation of Ganibi Hatao which was conceived by the late Prime Minister Smt Indira Gandhi. This programme was implemented with a pragmatic success during 1975-76 and 1976-77 Annual Plans. The Sixth Five Year Plan (1980-85)) incorporated these programmes as guiding factors in the planning process. Taking the past experience, the original 20-Point Programme was further re-defined, revitalized and announced to the Nation on 14 January 1982.

— Increase irrigation potential, develop and dissemiinate technologies and imputs for dry land agriculture;

— Make special efforts to increase production of pulses and vegetable oilseeds;

— Strengthen and expand coverage of integrated rural development and national rural employment programmes;

— Implement agricultural land ceilings, distribute surplus land and complete compilation of land records by removing all administrative and legal obstacles;

— Review and effectively enforce minimum wages for agricultural labour; (vi) Rehabilitate bonded labour;

— Accelerate programmes for the development of scheduled castes and scheduled tribes;

— Supply drinking water to all problem villages;

— Allot house sites to rural families who are without them and expand programmes for construction assistance to them;

— Improve the environment of slums, implement programmes of house building for economically weaker sections and take measures to arrest unwarranted increase in land prices;

— Maximise power generation, improve the functioning of electricity authorities and electrify all villages;

— Pursue vigorously programmes of afforestation social and farm forestry and the development of bio-gas and other alternative energy sources;

— Promote family planning on a voluntary basis as a people's movement; (xiv) Substantially augment universal primary health care facilities and control of leprosy, TB and blindness;

— Accelerate programmes of welfare for women and children and nutrition programmes for pregnant women, nursing mothers and children, specially in tribal hill and backward areas;

— Spread universal elementary education for the age group 6-14 with special emphasis on girls and simultaneously involve students and voluntary agencies in programmes for the removal of adult illiteracy;

— Expand the public distribution system through more fair price shops, including mobile shops in far flung areas and shops, to cater to industrial workers, students' hostels, and make available to students textbooks and exercise books on a priority basis and to promote a strong consumer protection movement;

— Liberalise investment procedures and streamline industrial policies to ensure timely completion of projects. Give handicrafts, handlooms, small and village industries all facilities to grow and to update their technology;

— Continue strict action against smugglers, hoarders and tax evaders and tax evaders and check black money; and

— Improve the working of the public enterprises by increasing efficiency, capacity utilisation and the generation of internal sources.

Various programmes were formulated to achieve the above objectives focussing mostly on the critical socio-economic constraints on development. The existence of human poverty was considered the single most adverse constraints to human development.

Therefore, breaking the vicious circle of poverty which was both the cause and the effect of under development in the country was central to the formulation of 20-Point Programme. The Sixth Five Year Plan was designed taking note of the micro-objectives of 20-Point Programme in the critical sectors which were accorded high priority in the planning process.

The emphasis on agricultural productivity, rural employment, provision of safe drinking water, allotment of houses sites to the rural families, improvement of slums, voluntary family planning, provision of basic health care, concern for environmental degradation, spread of elementary education, accelerating welfare programmes for the women and children were the most positive features of the revised 20-Point Programme which were spelt out keeping in view the basic objective of the development planning that the fruits of planning mustensure the 'basic needs' of human beings if development process is at all to be sustainable.

While the various evaluation reports indicate different positive impacts, the major impact of the 20-Point Programme in the country was the re—distribution of productive assets in favour of the less privileged who are the backbone of the economy. From the point of view of a sustainable growth, these programmes not only improve the productivity in the rural sector but also increased the overal quality of life in the villages to a perceptible degree.

In the light of the experience and achievements of the revised 20-Point Programme 1982 and the emerging new socio-economic problems during the Seventh Plan (1985-90) the programmes were restructured in 1986 with the directions given by the then Prime Minister Shri Rajiv Gandhi which was popularly known as 20-Point Programme 1986.

The restructured programmes came into effect from 1 April 1987 along with Annual Plan of 1987-88. Briefly, the programmes are as under:

- Attack on Rural Poverty: (i) ensure that poverty alleviation programmes reach all the poor in every village; (ii) dovetail wage employment programmes with programmes for area development and human resource development and create national and community assets like school buildings, roads, tanks, fuel and fodder reserves; (iii) correlate the various rural development productivity and production-expand rural employment; (iv) promote handlooms, handicrafts, village and small industries and improve skills for self-employment; and (v) Revitalise Panchayats, cooperatives and local bodies.

- Strategy for Rain-fed Agriculture: (i) improve the technology for conserving moisture and ensure better management of land and water resources; (ii) develop and distribute appropriate and improved seeds; and (iii) reduce vulnerability to drought through suitable changes in droughtprone areas and drought-relief programmes.

- Better use of Irrigation Water: (i) Develop the catchment areas and improve drainage in basins and deltas; (ii) improve irrigation management in command areas; (iii) prevent water logging, salinity and wasteful use; and (iv) coordinate the use of surface and ground water.

- Bigger Harvests: (i) revolutionise rice production in the eastern region and other areas of low productivity; (ii) achieve self-reliance in edible oils; (iii) secure greater production of pulses; (iv) intensify the cultivation of fruits and vegetables; (v) augment facilities for modern storage, processing and marketing of agricultural produce; (vi) help livestock and dairy framers to increase productivity; and (vii) develop fish farming and sea fishing.

- Enfrocement of Land Reforms: (i) complete compilation of land records; (ii) implement agricultural land ceilings; and (iii) distribute surplus land to the landless.

- Special Programmes for Rural Labour: (i) enforce minimum wages for unorganised labour in agriculture and industry, (ii) fully implement laws abolishing bonded labour; and (iii) involve voluntary agencies in prigrammes for the rehabilitation of bonded labour.
- Clean Drinking Water: (i) provide safe water all villages; (ii) assist local communities to maintain the sources of such water supply in good condition; (iii) pay special attention to water supply for SCs and STs.
- Health for All: (i)Improve the quality of primary health care; (ii) fight leprosy, TB malaria, goitre, blindness and other major diseases; (iii) provide immunisation for all infants and children; (iv) improve sanitation facilities in rural areas, particularly for women; and (v) pay special attention to programmes for the rehabilitation of the handicapped.
- Two Child Norm: (i) bring about voluntary acceptance ofthe two child norm; (ii) promote responsible parenthood; (iii) reduce infant mortality; and (iv) expand maternity and child care facilities.
- Expansion of Education: (i) universalise elementary education with special emphasis on girls' education; (ii) improve the content of education at all levels; (iii) promote non-formal education and functional literacy programmes, including promotion of skills; (iv) stimulate adult literacy programmes, with the participation of students and voluntary agencies; and (v) emphasis on national integration and social and moral values and instil pride in our heritage.
- Justice to Scheduled Castes and Scheduled Tribes: (i) ensure compliance with the constitutional provisions and laws for the SCs and STs; (ii) ensure possession of land allotted to SCs and STs; (iii) revitalise the land allotment programme; ()iv) organise and assist

special coaching programmes to immprove educational standards, (v) eradicate scavenging and undertake special programmes for the rehabilitation of Safai Karamcharis; (vi) provide better direction and adequate funds for the special component programmes; (vii) pursue programmes for the fuller integration of SCs and STs with the rest of the society; and (viii) ensure the rehabilitation of tribals displaced from their habitat.

- Equality for Women: (i) raise the status of women; (ii) enhance awareness of the problems of women; (iii) create mass consciousness about women's rights; (iv) implement a national programme of training and employment for women; (v) enable women to participate with equality in socio-economic development and nation-building; and (vi) rouse public opinion against dowry and ensure effective implementation of anti-dowry legislation.
- New Opportunities for Youth: (i) enlarge opportunities for youth in sports, adventure and cultural activities; (ii) promote physical fitness; (iii) involve youth on a massive scale in projects of national development such as the cleaning of the Ganga, the conservation and enrichment of the environment and mass education; (iv) identify outstanding young persons in all fields to encourage and develop their talents; (v) involve youth in temper; (vi) expand the network of Nehru Yuvak Kendras; (vii) strengthen the National Service Scheme and the National Cadet Corps; and (viii) encourage voluntary agencies working for the welfare of rural youth.
- Housing for the People: (i) make available house sites to the rural poor; (ii) expand programmes of house construction; (iii) lay special emphasis on construction of houses for SCs and STs; and (iv) develop low cost building materials.

- Improvement of Slums: (i) restrict the growth of slums; (ii) provide basic facilities in existing slum areas; and (iii) encourage planned house building in urban areas.
- New Strategy for Forestry: (i) grow more trees and raise more firest, with the full involvement of the people; (ii) protect the traditional rights of tribal populations and local communities of access to fuel wood and forest produce; (iii) reclaim wastelands for productive use; and (iv) plant appropriate vegetation in hilly, desert and coastal areas.
- Protection of the Environment: (i) enhance public awareness of the dangers of environmental degradation; (ii) mobilise popular support for environmental protection; (iii) promote recognition that enduring development demands preservation of the ecology; and (iv) ensure judicious site selection for projects and proper choice of technology.
- Concern for the Consumers: (i) bring essential consumption goods within easy reach of the poor; (ii) build a consumer protection movements; (iii) restructure the distribution system so that subsidies reach the most needy; and (iv) strengthen the public distribution system.
- Energy for the Villages: (i) expand the supply of electricity for productive use in the villages; (ii) develop alternative sources of energy, particularly biogas; and (iii) promote integrated area specific programmes for rural energy.
- A Responsive Administration: (i) simplify procedures; (ii) delegate authority; (iii) enforce accountablility; (iv) evolve monitoring systems from block to national level; and (v) attend promptly and sympatherically to public grievances.

While the restructured 20-Point Programme renewed the nation's commitment to eradicate poverty, it laid balanced emphasis on how to raise overall procductivity, reduce income inequalties and remove social and economic disparities so that the ultimate fruits of development resulted in improvement of quality of life of human environment.

The coverage of the programme was broadened to bring within its ambit a number of lmajor areas of social concern for fulfiling not only the 'basic needs' like adeauate provison of food, clean drinking water, housing and health facilities, it laid more emphasis on human dignity and individual rights by encouraging 'responsible' parenthood, equality for women, opportunities for the youth, rights of consumers, justice to scheduled castes and scheduled tribes, etc.

The inherent philosophy behind the restructured programme was that the development has no real meaning without human dignity and individual rights.

The departments/ministries concerned on the subject of 20-Point Programme, 1986 set the annual targets in consultation with the states and the Department of Programme Implementation (DPI). DPI monitors the implementation of the 20-Point Programme. The management information system developed by this Department for implementation of the programmes consists of (i) Monthly Progress Report; (ii) Capsule Report; (iii) Half Yearly Progress Report; and (iv) Annual Report.

Under 20-Point Programme-1986, there are 119 items identified for monitoring. Of these, 54 are monitored on an evaluatory basis and 65 items are retained for physical targetting/monitoring. Again of the 65 items identified for quantitative assessment, 28 items have been identified for monitoring on a monthly basis. Only 19 items, out of the 28 items of the Monthly Report, are taken for the purpose of ranking. The Half Yearly Report covers majority of the items of 20-Point Programme indicating qualitative performance.

A three-tier system of monitoring has been established in the states/UTs, as follows:

- at the agency level which are entrusted with the execution of the programmes in the field level;
- at the state level which provides infrastructure and direction for programme execution; and
- at the Central Government level not only by the sectoral ministries and departments but also by the Department of Programme Implementation under the Ministry of Planning and Programme Implementation, which oversees the monitoring and evaluation system on a contiuous basis and reports to the Cabinet Secretriat and the Prime Minister's Office.

A statement showing the targets and achievements of major items of the 20-Point Programme on all India basis for the years 1992-93,1993-94 and 1994-95 is given in table 19.

A common symptom of rural poverty which India shares along with other developing countries is the existence of underutilized resources, such as land, water and endemic underemployment of labour. Poverty itself is the lot of about 39 per cent of the population as against about 20 poer cent as per calculations of theearlier government. During the period 1983—84 to 1987—88, rural poverty fell from 45.6 per cent to 39 per cent while between 1987—88 and 93—94, it fell only by a further 1.7 per cent.

In 1987—88, unemployment inperson—years was estimated to be 12.43 million in usual principal status,

15.30 million in weekly status, and 18.95 million on daily status. Even causal labour employment is 38.4 per cent among rural males and 31.4 per cent among rural females.

The above phenomenon has been interpreted from different perspectives. It is regarded as due to the fickleness of the poor and, therefore, the total literacy campaign in India seeks to encnouraged the poor to come together and improvve their lot. It can also be seen as an inherent attribute of the socio—economic structure retarding growth and perpetuating poverty.

Land reforms is the answer to this situation. A third perspective is to look at it as a potential for local resource mobilization and its concomitant local—level planning. In this context , the 73rd constitutional amendment conferring constitutional status to local bodies and for greater decentralization in the country is worth noting.

It is this point of view that the present paper has adopted. It is noted that there is an enormous potential for alleviating poverty which such underutilized resources represent.

Along side with the resource augmenting aspect, the mobilization of local resources also promises the simultanneous attainment of other adjectives which are apecial to rural development like greater decentralization in planning, increasing popular paraticipation and ensuring a greater degree of self—reliance on the part of local communities. Macro planning embodied in the Ninth Plan alone cannot cope with the highly particularized and the localized problems of identifying development potentialities in the rural communities. Even though the basic criteria of rural development are participation, production, distribution and consumption, participation takes on a different meaning.

The disadvantaged people are not to be cast inthe role of the objects of participation, but they are to be integrated as the subjects of the operation. Both human ıesource development and human development are the objectives in rural development and a World Bank study has shown that there will not be adequate resources for human development if government funds alone are to be depended upon. It is imperative to use local resources and community resources will have to be mobilized. Also the interdependence between eduction, health, sanitation and other social development sectors has to be taken care of because all of them jointly promote rural development.

Secondly, the interdependence between agriculture and rural development is noted and it is concluded that there is no alternative except to mobilize local resources. Reference in this context is not only to mobilization of financial resources through imposition of appropriate taxes in agriculture, but also more importantly to mobilize non-financial resources like labour, locally available material and technical expertise.

Indeed at the local level, resources like land, labour and human and physical resources—physical capital to a limited extent are available. Techno—economic surveys can identify the potential resources. But will all the labour force be mobilized for gainful and productive employment? This is a more important task and accompllishing ths depends on the integration of the techno—economic approach with other aspect of the social system and development process.

This is the concern of many mono—disciplines like economics, engineering, sociology, psychology, etc. All such studies have pointed out that only at the local level, the basic needs, particularly of vulnerable sections can be identified and they justify larger investment in primary education for promoting health, nutrition, rural development, family size, fertility, literacy and awareness of national culture.

It is true that rural development is in the main equivalent to the development of food and cash croops and their needed inputs—irrigation, fertilizer, seeds and other resource inputs—animal husbandry, dairying and poultry farming, fisheries, forestry and agro—industries.

But such investments in agricultural developmentare bound to be more effective when there is adequate investment in human resource development, particularly in literacy and primary education. Between the I and VII Five Year Plans, there has been a decline in agriculture, forestry, animal husbandry, fisheries irrigation, rural development and village and cottage industry from Rs. 45,924.70 crore to Rs. 45,523.02 crore (ie from 54.92% to 23.62% of the total public sector outlay). But in spite of the decline in agricultural outaly, rural development culd have been quickened if only there had been more investment in human resources and human developmen.

Local resource mobilization with local planning seems to be a promising vehicle for promoting rural development and alleviating poverty.

Local resource mobilization and substitution of human capital as well as physical capital is in conformity with the experience of some of the Scandinavian countriesand Japan in this context.

They have been able to substitute the scarce resources with resource mobilizaton at the local level in rural and agricultural sectorsin particular. Such local resources cannot flow to higher levels but can improve productivity at the local level. This resource augmenting effect has the advatage of accelerating agricultural growth.

In such an effort, equity will have to be given special consideration. The disadvantaged population has to be seen not in therole ofobjects of participation but they are to be integrated as the subjects ofoperation. There should be also anb organizational structure which promotes the effective participation of the disadvantaged population. The emergence of local bodies with elected representatives, one hopes, will make it possible to privide thisinfrastructure.

There should be sound planning at the three levels of District Panchayats, Panchayat Samithis and Village Panchayats.

To achieve the ambitious objectives of the Ninth Plan (1997-2002), the government has to face hard realities in mobilizing the required amount of huge resources. The Prime Minister and Chairman of the Planning Commission has called for collective efforts to raise resources of the order of Rs. 8,75,000 crore to finance the Plan.

The approach paper urges that the country has to take 'difficult decisions' which, as Mr. H.D. Deve Gowda explained, would in include reduction of fiscal deficit, rational user charges for power and irrigation, disinvestment of public sector and transparent and focused subsidies.

The Deputy Chairman of the Planning Commission, Prof Madhu Dandavate has rightly emphasized that the much needed public investment in various sectors could be available only if the required will is demonstrated in exploring new sources of revenues at all levels—the Centre, the States and local governments. He also noted that serious efforts are necessary to ensure better tax compliance and also to bring presumptive incomes computed from high expenditures of creamy layers under the tax net. Disinvestment of PSUs: Insofar as disinvestment of public sector undertakings as a source of revenue mobilization is concerned, the earlier experience is not at all encouraging. The failure of the disinvestment programme in 1995-96 and all indications of its repetition in regard to the target of mopping up Rs. 5,000 crore in the current fiscal year amply shows that the Ninth Plan should not bank much on this source prior to restructuring of the PSUs.

It may be noted here that an important reason for the inefficiency of PSUs is the defective MOUs which fix responsibilities of the organisations but remain silent on the responsibilities of government and administrative ministries.

This needs to be corrected and efficiency enhanced since the government has to justify the existence of this sector and make the enterprises commercially viable.

Need for political will: Insofar as the States' efforts are concerned, there is room fro enhancing revenue collection provided political will is mobilized, administrative machinery for taxation is properly cleaned and temptation of the government for populist spending is arrested.

There is huge amount of tax arrears, under assessment of levy, tax evasion through foul means, complete absence of or unjustifiably low rates of tariffs and charges against public services rendered and inefficiently managed State PSUs running on heavy government subsidies. Bold steps to reverse the trend is urgently necessary. This also applies to the Union government by and large.

Savings: The approach paper aims at an annual rate of savings at the rate of 26.2 per cent as against the peak of 24.6 per cent in 1989-90. Since the biggest source of savings in the household sector which mobilizes around one-fifth of GDP, there is ample opportunity of raising this source through tax-related saving incentives and stability of the capital market for shares and debentures. Proper incentive pattern is also necessary for saving in physical assets which alone comprise more than 55 per cent of the total household sector savings. The savings of the private corporate sector is only 2.7 per cent which may be easily raised to three per cent of GDP through incentives and better collection.

The lowest is the public sector savings which are stagnating at around Id. 7 per cent. The savings from government companies and statutory corporations have started declining since 1990-91 and presently accounts for less than three per cent of GDP. Unless the negative savings on account of government administration and departmental enterprises are checked effectively, one could nolt expect larger savings from the public sector.

At the same time, the huge amount of government subsidy on account of food and fertilizers, petroleum and petroleum products, sugar and other selective items should be withdrawn from those who have the capacity to pay at the rate of open market prices. The oil pool deficit alone has reached public destribution system would claim a whopping Rs. 2,000 crore. There is no justification of suppresssing the administered prices since its substitute is only a resort to deficit financing that would come in the way of macro-economic adjustment in the country.

Inequitable income tax system: The system of income taxation in India has remained utterly inequitable as millions of highly rich people go untaxed due to fear of unpopularity among politicians. Thus, the much talked about unexploited source of agricultural income tax has remained a forbidden fruit. In spite of the fact that the

Green Revolution and the new agricultural strategy with all kinds of agro-mechanisation subsidy together with a price support programme for farm products have placed more and more wealth in the hands of rich farmers, no political decision has yet been taken to bring the wealthy section of farmers under the income tax net.

The K.N. Raj Committee recommended long ago a progressive tax structure for agricultural incomes along with the incomes from non-agricultural sources and also from allied activities of the farm sector. Some members in the NDC while approving the Ninth Plan approach paper, urged upon mobilization of black money as a revenue raising device.

Since the agricultural sector offers a golden opportunity to earners of illegal incomes to conceal black money and black wealth under the veil of untaxed farm incomes and since the gap between poverty and prosperity in the farming community has greatly widened as a result of the emergence of highly rich agriculturists, the imposition of agricultural income tax along with non-agricultural income will not only fetch huge funds to the resource-starved exhequer, but will also reduce considerably the prevailing inequality of incomes in rural areas on the one hand and mop up a large part of black money on the other.

The other areas of unequal treatment lies in the complete absence of income tax among Scheduled and backward classes, where, too a large section of people has become millionaires due to business activity, government contracts, construction works and heavy development expenditure incurred in backward regions by the government in course of the five year plans, These rich people also go untaxed.

In order to remove such utter discrimination, it is

urgently necessary that these creamy layers be invariably brought within the income tax net.

Thus, what the foregoing discussion implies is that bold decisions and hard determination are necessary to give a proper shape to the economy after the aspirations of the Ninth Plan approach paper. While political will is a pre-condition, the States' unqualified co-operation will be the most basic factor.

However, the aspirations of resource-starved States will urgently need attention particularly with respect to their autonomy and larger access to Central tax sharing which has been the main irritant in the Centre-State relationship. The Centrally-sponsored schemes which have remained only half-hearted attempts for all these years should be left to the responsibility of the States with hundred per cent resource disposal to them.

The declining trend of the share of the State' Plan in the total public sector plan outlay needs to be reversed in the Ninth Plan and the decentralized planning should call for strengthening of the administrative set-up of Panchayati Raj institutions at all levels.

Accountability and monitoring of activity must be ensured at every step so that development plan does not degenerate into expenditure plan. If all revenue sources are properly exploited, implementation of programmes is carried out in the right perspective and utmost care is maintained in government consumption expenses, there is no reason why the aspirations of the approach paper should not come into reality.

Underutilization may be in the intensity of land use and agricultural productivity or the levels of utilisation of labour force. Measures ofunderutilization can be:

- a straightforward measure of idle resources, of production capacity at a given level of technology and organization, eg fallow land, unemployment and underemployment according to atime measure;

- misallocation of resources due to lack of knowledge of superior alternatives or distortion in the structure of incentives; and
- underutilization in terms of productivity. According to Prof. Brahmananda, even though aggregate capital may be adequate potentially at the macrolevel, capital in the form of wage goods capacity may be deficient.

It is in the process of production of wage goods at the local level through local planning that local resource mobilization can take place and productivity can be improved and social change brought about. At the grass roots level in the rural areas, there is urgent need for improving productivity and promoting social change with better education.

Rural development refers to a number of development programmes. Earlier it was linked only with agricultural development but on the basis of the experience during the last few decades we can speak of holistic rural development which includes agriculture, rural development, rural indutries, and hollistic self—supporting development.

In order to accelerate such a holistic rural development there are three major potential areas for integration which are: (a) stepping up the existing wage employment programme in rural areas ofor capital construction in agriculture and for ecodevelement; (b) stimulating the growth of households by intergrating them with the existing self—employment programmes like IRDP; and (c) accelerating the pace of social development.

In sum, we will emphasize that poverty alleviation

programmes should be properly integratd with over—all development. No rural development is possible without wipping out poverty or reducing it in stages. The integration of poverty alleviation objective with the over–all development strategy has to be distinguished from the issue of integrating poverty alleviation programmes with the over–all development strategy.

The over—all development strategy is concerned with questions like investment priorities, choice of technique and location of projects through trickle down effects. It tries to reduce poverty. A greater and more specific role has to be given to investment in agiven resources, eg bringing down the capital output ratio to a certain level sector by sector). But integration of poverty alleviation programmes with over–all development strategy tries to ensure that poverty alleviation programmes subserve the goals of over—all development. At present, the schemes for increasing incomes and employment do not adequately take care of it. In this also there should be a greater role both for human resource development and human development.

In India, as in most traditional societies, people lived a life that rarely, if ever, threatened their environment. For centuries populations were more or less steady and local resources were sufficient to meet the demands of food, fuel, shelter and other basic requirements of life. Practices specifically suited to each area evolved over hundreds of years. Practices that ensured utilization of natural resources without degrading them.

While these systems were environmentally sound, life was vulnerable to many externaly factors. This was reflected in the low life-expectancy at birth, which was about 30 years at best. Communities were highly vulnerable to disease, epidemics and calamities like floods and drought. It is estimated that about 2.5 million people died during the Bengal famine of 1943. During the decade 1911-1921, the great influenze epidemic took a toll of 12 million lives. In fact, during this period the number of deaths exceeded the number of births, resulting in a population decline.

At the time of independence in 1947, the challenges before the new nation were many. Prime in importance was the task of decreasing human vulnerability to natural calamities. India needed not only to become self-sufficient in food production, but also to build enough reserves to tide over a drought year. Changes were also required in policies laid down during colonial times which dealt with the use and distribution of basic requirements.

With better health services and sanitation, increased food production and better nutrition, life expectancy at birth went up from 32 years at Independence to 64 years in 1991. Death rate decreased rapidly from 22.8 per thousand in 1951 to 10.9 in 1988. Birth rates have also decreased with overall development, but these have been slower in coming down. The net effect was a rapid increase in population from 361 million in 1951 to 844 million in 1991, a 134 per cent increase.

To meet the challenge of sustaining this increased population, nes land was brought under the plough. The total cultivated area went up from 118.75 mha in 195-51 to 140.90 mha in 1984-85, levelling off thereafter. Irrigation potential went up from 22.6 mha in the '50s to 74.3 mha by 1989-90. New seeds and higher inputs brought about the Green Revolution, and India's agricultural growth rate went up from a mere 0.3 per cent in pre-Independence years to 3.5 per cent after 1977. Between 1950-51 and 1988-89, the country's foodgrain production rose from 50.8 million tonnes per annum to 170.2 million tonnes per annum, an increase of 235 per cent. Milk production has gone up from 17,406 thousand tonnes in 1950 to 44,300 thousand tonnes in 1986—an increase of 180 per cent. Largely operating through producers cooperatives, India has a sophisticated dairy industry. However, despite a livestock population of over 400 million—the world's largest—India milk yield per animal is still very low. Bullocks are used for traction in fields and for rural transport, making for a close relationship between cattle and agriculture. Animal dung acts as a source of fertilizer as well as fuel.

India is no longer dependent on import of foodgrains. While gains in food production have taken India towards self-sufficiency, the country still depends on imports of certain agricultural inputs. While floods and drought are a recurrent reality, no longer do they lead to mass starvation deaths. A buffer stock of foodgrains, with rice and wheat amounting to about 15 million tonnes, has been built up.

While achievements have been considerable, the gains in the quality of life have been slow. The increasing population continues to erode the net benefits. Although they spend 85 per cent of their income on food, the poorest 20 per cent of the population are still unable to consume more than 1,500 calories a day, as against the 2,300 considered a necessary minimum by the Planning commission.

Efforts are on to ensure that all 600,000 villages in India, have a safe and protected source of drinking water. The implications of this on health and sanitation, and on the amount of time and energy spent by women on fetching water are enormous. While the challenge of vulnerability has been met, poverty remains an issue central to India's development.

But while the effect of population increase in decreasing the net benefits of development was understood, there was something else, less noticed, which was threatening the gains of development. This was the erosion of the biological and environmental base of the country. Many of the gains of the first few decades had come at the cost of India's biological and environmental 'capital'. Intensive agriculture led to problems like land deterioration, water depletion, pest infestations and loss of genetic diversity of crops. Excessive use of chemical fertilizers and pesticided, and poor drainage have led to pollution in several rural areas.

Land, water and the biological resources which support agriculture and animal husbandry and provide the essential requirements of food, drinking water and fuel are all under severe pressure. Protecting and reclaiming these and managing them more carefully is essential to sustaining India's life-support systems.

It is estimated that 175 mha of India's land is degraded. This includes 85 mha under agriculture and 35 mha of forest land. Among the various reasons for the land losing its productivity are the over-application of chemical fertilizers in agriculture, waterlogging as a result of over-irrigaiton, canal seepage, poor drainage, overgrazing of common grazing lands and deforestation. The seriousness of deforestation has been dramatically brought out through the use of modern monitoring and mapping thechnologies.

Land, water and biological resources are intricately linked to one another. With excessive pressure on the biomass, the vegetative cover starts to disappear. As a consequence, the runoff of water during the rains increases and groundwater recharge is diminished. Without vegetation, the topsoil that has taken centuries to form is washed away and the land gets eroded. In hilly areas, the process starts an almost irreversible cycle of degradation.

Two of the main pressures on the vegetative cover are the need for fuelwood and fodder. In India almost 87 per cent of energy for cooking is obtained from firewood, agricultural wastes and cow-dung, and only 13 per cent cooking energy is from commercial sources.

Firewood alone provides 50 per cent of the cooking energy in cities and 70 per cent in villages. This dependence on firewood has put a great pressure on forest, and in fact on all vegetative matter. The demand, estimated at 157 million tonnes in 1986-87, is far in excess of the supply. With the consequent disappearance of trees and other vegetation, women, who are the principal collectors of fuelwood, have to spend a much greater amount of time on collection thereby putting up the 'cost' of fuelwood.

The other pressure is the need for fodder. With the world's largest cattle popultion of over 400 million animals, fodder availability in India is grossly inadequate. Pasture land only constitutes 3.9 per cent of the land and as a result is degraded. The pressure on forests is once again heavy. The cattle which are undernourished produce low quantities of milk. In degraded environments people find it easier to keep goats, and the increase in te goat population has been much more rapid than that of cattle, buffaloes and sheep. But goats in fragile ecosystems are as much a problem as a solution and, unless properly managed, can further degrade the environment.

Realizing the urgent need to increase biomass production, social foresty programmes were started in the late 1970s. These included raising rural fuelwood plantations and village wood lots, starting tree nurseries, distribution of tree spalings, encouragement to plantations around agricultural fields, as well as promotion of farm forestry and strip plantation on roadsides and canel banks. But while there were many successes, this programme was not able to arrest the increasing degradation of land caused by over-exploitation.

By 1985 about half of India's land was estimated to be wasteland—land which had hardly any vegetation left on it. Rajiv Gandhi, who was then Prime Minister, announced the development of wastelands as a major thrust area. The social forestry experience had shown that such programmes were more effective if carried out with the participation of the local communities at every stage.

Without this it would not be possible to protect the plantations. The National Wastelands Development Board was set up to encourage wastelands development and, working with a number of voluntary agencies, to involve people in this process.

While these programmes were being initiated several experiments were underway, including the one at Arabari in West Bengal, in which people were being involved in managing forest areas along with the Forest Department. The cumulative experience of such efforts led to a Government circular in 1990, asking all state forest departments to try the Joint Forest Management model. It will be some time before such a concept can be fully implemented, but the circular itself represents a significant recognition regarding the management of forests.

When the forest regulations, and indeed the Forest Department, were established during the colonial period, they were seen as agencies for the controlled exploitation of forests for wood and revenue. The growing pressure on forests has seen the gradual transformation of the Department into a conservation agency.

The recent circular speaks not of protecting forests

from the people, but rather of conserving forests for the people, with the help of the people. While there is a long way to go in strengthening this partnership, the new initiative marks the beginning of a new era in the management of forests India's largest publicly held biological resource.

The initiatives for conserving biological resources have not come from Government alone. The Bishnoi example and movements like Chipko have been based on local communities protecting these resources and taking up afforestation programmes. people are involved in selecting the species most relevant to them, and take the responsibility for their protection which leads to high survival rates of the saplings.

While greater generation of biomass is one way of dealing with the pressure on this resource, its more efficient use is another. Several initiatives have been taken in this direction by both NGOs and the Government. But changing practices is a slow process. New technologies need to be explored while certain old practices need to be reaffirmed. There are practices that were once beneficial but are no longer sustainable. An example is that of shifting cultivation, practised in north-east India, parts of Andhra Pradesh etc. This used to operate under cycles of 20-30 years or more, but with increased population and reduced availability of land the cycle has been shortened, making the practice unviable today.

New improved chulhas (wood-fuelled stoves) can, if used properly, reduce the requirement of firewood by as much as 40 per cent. New experiments such as those under the Programme of Integrated Energy Systems for Villages of the Department of Non-Conventional Energy Sources go even beyond this. their aim is not only to make the village self-sufficient in cooking energy but also to fulfil its energy requirements for agriculture, pumping, lighting and heating.

Experiments such as those by the Gujarat Energy Development Agency (GEDA) have made villages like Methan and Kalyanpura self sufficient in energy. The strategy is based on growing biomass on village fallow land and using a wood gasifier to generate motive power. This is combined with direct solar-thermal power for heating water. The gasifier uses the biomass five times as efficiently as conventional methods. The key to this success story, as in the case of forest management, is a self-managed system controlled by the local community.

Biogas is a low-cost appropriate energy technology with major potential in rural areas. The National Biogas Development Programme has, as its main objectives, the maximisation of recycling of organic wastes in order to provide gas for cooking, and small decentralized power generation systems for operating water pumps, flour mills and other rural industries.

At present 1.4 million family-size biogas plants generate energy for cooking in village households across the country. The progress with community biogas plants has been less encouraging, with only around 300 such plants operating in the country today.

The shortage of fodder would similarly have to be dealt with through a combination of more production and better utilization. The current estimate of availability of green and dry fodder in the country is 250 million tonnes and 440 million tonnes respectively, while the requirement is about 932 million tonnes and 780 million tonnes respectively. About 100 million head or 25 per cent of the cattle population is estimated to be grazing on forest land. To close the gap between demand and supply and to reduce pressure on grazing land, practices like stall feeding of cattle need to be promoted.

The problem is, however, that with a large number of unproductive cattle, stall feeding is not always viable. The livestock issue is complex because of the very intricate relationship cattle have with life in rural India. The cow-dung is used for manure or as fuel. Bullocks are used as drought animals. The social status of a family is often linked to the number of animals owned by it. Cows are not slaughtered for meat. The unproductive animals graze on public lands, and are maintained at virtually no cost to the owner. But the price is paid in terms of the pressures on the local environment. Excessive grazing leads to land deterioration, soil erosion and the suppression of the regeneration of useful species.

Just as excessive pressure on bio-resources leads to land denudation and decline in groundwater recharge, the excessive demand for water leads to a decrease in land and agricultural productivity due to waterlogging and salinity. In addition, the large projects to supply such quantities of water can lead to several environmental problems.

Harnessing the water resources of India was identified as a major task at the time of Independence. Large dams were seen as a solution. But India's first Prime Minister Jawaharlal Nehru in 1957 cautioned. "We have many large scale river valley projects which are carefully worked out by engineers. I wonder, however, how much thought is given before the project is launched to having an ecological survey of the area and to find out what the effect would be to the drainage system or to the flora and fauna of the area.

It would be desirable to have such an ecological survey of these areas before the project is launched and thus avoid an imbalance of nature.

Nehru's apprehensions have today become major environmental issues. They are central to the debate over large dams. Issues of resettlement of affected persons and rights of tribal communities, the impact on biodiversity and fragile ecological systems, the correctness of assessment of parameters like siltation rates, drainage and waterlogging are at the centre of the debate. The imbalance perceived as to who pays the cost and who benefits has led to arguments on equity. The whole issue of scale, of small irrigation projects compared to large projects, is a major environmental debate in India.

Sustainable utilization of groundwater resources necessitates a shift from extraction-focused development to conservation and creation of management systems. To date, most development efforts have concentrated on ways to increase groundwater extraction. Nationwide the number of diesel and electric pump sets have grown from 87,000 in 1950 to 12,581 million in 1990.

Over 20 per cent of the electricity generated in India is currently used for pumping. Groundwater accounts for 42 per cent of India's irrigation potential and for nearly 48 per cent of the net area actually irrigated. Over exploitation of groundwater is causing the water table to drop in most hard-rock and aridzones, and saline intrusion is occurring in extensive areas along the coasts.

Ecologically sustainable economic development has become a policy issue of major significance. conceptualizing and analysing sustainable development is very important at the regional level. This paper investigates sustainable in a practical planning context and seeks to highlight the notions of sustainable resource use. Economics provides some guidelines for planning responsibilities, although ecological considerations should also be taken into account. A region is a geographical area consisting of a coherent entity from the standpoint of description, analysis, administration, planning, or policy.

Among the various types of regions are homogenous and functional regions. Functional environmental regions are often based on the interactions between environmental resources like ground-water, river, and meteorological systems within a particular region. Homogenous environmental regions are based on the existence of common resources in the area concerned. Regions can also be distinguished as natural regions, economic regions, administrative regions, etc.

Regional development is often critically dependent on the regional availability of resources. A region's economic development may be directly dependent on the resources in the region. Usually, in such cases the dependence is on resources that may serve as essential and cheap productive inputs for economic activities. Concomitantly, the environmental capacity to absorb waste materials and pollution can restrict economic activity. Some regions may depend on export of resources as the main source of income.

A regional resource sector may have several effects on the activities in a region such as increased demand for public services, utilities, and infrastructure; demand for labour; capital, space and spin-offs to other private sectors. Thus, the development of a resource sector might lead to shifts in sector allocation, income levels, distribution, and exchange rates.

Aims of Development: From the standpoint of welfare, regional sustainable development ensures that the regional population attains an acceptable level of welfare both at present and in the future and that this regional development is not only compatible with ecological circumstances in the long run but also tries to accomplish a globally sustainable development.

Consequently, regional sustainable development has to fulfil the following goals:

- It should ensure the regional population a sustained acceptable level of welfare;
- It should not have conflict with sustainable development at a supraregional level;
- It should ensure economic progress and/or developoment of potential of the region concerned;
- It should maintain ecological values and/or relieve constraints of the area concerned; and
- — It should ensure the economic and environmental interest of the parties involved.

The Conflict: The economic-ecological interactions arise in general, because concerted socio-economic development requires a compromise between material growth and environmental parameters, including environmental quality and vital natural resources.

Although in the short run, the conflict between material growth and environmental quality may be severe, in the long run, a mitigating effect may emerge, because continued economic growth needs a sound resource base and structural protection and upgrading of environmental quality.

Such a coevolutionary development, in both the developed and the developing countries takes for granted that the economy and the ecology ultimately do not conflict with each other.

Such coevolution is also based on equitable development options for the present and future generations. It does not necessarily require mutual positive spill-over effects between the economy and the ecology. This idea is echoed in the notion of ecologically sustainable economic development. This paper, investigates sustainable development in a practical planning context and seeks to highlight the notion of sustainable resource use.

An attempt has also been made to provide a practical framework, as renewable stocks of natural resources are key factors of sustainable development.

The following five committees of the National Development Council were constituted to go into some of the critical areas of development: (i) Committee on Austerity, (ii) Committee on Population, (iii) Committee on Employment, (iv) Committee on Micro-Level Planning; and (v) Committee on Literacy.

The meeting of the National Development Council held on 5 April 1993 considered the report of the NDC Committee on Austerity. The Council generally endorsed the recommendations of the report of the Committee. It was also decided to set up a NDC Committee on Power.

Accordingly, NDC Committee on Power under the Chairmanship of Chief Minister, Maharashtra, was constituted to examine measures to make state electricity boards economically viable by recasting tariffs, improving efficiency and considering delinking of distribution from generation.

A Committee headed by Deputy Chairman, Planning Commission was constituted to evolve a suitable formula for distribution of Central assistance to Non-special Category States. The suggestions made by the Committee were discussed by the NDC in its meeting on 23-24 December 1991, wherein a consensus emerged and a revised formula evolved which was made the basis for allocation of Central Plan assistance to the states for the Eighth Plan.

Under the criterion of the progress in respect of national objectives, the approved formula highlights four objectives, viz., (a) population control and maternal and child health; (b) universalisation of primary education; (c) on-time completion of externally aided projects; and (d) land reforms.

During the 43 year period (1950-51 to 1993-94), Net National Product (NNP) at factor cost at 1980-81 prices increased from 40,454 crore to Rs. 2,02,670 crore implying compound growth rate of 3.8 per cent per annum. Advance estimates of GDP for 1994-95 project a growth rate of 5.3 per cent over 1993-94.

During the First Five year Plan (1951-56), national income increased by 3.6 per annum. In the Second Five Year Plan (1956-61), however, the growth rate actually achieved was four per cent annum against the target of 4.5 per cent per annum.

In the Third Plan (1961-66), there was a sharp decline in the growth rate at 2.3 per cent per annum and fell well short of the target at 5.6 per cent per annum. This was primarily due to the steep fall in agricultural production and consequent decline in NNP at factor cost of 4.65 per cent in the last year of the Third Plan. However, during the subsequent three Annual Plans, the economy picked up and the growth rate during 1965-69 was 3.7 per cent per annum. Fourth Five year Plan (1969-74), the growth rate target was fixed at 5.7 per cent in terms of NDP at factor cost. However, the actual growth rate achieved was only 3.3 per cent per annum.

The economy took an up-turn during the Fifth Five Year Plan (1974-79). The growth rate fixed in terms of GDP at factor cost of 4.4 per cent per annum was over-achieved at 4.8 per cent annum for the Fifth Five Year Plan. In 1979-80, however, the economy faced a severe drought resulting in the decline of GDP at factor cost by 5.2 per cent over the previous year. The economy bounced back on the track during the Sixth Plan (1980-85) period when the rate of growth in GDP at factor cost at 5.6 per cent per annum surpassed the target of 5.2 per cent per annum. Despite successive drought condistions during the first three years of the Seventh Plan (1985-90), the economy has fared exceptionally well. The growth rate achieved during Deventh Plan period was six per cent per annum and this surpassed the target of five per cent per annum in GDP at factor cost for the Seventh Plan.

During 1991-92, the country faced a severe fiscal crisis and the balance of payment situation became so critical that exceptional measures had to be restored to. While the growth momentum enabled an increase in GDP by 5.4 per cent in 1990-91, the growth in 1991-92 was only 0.9 per cent. In 1992-93 the economy registered the growth of 4.3 per cent and this had been mainly due to high growth in agriculture and improvement in sectors of trade, hotel and restaurants, transport by other means, storage, communication and the public administration and defence, despite railways and banking and insurance sectors registering a decelerated growth. The GDP from agriculture and allied sectors recorded a growth of 5.1 per cent in 1992-93 as compared to 2.3 per cent in 1991-92.

Important policy reforms had been made during June 1991 towards liberalisation and structural adjustment of the economy. These measures have started showing results. The annual rate of inflation as measured by the wholesale price index declined from 13.6 per cent at the end of 1991-92 to seven per cent in 1992-93. The inflation rate stood at 10.8 per cent in 1993-94. The Eighth Plan has targeted for a GDP growth of 5.6 per cent per year, a substantial reduction in the average annual inflation rate, about five per cent and the average current account deficit of about 1.6 per cent of GDP.

Index of agricultural production with the triennium ending 1969-70 as base, rose from 71.9 at the end of First Plan to 86.7 at the end of Second Plan. During Third Plan performance of agriculture was not quite satisfactory. Widespread drought during 1965-67 slowed down the rate of growth in agricultural production and led to increased import of foodgrains and other items. Index of agricultural production reached the level of 80.8 in 1965-66 and 80.7 in 1966-67. These drought years also witnessed introduction of the best available agricultural technology for the first time in India in the form of high yield variety programme and multiple cropping programme. The folloeing years recorded substantial improvement in agricultural production. As a result, the index, after recovering to 98.9 points in 1967-68 increased steadily to 112.4 in 1973-74. The next year 1974-75 again a bad year for agriculture when the index declined to 108.6. This was followed by considerable improvement in 1975-76 when it touched 125.1. In 1976-77, the index registered a decline of 8.8 points and stood at 116.3 but again shot up to 132.9 in 1977-78 and 138 in 1978-79. The year 1979-80 witnessed a fall by 21 points when index number of agricultural production slipped to 117. It recovered to 135.3 in 1980-81.

The index number of agriculture production steadily rose to 158.4 in 1985-86. There was decline during 1986-87 to 152.5 and 151.3 in 1987-88.

Thereafter it picked up steadily to 192 in 1990-91 and came down to 188.5 in 1991-92 and recovered to 195.8 in 1992-93. According to the revised triennium ending 1981-82 as base, the index numbers of agriculture production which stood at 85.9 in 1970-71 rose to 154.8 in 1993-94. During 1982-83 Kharif production was adversely affected due to wayward monsoon which was inadequate, uneven and untimely. Even so, fall in foodgrains production was only marginal, indicated by a drop of 5.4 points in the production index.

Agricultural production registered significant improvement in 1983-84 which was near normal year from the point of view of weather conditions. Index of agricultural production increased from 137.5 in 1982-83 to 156.4 in 1983-84 and production of foodgrains touched a record level of 15,237 crore tonnes. Weather conditions during 1984-85 were not very satisfactory. As a result, production of foodgrains declined to 14,554 crore tonnes and index number of agricultural production also declined marginally to 154.6.

During Kharif 1985, onset of the south-west monsoon was delayed over central and northern states and its behaviour during the season was erratic over many states. However, weather conditions during the rabi season were on the whole rather favourable to crop production. Consequently, foodgrains output during 1985-86 stood at 15.044 crore tonnes. Weather conditions during 1986-87 continued to be unsatisfactory.

Monsoon was delayed over eastern states, while southern states experienced dry spells leading to moisture stress conditions. As a result only 14.342 crore tonnes of foodgrains production could be achieved during 1986-87. The year 1987-88 witnessed severe drought conditions in most parts of the country and the incidence of heavy floods in the eastern states.

The foodgrains production consequently further fell down to 14.035 crore tonnes. During 1988-89 production of foodgrains recorded a new peak of 16,982 crore tonnes indicating a substaintial increase of 1.775 crore tonnes over the previous peak of 15.237 crore tonnes achieved in 1983-84. With the rainfall and weather situation being favourable during south-west monsoon 1989, the total foodgrains production reached another record level of 17.065 crore tonnes.

On account of erratic behaviour of south-west monsoon, foodgrains production in 1991-92 fell by 4.6 per cent to 16.337 crore tonnes from a record level of 17.64 crore tonnes in 1990-91. Production of rice and wheat was 7.467 crore tonnes and 5.676 crore tonnes respectively.

There was a substantial decline in the production of coarse cereals and pulses. Production of oilseeds in 1991-92 was less than previous year's production of 18.60 crore tonnes. Production of foodgrains during 1992-93 was 17.948 crore tonnes and the production was recorded at 18.212 crore tonnes in 1993-94. Production of foodgrains during 1994-95 is expected to be of the order of 18.636 crore tonnes. Production of oilseeds is expected to be around 2.251 crore tonnes. The thrust has been given for the growth and diversification of agriculture to achieve self-sufficiency in food and generate surpluses for exports during the Eighth Five year Plan Period (1992-97).

On the irrigation side the potential created on major, medium and minor schemes increased from 22.6 million ha in 1950-51 to 26.25 million ha at the end of the First Plan, 29.08 million ha by Second Plan, 33.57 million ha at the end of Third Plan 37.1 million ha by 1966-69. At the end of 1969-74 the potential created was 44.10 ha. By 1979-80, it touched 56.61 million ha and by 1984-85, it reached 65.22 million ha. Potential created by 1989-90 was 76.52 million ha by 1991-92, 81.09 million ha and by 1992-93 achievement was 83.01 million ha. The anticipated achievement by 1993-94 is 85.05 million ha. The target for 1994-95 isto create additional irrigation potential of 2.62 million hectare.

Under power sector, total installed capacity (including non-utility), which was only 2301 mw in 1950, increased to 78,367 mw by the end of March 1992. Against the capacity addition of 30,538.7 mw in public utilities envisaged during the Eighth Plan period (1992-97), the actual addition during the first three years (1992-95) were 12,674 mw.

Under the rural electrification programme, 4.70 lakh villages had been electrified out of 5.79 lakh villages (as per 1981 Census) by the end of the Seventh Plan, achieving 81.3 per cent level of electrification. Upto December 1994, 4.94 lakh villages were electrified.

Universal elementary education, eradication of illiteracy in the age group of 15-35 and development of vocational education to act as viable alternate stream have been the focal points of all programmes in the education sector during the Eighth Plan. Major initiatives in the form of Operation Black-board, non-formal education programme, Teacher Education, and District Primary Education Programme have been undertaken to achieve the goal of 'Education for All'. As on September 1993, 108.20 million children have been enrolled in primary schools and 39.91 million in upper primary schools.

The Eighth Plan during its first three years could achieve an additional enrolment of 11.69 million in the primary schools and 7.06 million in upper primary sections making a total enrolment of 18.7 million during the Eighth Plan.

The emphasis of adult literacy programme has been on sustainability of literacy skills and the achievement of goals of rmediation, continuation and application of skills of actual living conditions. Total Literacy Campaign (TLC) and Post Literacy and continuing education programmes are designed to cater to the above objectives. The Eighth Plan target was to cover 100 million adult illiterates by 1991. About 41 million people have been made literate so far under various programmes.

Under Vocational Education, the Eighth Plan target is to divert about 11.63 lakh higher secondary students to the vocational stream. Upto the end of 1993-94, 9.12 lakh students were enrolled in 16,450 vocational sections approved in 570 schools. In order to boost .he programme and activities in Vocational Education, Pt. Sunder Lal Sharma Central Institute of Vocational Education (PSSCIVE) has been established under NCERT at Bhopal on 1 July 1993.

In the higher education sector as on 1994, there are 153 universities, 34 demand universities, 7,958 colleges and total enrolment in the higher education system is about 48 lakh. In addition, there ia a vast network for technical education, including colleges and institutions offering courses in engineering, medical science, management, etc. In the technical education sector new initiatives like Technology Development Missions, establishemnt off corpus fund in the case of IITs, IIMs and IISc, Banglaore have been taken up recently.

Large investments in the industrial and mineral sector particularly from the beginning of the Second Plan have brought about a significant transformation in the industrial scene. This rate of industrial growth has not been uniform during this period. After a steady growth of about eight per cent during the initial period of 14 years, there was fluctuating trend in the industrial growth rate approaching near stagnancy in 1960-68, going upto a level of 9.6 per cent in 1976-77 and dropping to -1.6 per cent in 1979-80.

During the last decade (1970-71 to 1979-80) the average growth rate has been about four per cent per annum. The average growth rate of industry in the Sixth

Plan period (1980-85) amounts to nearly six per cent which is a small improvement over the average of about 5.3 per cent in the preceding five years.

Seventh Plan envisaged an average annual growth rate of 8.7 per cent in the output of industry sector. In the first year of the Seventh Plan i.e. 1985-86, the actual growth rate achieved was 8.7 per cent as per revised Index of Industrial Production (IIP) (Base 1980-81=100). In 1986-87, second year of the Seventh Plan, growth rate achieved was 9.2 per cent.

However in 1987-88, the growth rate declined to 7.3 per cent due to decline in production towards the end of the year following unprecedented drought. In 1988-89, there was agian a recovery in the growth rate and the IIP recorded an increase to 8.7 per cent. In the last year of the Seventh Plan, there was slight deceleration in the growth rate, which was only 8.6 per cent due to sharp decline in growth rates of mining and electricity sectors. During 1990-91, the growth rate was 8.3 per cent and during 1991-92, the growth rate was 0.6 for industrial production. The industrial production registered an increase of 2.3 per cent in 1992-93 and 4.1 per cent in 1993-94.

Government initiated a number of measures late in Sixth Plan and in early years of Seventh Plan with the objective of removing constraints on industrial growth and providing a more liberal and congenial environment for development of industries. A number of steps were taken to liberalise industrial procedures relating to creation of capacity, imports of technology, etc., to encourage competition in Indian industry so as to ensure reasonable prices and improvement in quality.

These include re-endorsement of capacities, delicensing of industries including specified MRTP and

FERA industries and broad-banding of a large number of industries especially in areas of high technology industries linked with energy production and utilisation, as well as mass consumer goods industries. Provisions of the MRTP Act and FERA regulations were rationalised to facilitate entry into industrial areas of high priority. Expansion of existing units has been liberalised and investment in moderanisation/renovation/replacement as well as export production, has been exempted from industrial licensing. Licensing of new capacity has been liberalised and concept of minimum economic scale introduced to promote production efficiency, taking advantage of economics of scale.

A number of policy measures have been initiated for development of specific industries like textiles, sugar, steel, electronics, etc. Steps have also been taken to tackle the problem of industrial sickness. These include (i) system for early detection of industrial sickness introduced by Reserve Bank of India' (ii) various steps for checking industrial sickness and promoting industrial revival evolved by Industrial Reconstruction Bank of India; (iii) setting up of Board for Industrial and Financial rreconstruction, and (iv) setting up of Small Industries Development Fund in IDBI to provide refinancing assistance not only for development, expansion and modernisation but also for rehabilitation of sick industrial units in small scale sector. The statement on industrial policy announced in July 1991 is being implemented. The new industrial policy emphasises delicensing and technological dynamism. Government has also set up modernisation funds for textiles and jute industries to cater to problems of those industries which account for major share of industrial sickness.

The Government is to establish 70 growth centres to act as a nucleus for industrial growth and promote accelerated development especially in backward areas. Sixty nine centres have already been identified.

The process of setting up of the growth centres has been started. There has been an important milestone in the public sector steel capactiy with most of the main units of the Stage-I of the Visakhapatnam Steel Plant having come on stream in 1990-91. The 4 MT expansion programmes of Bhillai Steel Plant and Bokaro Steel Plant have also fully materialised during the year.

7

Other Programmes and Activities

Under the scheme of 'Grant-in-aid for Research and Publications', Universities, Research Institutes, Professional Bodies, NGC)s are given grants to meet the project cost as per the approved norms for conducting research / evaluation studies. The Scheme covers (i) grants for research including action research; (ii) grant to individual scholars for research studies; (iii) grant for sponsoring publication; (iv) grants for organising workshops, seminars, conferences. A Departmental Screening Committee approves the research projects for sponsorship. Under the Scheme, research/evaluation studies on various aspects of women and children are being sponsored by the Department. Priority is given to research projects of an applied nature keeping in view the plan policies and social problems requiring urgent public interventions, this includes diagnostic studies and evaluation studies. Emerging social problems related to, for example, destitute women/widows, child abuse, etc., are enquired into under diagnostic studies. Evaluation studies of ongoing programmes are made to assess the strength / weaknesses of these programmes for possible corrections. The results of these studies are made use of as intervention strategy both at the policy level as well as implementation.

The scope of this Scheme is also extended in strengthening monitoring of women's programmes by this Department Support to multi-centric studies, state, national and international level workshops/seminars and conferences on emerging problems and gender issues are done on preferential basis.

Monitoring process is further supplemented by supporting research on emerging problems and evaluation studies on the ongoing women's programmes of the Department. The information gaps are bridged through such studies, for strengthening the existing schemes and for evolving appropriate intervention strategies. Besides, exchange of ideas among scholars and activists on gender development issues are supported by sponsoring conferences workshops and seminars.

Funds under this Scheme are being utilised to conduct important studies like baseline survey of adolescent girls, credit facilities for women, evaluation of Working Women's Hostels, STEP and NORAD Schemes, and girl child and family (all multicentric studies), etc.

During the year under report, a study has been sanctioned to evaluate "Apna Beti Apna Dhan" scheme of Haryana, Tamil Nadu and Andhra Pradesh. The findings of this study would be made use for intervention in the National Programme of Balika Samriddhi Yojana which was launched in 1997.

To widen its scope to cover additional activities by amalgamating the research activities now being funded through the Research & Development of FNB and Monitoring Scheme of the Department, the scheme of Grant-in-aid for Research and Publications is being revised by the Department.

The Budget provision for the year 1998-99, under the Scheme is Rs. 50.00 lakh, of which Rs. 8.00 lakh has been approved upto December, 1998. The Department has sanctioned one evaluation study and one workshop till December, 1998. The entire plan provision of Rs. 50.00 lakh will be spent during the year to sponsor the research proposals which are under consideration of the Department.

Monitering of women beneficiary scheme

The Monitoring Cell set up in 1986, continues to monitor the 27 Beneficiary Oriented Schemes for Women being implemented by different Central Ministries/ Departments, as identified by the Prime Minister's Office. The progress of implementation of these schemes are reviewed on the basis of inter-ministerial meetings and remedial actions for removing the bottlenecks are suggested. The status of implementation of the scheme is apprised to PMO at an interval of six months.

The qualitative monitoring of the schemes and widening the scope by covering other women is schemes will help in implementation, quantifying benefits flowing to women from these schemes and for advocating higher outlays for women in the plan schemes, women.s needs issues and perspectives in the plans, policies. Other schemes, including schemes having women component, being implemented by Central Ministries/Departments are being studied for monitoring purposes.

The achievements under Point No . 12 of the Twenty Point Programme 1986 viz. 'Equality for Women' are being monitored. An Annual Evaluatory Report focusing on the achievements in raising the status of women through various developmental programmes is prepared. Further, monthly, quarterly, half yearly progress reports on achievements of ICDS Scheme under Point No. IX of TPP are also prepared. These are sent to PMO, Ministry of Programme Implementation, Planning Commission, etc.

To gender sensitise 2001 Census, a Core Group on Gender Sensitisation was set up up in the Department to consider various matters relating to engendering the 2001 Census. Based on discussions, it made several recommendations which were sent to Registrar General of India for implementation. Core Groups have been set up for suggesting training and media strategies for engendering Census 2001.

The Department is also working on construction of Gender Development Index (GDI) and Gender Empowerment Measure (GEM) for state and district levels. This Is being done with a view to monitor the status of women at State and District levels and for assisting policy makers and implementing agencies.

A workshop on "Developing GD1 for State and District levels" was conducted by the Department on 6-7 November, 1998 for development of a common methodology for construction of GDI/GEM. Another workshop was conducted on 2-3 December, 1998 to short list the indicators, and conducting pilot studies.

Collection of gender-wise data in different sectors is being taken up with CSO/NSSO.

Details of different schemes benefiting women are being compiled for publication of a brochure for reference and use of potential beneficiaries.

Work on compilation of district-wise information on the schemes for women being implemented through NGOs is in progress. This would help in monitoring of the projects sanctioned by the Department.

Scheme of Organisational assistance to voluntary orgar isation

Under most schemes of this Department, grant is given to voluntary organisations only for the purpose of implementing projects. However, many voluntary organisations also need some support to maintain their central office so that their activities can be carried out smoothly and efficiently. The Department of Women and Child Development therefore has a scheme for extending maintenance grant to voluntary organisations expressly for their central office.

Under this Scheme, grant not exceeding Rs. 50,000/- per annum can be given to an organisation subject to certain conditions for maintenance of central office to co-ordinate various activites for women, Social awareness, sanitation and hygiene and nutrition education with special emphasis on pre-school children, dissemination of knowledge of family welfare, immunisation, nutrition, etc.

Information and mass educational activities

The Media Unit of the Department aims to create awareness about issues relating to the development of women and children by giving wide publicity to the policies, programmes and developmental activities being formulated and implemented by the Department. This objective is being achieved through multi media publicity campaigns for which the electronic and print media are being effectively used. Outdoor publicity activities are also undertaken to inform, educate and motivate people for bringing about attitudinal changes to achieve social development goals. Specific objectives include the mobilisation of public opinion on issues pertaining to the girl child, the holistic development of children ' women's empowerment, early child development , nutrition, equal status for women and social evils like child marriage, dowry, sexual harassment, status for women and social evils like child marriage, dowry, sexual abuse of the girl child, exploitation of women and children, etc. Media activities are also undertaken to promote positive social attitudes such as better pre-natal care, health and nutritional needs of the child as well as care of expectant women and nursing mothers, etc.

Radio programmes

The widely acclaimed weekly radio programme 'Naya Savera' produced and sponsored by this Department has completed 16 years of its broadcast. This programme is broadcast in 12 regional languages by 30 stations of All India Radio in the commercial channels of "Vivid Bharati". The duration of each programme is 10 minutes. The programme is produced in a story format through which messages relating to issues on women and child , development are disseminated. Favourable reactions of public to this programme are received from various parts of the country. It has also been decided to conduct survey on the listenership of this radio sponsored programme by the Audience Research Unit of the All India Radio so as to consider changes in the format.

Dissemination Services

Copies of various schemes administered by the Department were issued to various Non -Governmental Organisations and Institutions working for the developmental activities for women and children.

A proposal has also been approved for dissemination of messages on postal stationery.

Financial allocation

An amount of Rs. - 125 lakh has been allocated for multi-media activities during 1998-99 and the entire amount will be utilised on various activities.

Administrative improvement

Due priority was given to the administrative improvement in the Department. The position regarding the various O &M activities viz. reports/returns, review of rules/regulations, consolidation of orders/ instructions, allocation of work among different sections/desks, channel of submission and final level of disposal and time limits of cases are being reviewed. An action plan of the 0 & M activities was drawn up and scrupulously followed.

The computerised Information & Facilitation Centre, which started functioning during the last year in the Department, continued working successfully. The necessary computerisation support has been provided by the NIC. The Centre aims to provide information on matters relating to the schemes being dealt with in the Department, to the members of public/representatives of NGOs on various concerned issues under one roof,

Public and staff grievances

As regards the Public grievances received in the Department, the same were attended to on priority and regularly monitored through a monthly return to Department of AR & PG. Instructions to set up public grievances redressal machinery have also been issued to the sub-offices of the Department.

The Department has initiated various steps to redress staff grievances. A suitable mechanism exists in this Department to redress grievances of staff at all levels and at regular intervals. Being a small Department, the inter-personal communication is very informal which also substantially helps in speedy redressal of grievances.

15-Points programme for the welfare of minorities

The department is implementing various schemes in .41 districts of 11 educationally backward states having minority concentration areas as given in Annexure XIV. The schemes/ programmes in the minority concentration areas are:

- — Socio-Economic Programme
- — Schemes for Creches for Working and Ailing Mothers
- — Condensed Courses of Education a Vocational Training (CCE&VT)
- — Awareness Generation Programme
- — Early Childhood Education
- — Balwadi Nutrition Programme

Environmental awareness

While implementing the ICDS programme for women and children, environmental dimensions receive special attention.

The following topics on Environment Pollution have been included in the curriculum of training of ICDS functionaries

- — Environmental Awareness;
- — Use of environmental resources in organising pre-school activities;
- — Audiovisual presentation for use of environmental resources;
- — Planting trees and plants in the training centres;
- — Cleanliness and sanitation of the home environment;
- — Role of the community in creating a healthful environment for children.

Outstanding audio objections

As per the Audit Inspection Report for 1996-97 on the Grant-in-Aid of the Department of Women and Child Development, there are 70 audit paras relating to various schemes of the Department which are being attended to by the concerned Divisions.

Computer based management information systems

National Informatics Centre (NIC) has established a computer centre in the Department of Women and Child Development and has installed a Pentium Processor based Windows NT Server and a Pentium Processor based Unix Server. Local Area Network has been established in the Department and various facilities like information sharing, electronic mail, graphical user interface (GUI) based INTERNET surfing have been provided. NIC continued to provide software, hardware and consultancy support to Department of Women and Child Development in developing computer based Management Information Systems. A team of officers of NIC is working in close coordination with the officials of the Department. Highlights of the year 1998-99 are as follows :

Local area network

Local Area Network has been established in the Department. Existing computer systems in the Department with compatible network card (Ethernet card with UTP port) have been configured and put on LAN. Necessary training regarding surfing INTERNET sending electronic mail and sharing of files has been provided to senior officers of the Department. Network Interface Card has also been purchased by the Department and installed in systems in which the same was not available and these systems have also been configured. In all, 15 computer systems have been put on LAN.

IT induction plan

The five year plans of the Department have been studied and priority areas for growth in the sector have been identified. Hardware, software and networking requirements have been worked out. Budgetary estimates for IT induction plan during the Ninth Plan period with yearly phasing has been worked out. Report on IT induction plan for the Department is in final stages of preparation.

Y2K Compliance

Various software packages developed and implemented in the Department of Women and Child Development have been thoroughly examined and made Y2K compliant.

Integrated Child Development Services (ICDS)

Software package developed in Foxplus for monitoring the scheme of Integrated Child Development Services (ICDS) has been taken up for conversion in DB2 at the back end. The same is in progress.

Presentation to delegation from Bangladesh

Management Information Systems developed for the Ministry of Human Resource Development have been organised in a presentable format using power point. A presentation of the same has been made to a delegation of high level educationists from Bangladesh on 23 June 1998.

VIP references information system

VIP references information system and file monitoring system have been developed in DB2. The same will be implemented in all sections of the Department after thoroughly testing the software in one or two sections.

Personnel information system

Development of Personnel Information System has been taken up. Information requirements of the users have been chalked out. Design of necessary input/ out proformae is in progress.

Website for the department

A Web page for the Department of Women and Child

Development has been created. Various schemes and activities of the Department, organisational structure, role of various agencies in national development have been briefly described. The same has been demonstrated to senior officers of the Department.

Hardware and Software requirements

Hardware and software requirements of the Department for providing client computer system upto Section Officer level and to PA/PA to Deputy Secretary and above have been worked out in connection with the introduction of office automation. A proposal has been sent to the Department for taking necessary action.

Fifth Pay Commission Arrears

In connection with the payment of 2nd instalment of arrears to the employees of Department of Women and Child Development, NIC worked on the software for calculation of balance of arrears and prepared a detailed statement giving arrears to be paid to each employee.

Software Maintenance

Necessary support has been provided in the maintenance and smooth functioning of packages viz. Stores Inventory System, Payroll, Public Grievances Information System, Mahila Samriddhi Yojana, Balika Samriddhi Yojana, Budget Information System, etc.

Technical consultancy and guidance

NIC provided technical consultancy and guidance to various organisations like National Commission for Women (NCW), National Institute of Public Cooperation and Child Development (NIPCCD), Rashtriya Mahila Kosh (RMK), Central Social Welfare Board (CSWB), etc.

Training programmes conducted

On-the-job training programmes have been organised

from time to time. Necessary training has been imparted to senior officers of the Department in surfing INTERNET, sending electronic mail, sharing of information, etc.

Financial assistance to voluntary organisations

A list of voluntary organisations who have received a recurring grant of Rs. 1 lakh and above from the Department for various activities in the field of women and child development during the year under report is given at Annexure XV.

8

National Institute of Public Cooperation and Child Development

The National Institute of Public Cooperation and Child Development (NIPCCD) is an autonomous organisation with its headquarters at New Delhi. It functions under the aegis of the Department of Women and Child Development, Ministry of Human Resource Development.

The objectives of the Institute are to develop and promote voluntary action in social development; take a comprehensive view of child development and develop and promote programmes in pursuance of the National Policy for Children; develop measures for coordination of governmental and voluntary action in social development; and evolve a framework and perspective for organising children's programmes through governmental and voluntary efforts.

With a view to achieve the above objectives, the Institute conducts research and evaluation studies, organises training programmes, seminars, workshops, conferences, and provides documentation and information services in the field of public cooperation and child development. The Institute is the apex body for training of functionaries of the Integrated Child Development Services (ICDS) programme. It provides technical advice and consultancy to government and voluntary agencies in promoting and implementing policies and programmes for child development and voluntary action. In addition, it collaborates with regional and international agencies, research institutions, universities and technical bodies.

The General Body and the Executive Council are its two main constitutional bodies, The General Body formulates policies for management and administration of the Institute. The Minister for Women and Child Development is President of the General Body and Chairman of the Executive Council. In addition, there are committees to oversee academic programmes and administrative matters.

The Institute at its headquarters functions through six divisions, namely, Public Cooperation, Child Development, Women's Development, Training, Monitoring and Evaluation and Common Services. The Divisions are grouped under two Departments, namely, the Department of Mother and Child Development and the Department of Training and Common Services.

Recognising that in a country of such vast dimension, an Institute located in Delhi will not be able to cater to the specific field level regional requirements in terms of training, research, consultancy, etc., the Institute has set up its Regional Centres at Guwahati, Bangalore, and Lucknow. It has also identified a number of institutions to cater to the training needs of child care workers in different states and Union Territories.

Programmes and activities

In the pursuance of the recommendations of the committee on reorganisation of the Institute approved by the Executive Council in February 1998, for the prioritisation of its programmes and activities, the central focus of the Institute is the integrated development of the child and the mother in its most comprehensive and varied form. This recommendation of the Committee has been kept in view while planning programmes for the year 1998-99.

The programmes and activities of the Institute may be grouped under the broad categories of regular programmes of training, research and documentation in the area of Public Co-operation and Child Development; and functionaries.

Regular training programmes

Under regular programmes, the institute organises orientation/training courses for representatives of voluntary organisation and officials of government departments engaged in implementation of programmes of mother care, child development and women's development. The Institute also conducts programmes on subjects of topical interest in these fields to highlight the role of voluntary organisations and government departments in tackling emerging social problems including problems having a bearing on welfare and development of children and strengthening the service delivery system. These programmes are aimed at creating consciousness in the community about the needs of the child and mother and help channelising it into concrete action.

The institute has been consistently trying to maximise the outreach of its regular programmes for officials and non-officials engaged in the area of women and child development with the resources available with it. During the year 1997-98, the Institute organised 75 programmes against the target of 60 programmes. These programmes were attended by 3236 participants against a target of 1800. During the year 1998-99, the Institute organised 77 programmes upto January 1999 against the target of 60 programmes for the year. 2657 participants attended these programmes against the target of 1800 participants for the year. The Institute proposes to organise about 40 more programmes during the remaining year.

In the year 1998-99, the Institute has undertaken several new initiatives in making its training programmes more interesting and effective by laying more emphasis on the participatory method of training. Its training programmes have covered some new areas in terms of subject matter of the courses.

New Initiatives in Methodology and Contents of Regular Training programme:

— Changing family, emerging patterns of care and protection of human development services
— Management of child programmes Laws relating to welfare of children development
— People's participation for sustainability of child welfare and development programmes
— Holistic approach to the development of adolescent girls Prevention and early detection of childhood disabilities
— Early childhood care and education Family life education—emerging challenges Stimulation for children below three years Prevention of Hepatitis B in children
— Training on micronutrients for personnel of voluntary organisations engaged in maternal and child health
— Nutrition and health of young children
— Women's empowerment—their role in governance and decision making Negotiation skills

- — Training the faculty of the Institute on application of computer knowledge and techniques
- — Qualitative methods in social sciences research
- — Training women members of Jilla Panchayats on issues concerning children's rights, needs, problems and management of children in institutions
- — Alternate strategies for reaching adolescent girls
- — Review training material on Meena— the girl child initiative
- — Stress on participatory training method
- — Introduction of more skill-based and field-based training and practicals. Emphasis on innovative methods of training such as group discussion, case presentations, mock sessions, etc.
- — Greater use of audiovisual aids in training sessions
- — Preparation and supply of relevant training material for the participants

Training for ICDS functionaries

As the apex body for the training of ICDS functionaries of Integrated Child Development Services (ICDS) programme, the Institute has been entrusted with the responsibility of planning, coordination and monitoring the training of ICDS functionaries; building up training infrastructure and capabilities of institutions engaged in training of ICDS functionaries; organising training of trainers; designing, revising, standardising and updating syllabi for training of various categories of functionaries; preparation of model programme schedules; and preparation, procurement and dissemination of training materials including audio visual aids. The Institute also provides feedback to the Department of Women and Child Development, Government of India and the concerned departments of State Governments on matters pertaining to the training of ICDS functionaries.

In addition, the Institute is shouldering the responsibility of training of functionaries of World Bank Assisted ICDS Projects since 1992-93. This includes preparation and revision of syllabi for training of CDPOs, supervisors, Anganwadi Workers and helpers of these projects; training of CDPOs and instructors of AWTCs and MLTCs; and building up infrastructure for training of Anganwadi Workers and middle level functionaries in the states of Andhra Pradesh, Bihar, Madhya Pradesh and Orissa.

The training of Child Development Project Officers (CDPOs) is conducted at the Institute's headquarters in New Delhi and its three Regional Centres located at Bangalore, Guwahati and Lucknow. The training of supervisors takes place at selected training centres known as Middle Level Training Centres (MLTCs) which are located in different states. The Regional Centres of the Institute also function as MLTCs for the states/regions in which these are located. While the training of trainers of CDPOs and supervisors is imparted at the Institute's headquarters, the training of trainers of Anganwadi Workers (AWWs) is given through the MLTCs. The Institute also provides skill specific training in the areas of pre-school education, growth monitoring, nutrition and health education, community participation, 'etc. to trainers of AWTCs and MLTCs.

During the year 1997-98, the Institute imparted job training to 386 CDPOs/ ACDPOs and refresher training to 202 CDPOs/ACDPOs. The number of Supervisors of ICDS who were trained in Job Training and Refresher Training during the above period was 921 and 750 respectively. 278 instructors of AWTCs/MLTCs received training in different courses. A total of 238 senior officers participated in review meets/training programmes during the period under report. 16 Executive Heads of AWTCs were given orientation training, 50 CDPOs attended the orientation course.

New Initiatives in Training of ICDS Functionaries

— Skill training on communication for instructors of AWTCs/MLTCs
— Greater emphasis on making training programmes more participatory, skill-based and practical by using audiovisual aids, role-plan, exercises in groups, demonstrations, etc.
— Adoption of new approaches and strategies such as utilisation of additional training centres, and using alternative methodology for training to minimise the training backlog.
— Revision of curricula and syllabi for training of ICDS functionaries
— Incorporating changing requirements of ICDS programme and its convergence with other schemes such as WILL, IMY, MSY and community based monitoring.

A comparative status of programmes organised by the Institute in 1997-98 and 1998-99 is at Annexure XVII.

A list of training/orientation programmes organised by the Institute and its regional centres in 1998-99 (upto January 1999) is at Annexure XVII.

Research/Evaluation studies and other projects

The Institute undertakes research and evaluation studies as an integral part of its work. It has adopted a policy on research which has the approval of its Executive Council. The following areas identified in the policy provide a broad framework for research work of the Institute:

(a) research for policy formulation and programme development; (b) research and surveys for identification of needs and problems in the areas of voluntary action and mother care and child development; (c) assessment of efficacy and impact of on-going programmes for promotion of voluntary action and mother care and child development and identification of bottlenecks in the implementation and service delivery of various programmes and mid-course corrections; and (d) research, surveys and evaluation studies for identification of training needs in the areas of voluntary action and mother care and child development, development of curriculum and training materials and aids.

During the year 1998-99, the Institute completed the following research/ evaluation studies and other projects:

i) Revision and Translation of the Source Book on Financial Assistance to Voluntary organisations

Voluntary organisations, who have come to play a pivotal role in the process of social development, always face the problem of limited resources which bar them from performing their legitimate role. In this context, the provision of grant-in-aid to voluntary organisations forms one of the important measures for promotion of voluntary action in the field of social development. Today, there are number of Ministries/ Departments of the Central Government which give grants-in-aid to voluntary organisations for carrying out numerous activities for the needy and deprived. In addition, there are number of private funding bodies which, too, provide financial assistance to voluntary organisations for implementing social development programmes. However, information about the availability of such funds is often scattered and not always accessible to voluntary organisations, especially those working in remote parts of the country. With a view to filling up this information gap, the Institute, in 1981, for the first time, brought out a Source Book containing information on various government and non -governmental sources of funding for activities of voluntary organisations. The Source Book was well received by voluntary organisations and revised editions were brought out in the years 1984, 1987 and 1991. Continuing demand for the Source Book has resulted in the Institute' bringing out the fifth edition incorporating recent changes in the schemes and programmes for financial assistance. This edition contains 50 new entries apart from modification in some of the schemes included in the fourth edition. In all, there are 130 schemes of various Ministries/ Departments, international agencies and other funding agencies whose grant-in-aid programmes have been included in the present edition.

ii) Evaluation of Tamil Nadu Integrated Nutrition Project: A Study

The main objective of this study conducted by the Regional Centre Bangalore was to assess the extent to which the Tamil Nadu Integrated Nutrition Project (TINP) achieved its objectives. The study examined the strategies adopted in accomplishing the objectives of TINP. The study covered 90 villages in 30 blocks spread over 10 districts of Tamil Nadu. A total of 1220 respondents who comprised TINP functionaries and target beneficiaries were interviewed.

Some of the important on-going studies/projects approved by the Academic Committee earlier and which are at different stages of progress are listed below:

i. Girl Child in Adoption - A Study
ii. Child Marriage Restraint Act-A Study of its Implementation in Gujarat
iii. Revision of Guidebook for Creche Workers

iv. Scholastic Problems of Children

v. Information, Education and Communication (IEC) in ICDS Programme: Research And Effectiveness

vi. Evaluation of Utilisation of Medicine Kit provided to Anganwadi Workers

vii. Child Welfare and Development in Post-Independent India - A Profile

viii. A Study of Food Habits and Growth Pattern of Children in the Ecological Context

ix. Child Abuse in Guwahati

x. A micro level study on birth weight and neo-natal deaths of hospital born children in hospitals of Guwahati city

xi. Aggression in Children.

xii. A Comparative Study on Community Participation in ICDS Projects run by a Voluntary Organisation and Government.

Celebration of 50th year of India's independence

To commemorate the 50th anniversary of India's independence, the Institute planned and organised a series of programmes including Consultation Meet, essay competition for children and adolescents, cultural programmes, etc. These programmes were organised by the Institute's headquarters at New Delhi and its three Regional Centres located at Bangalore, Guwahati and Lucknow. Details of these Programmes are given below

Headquarters

Essay competition for children and adolescents in the age-group 10-14 years and 14-18 years. The theme of the essay was "My Vision about India for the year 2000 and beyond".

National Consultation Meet on Women's Empowerment-their Role in Governance and Decision-making.

Initiated preliminary work for bringing out the publication entitled "Child Development in Post. Independent India". The publication will give a comprehensive view of the history of child development in India.

Regional Centre, Bangalore

The Regional Centre, Bangalore celebrated the Golden Jubilee of India's independence. The theme of the celebration was "Folk Media and Mass Awareness". The Regional Centre invited four groups to make cultural presentations which had a bearing on development communication. The first two groups were represented by voluntary organisations, while the remaining groups were represented by the Songs and Drama Division, Ministry of I & B. The other activities included Angavikalana Sutta (Around the Handicapped)-a street play; Hennu Shishu (Girl Child)-a street play; Beesu Kamsale- a folk art presentation, Akashara Vijaya (Yakshagana)- a folk art presentation.

Regional Centre, Guwahati

The Regional Centre, Guwahati celebrated the event by organising a day long programme for children. The activities included organisation of an exhibition highlighting the achievements made by the country in the field of women and child development in the last fifty years, a drawing and painting competition for children, organisation of a Quiz programme on 'India: Land ana the People' and a cultural show by the children in the evening.

Regional Centre, Lucknow

The Regional Centre, Lucknow celebrated the occasion at

its premises in Lucknow. The theme of the celebration was 'National Integration and Communal Harmony'. The main objective of the celebration was to create general awareness about national integration and communal harmony among participants of training programmes.

The Regional Centre also organised a film show entitled 'Ladki Ke Naam, Kaam Hi Kaam' to draw the attention to the plight of the girl child. A singing competition was organised in which children of different Anganwadi Centres participated. A group discussion for the mothers was also organised to discuss issues suck as breast-feeding, immunisation, hygiene and diarrhoea. A lecture was also organised on detection and prevention of Childhood Disabilities. Participants in the above programme included Anganwadi children, their mothers, Anganwadi helpers, Anganwadi Workers, supervisors and CDPOs.

Documentation

Resource Centre on Children is a specialised research and reference centre on children, women and disadvantaged groups. It is actively involved in development, research and networking activities and provides a comprehensive perspective about the status, and needs of children and women. RCC Data Base has bibliographic details of documents received and indexed. The facility of 'on-line-search' in the Centre provides the users an easy access to information.

During the year 1998-99 (upto January 1999), RCC collected about 310 unpublished documents and added 234 books to the library. It subscribed to 197 journals/ magazines and 17 newspapers.

During the year, NIPCCD Newsletter (English) and NIPCCD Samachar (Hindi) continued to cover programmes and activities of the Institute as well as the latest developments in the field of voluntary action and women and child development.

Financial allocation

The expenditure incurred by the Institute during 1997-98 under 'Plan' and 'Non-Plan' heads was of the order of Rs. 161.20 lakh and Rs. 380.12 lakh respectively. The approved Budget Estimates for 1998-99 under 'Plan' and 'Non-Plan' was Rs.260.00 lakh and Rs.300.00 lakh respectively. The Revised Estimate for 1998-99 under 'Plan' and 'Non-Plan' is to the tune of Rs.2.60 lakh and Rs.4.10 lakh respectively. The expenditure incurred during 1998-99 (upto November, 1998) under 'Plan' and 'Non-Plan' heads was Rs. 173.95 lakh and Rs.372.83 lakh respectively.

A budget provision of Rs.180.00 lakh was approved for the year 1997-98 for project entitled 'Training of ICDS Functionaries and other Tasks connected therewith' and Rs.65.00 lakh for Training of Functionaires of World Bank Assisted ICDS Projects. Upto March, 1998 an expenditure of Rs.126.58 lakh and Rs. 41.51 lakh was incurred against these provisions respectively. The Revised Estimates of Rs.175.00 lakh under 'Training of ICDS Functionaries and other Tasks connected therewith' and Rs.35.00 lakh under 'Training of ICDS Functionaires of World Bank Assisted ICDS Projects and other connected Tasks' were proposed for 1998-99. An expenditure of Rs. 59.42 lakh and Rs.19.14 lakh respectively was incurred till January 1999.

Outstanding audit objections

There are 11 outstanding audit objections from 1990-97. Most of the observations are of procedural nature. The Audit of Accounts of the Institute for 1997-98 by Director General of Audit, Central Revenue has been completed in September, 1998.

Position of reservation

The Institute follows the reservation policy of Government of India for SCs, STs and OBCs.

Meetings of committee working

Academic Committee

This Committee deals with all matters concerning academic work and programmes of the Institute. The Twenty Sixth meeting of the Academic Committee was convened on 3 June, 1998 to consider proposals of training programmes for the year 1998-99.

Administrative Committee

A Meeting of the Administrative Committee of the Institute was held on 3 December, 1998 to consider various administrative and financial matters. The Committee, inter-alia, reviewed the Annual Report (Volume-1) consisting of information on programmes organised by the Institute during 1997-98, revised estimates 1998-99, budget estimates 1999-2000 and other financial and administrative matters.

The recommendations made by the Committee will be placed before the Executive Council in the forthcoming meeting. The Committee expressed its appreciation for the work done by the institute during 1997-98 and recommended the Annual Report (Volume-1) for 1997-98 for approval by the Executive Council.

Promotion of use of Hindi

In order to promote use of Hindi during 1998-99 several measures were taken by the Institute. These included cash award scheme for officers for giving dictation in Hindi, scheme for incentives allowance to stenographers/ typists for doing their official work in Hindi, nomination of officers for Hindi training, celebration of Hindi

Fortnight from I to 14 September, 1998, organisation of two Hindi Workshops from 9 to 13 November, 1998, convening of meetings of Official Language Implementation Committee at the Institute on regular basis and translation of important documents in Hindi.

9

Central Social Welfare Board

The development of welfare services and the growth of the voluntary sector in India from the early years after Independence have increased almost in tandem, as it was recognized that governmental intervention alone would not be able to provide succour and relief to all the deprived and disadvantaged sections of society.

The growth of the Central Social Welfare Board has kept pace with the development of the welfare and voluntary sectors in India since 1953, when it was first established.

In the words of Jawaharlal Nehru, the first Prime Minister of India, "This attempt that we are making to encourage social welfare activities, is in a sense, rather unique. It is not some central authority which is doing it all by itself, nor does the burden of this fall on the local social welfare organisation. It is a certain combination of the two, where the Central Social Welfare Board comes in as a helper and advisor and at the same time the local welfare organizations who are best suited for it, undertake the work. In this way we can utilise the energy, enthusiasm and initiative of vast numbers of persons all over the country."

Although founded on 13th August 1953 by a resolution of the Government, the Central Social Welfare

Board was registered as a Charitable Company under the Companies Act, 1956 in April 1969.

The stated objectives of the Central Social Welfare Board indicate inter alia the following thrust areas:

- To-promote social welfare activities for the general public such as welfare of the family, women, children and the handicapped and give assistance in cases of unemployment, old age, sickness, disablement and other similar cases.
- To render technical and financial aid, when necessary, to deserving institutions or organisations including Panchayati Rai institutions.
- To promote the setting up of voluntary organisations in places where they do not exist and to promote additional organisations wherever necessary.
- To study the needs of Social Welfare organisations from time to time and to evaluate the programmes and projects of the aided agencies.
- To organise emergency relief measures in times of calamity.
- To organise and promote training in social work and to organise pilot projects whenever necessary.

The objectives of the Central Social Welfare Board are sought to be translated into reality by the implementation of various schemes and programmes for women and children. The Central Social Welfare Board receives grants for the purpose from the Department of Women & Child Development, Government of India.

Programmes of the Board

The programmes and activities of the Central Social Welfare Board have undergone several changes from time to time in order to make them responsive to society's changing needs. Within the broad objective of empowering women and providing for the needs of children, the Board is implementing specific programmes.

Empowerment through education

The schemes of Condensed Courses of Education and Vocational Training Programme for needy women in rural, hilly and tribal areas were started in 1958 and 1975 respectively. These schemes were revised in 1988-89 in order to provide relevant educational qualifications and skills so that women can become eligible for paying work opportunities. The revised scheme is being implemented from 1990-91.

Under the Scheme of Condensed Courses, voluntary organisations are given grants to conduct courses of one to 2 years duration to enable women of the age of 15 plus to pass Matric/Secondary, Middle and Primary level examinations. Under the vocational training programme, grants are provided to give training to needy and deserving women in different vocations suck as dress designing, computer courses, handicrafts, batik, hand-loom weaving, nursery teacher training, stenography, etc.

During the year 1998-99, a total of 70 courses were sanctioned and an amount of Rs. 20.79 lakh has been released upto December 1998.

Awareness Generation Programme (AGP)

In order to raise the general awareness of rural and poor women, the Awareness Generation Programme was introduced by the Central Social Welfare Board in 1986-87. The broad aim of this Programme is to create awareness among rural and poor women on various social issues so that they can realise their potential in the family and society. Since 1993-94 special emphasis is being given to the participation of women in Panchayati Rai institutions and their role in national integration and communal harmony. Under this scheme, NGO's are provided with grants to hold awareness camps for women. An NGO can conduct camps of varying duration in each area according to local needs. The local panchayats are also involved in conducting the camps. The Central Social Welfare Board's emphasis has been on involvement of genuine grass-root level activist organisations in the implementation of the awareness programme. During the year 1998-99, Rs. 18.30 lakhs has been spent on the programme uptil December 1998.

Economic empowerment

Socio Economic Programme (SEP)

Under the Socio Economic Programme, initiated in 1958, women's organisations are given financial assistance to take up a wide variety of income generating activities which include the production of industrial components in ancillary units, handlooms, handicrafts and fishery and self-employment ventures like vegetable or fish vending, etc. During the year 1998-99, an amount of Rs. 7.93 lakhs has been spent under the Programme uptil December 1998.

Support services

The provision of support services to women is a major thrust area of the Central Social Welfare Board which has the following schemes under which different types of services are provided to working women:

— Creches for Children of Working and Ailing Mothers
— Working Women's Hostels.

Creches

The programme of Creches for Children of Working and Ailing Mothers provides day care services to the children of upto 5 years of age of mothers from lower income group families who are working or ailing. Financial assistance upto Rs. 18,480/- as recurring grant is provided per unit of 25 children. Continuation units are given Rs. 2,000/- every five years for equipment. In the year 1998-99 an amount of Rs. 777.77 lakh has been released for a total of 9225 creches.

Hostels

In order to provide accommodation for women who are working away from their homes, the Board gives assistance to voluntary organisations for running women's hostels. Under this programme, the Board assists in the expenditure on the salaries of a matron, and chowkidar, for provision of recreational facilities and for rent subsidy (for a hostel in a rented building). The annual grant to NGO's under this scheme varies from Rs. 40,000 to Rs. 50,000 to a unit, depending on the class of city or town. An amount of Rs. 43.65 lakh has been sanctioned as grant for 108 hostels in 1998-99.

Social empowerment

The main objective of the Voluntary Action Bureaux and Family Counselling Centres is to provide services to women (and children) who are victims of family maladjustments and atrocities.

The FCC program has served a vital function in mending family relations through systematic counselling. The Board provides assistance In the form of grants, which cover honorarium for counsellors and other contingencies. Grants upto Rs. 1 lakh can be provided to an NGO for running a FCC. During 1998-99, the Central Social Welfare Board has so far released grants of Rs. 136 lakhs for 290 FCCs.

Family Counselling Centres in Collaboration with Police Departments

The Central Social Welfare Board had also decided to assist Family Counselling Centres in police stations to handle cases. During 1998-99, 15 Family Counselling Centres have been sanctioned in 15 States/ Union Territories. These are Andhra Pradesh Assam, Gujarat, Karnataka, Manipur, Meghalaya, Orissa, Sikkim, Tripura, Uttar Pradesh, West Bengal, Del h I Goa, Maharashtra and Pondicherry.

During the year 1998-99, an amount of Rs.16.41 lakhs was sanctioned and Rs.7.83 lakhs was released for these Family Counselling Centres.

Since training forms an integral component of the Scheme, intensive orientation training is given to all new counsellors within six months of their joining the Centre, while trained counsellors are imparted refresher courses annually to update their professional skills. Training is also conducted for office-bearers of the institutions. 9.6.4 A need has been felt for professional monitoring and evaluation of the functioning of FCCs and also for regular training of counsellors posted in the FCC's.

Schools of Social Work have been involved in the implementation of the scheme as nodal agencies to provide monitoring, evaluation and training services. 17 nodal agencies were identified in different states and a sum of Rs. 3.53 lakhs has been released to them for this professional service.

Mahila Mandal Programme

The Mahila Mandal Programme came into being in 1961-62 to take up welfare services for women and children. These groups of women form an entry point for comprehensive welfare services at the grass-root level. Out of the total expenditure on Mahila Mandals, 75% is borne by the CSWB and the remaining 25% by the organisations themselves. This is a decentralised programme of the Board and it is being run by State Social Welfare Advisory Boards. For 1998-99 an amount of Rs. 217.06 lakhs was sanctioned and Rs.91.80 lakhs has been released to the various State Boards uptil December 1998 to cover 722 centres and 76,163 beneficiaries.

Area Projects

These schemes were started by the Board in the 50's and 60's. The provision of integrated services for women and children is being facilitated by CSWB through a number of specific area projects. The Welfare Extension Projects are multi-purpose projects that extend services such as pre-primary school education, craft activities for women, maternity services and recreational facilities in rural areas. At present there are 44 such projects in five States. Expenditure on the Projects is shared between the CSWB and State Governments in the ratio of 2:1. In 1998-99 an amount of Rs.53.89 lakhs has been released to the State Boards for the implementation of these projects uptil December 1998.

Expenditure on the Border Area Projects is also shared by the CSWB and the State Government in the ratio of 2:1. This scheme was initiated following the Chinese aggression in 1962 and the Pakistan aggression in 1971. Tension in the border areas prompted the initiation and strengthening of welfare services in these areas with a view to promoting their emotional and cultural integration with the rest of the country. At present there are 87 projects functioning in the remote border areas of the country for which an amount of Rs.269.65 lakhs has been released to 1 A State Boards uptil December 1998.

Innovative scheme

It was felt that there are certain areas and social sectors which have remained untouched and uncovered in the entire process of development and social welfare. The Central Social Welfare Board has identified priority areas where there is a need for policy intervention and programme inputs. The areas which are identified by the Board are:—

— Women, who are victims of atrocities and have been assaulted by antisocial elements, etc., widows, who need socioeconomic rehabilitation, counselling, etc.

— Children of prostitutes who need care and development.

— Help in education of mentally retarded.

Rehabilitation of prostitutes & their children

The following institutions are implementing the scheme of Child Development & Care Centres for the rehabilitation of prostitutes:

— Bhartiya Patita Uddhar Sabha, New Delhi.

— Centre for Development Studies & Action, New Delhi.

— Gram Niyojan Kendra, Ghaziabad.

— Indian Council for Child Welfare, New Delhi.

Assistance to needy children

The Central Social Welfare Board has assisted the Indian Council for Child Welfare to set up a Toy, Clothes and Book Bank for poor and needy children. A sum of Rs.1.55 lakh has been provided to the ICCW for this purpose.

Montering and Evaluation

There is a Research, Evaluation and Statistics wing in the CSWB which is responsible for functions related to monitoring and evaluation of various programmes and the maintenance of a data bank on various indicators. During the year 1998-99 the following monitoring and evaluation activities were undertaken by CSWB :

— Continuing monitoring of Scheduled Castes Components of Plan (SCP) & Tribal Sub -Plan (TSP) of the Annual Plan of the Department.

— Compilation of "Directory of Facilities & Services in Delhi" through Women's Feature Services, New Delhi.
— Coordination & facilitation of a study by NIC on "Institutional Strengthening, Study of Central Social Welfare Board" (a study by National Productivity Council).
— Compilation of a list of Voluntary Organisations funded by Central Social Welfare Board.
— Installation of Hindi software in the Computer Systems and training of the staff for using Hindi software.
— Regular updation of data bank.
— A Research Study "Identification of 24 most Backward Districts in terms of Status of Women" in India was brought out.

Publicity and Publications

During the year 1998-99 the programmes and functions of the Board received wide coverage in the print and electronic media. The Board continued to publish its monthly journals 'Social Welfare' in English and 'Samaj Kalyan' in Hindi.

'Social Welfare' which was founded in April, 195.4 soon after the inception of the Board brought out theme issues and special articles this year on subjects relating to economic reforms and Indian women, women workers, disabled women, empowerment, drug abuse, women's education, population control, ICDS and health.

'Samaj Kalyan' was introduced in August 1955 and has been focusing on topical issues. In the year 1998-99 Samaj Kalyan highlighted women's education, drug problem, child labour, environment, population increase, Panchayati Rai, disabled, crime against women, AIDs, etc.

Hindi

During the year 1998-99 (upto 30 November 98) official language Hindi has been used progressively in Central Social Welfare Board as done in previous years. During the period under report the meeting of Official Language Implementation Committee was held.

An incentive scheme for original Hindi noting and drafting in official work was implemented for the propagation and spread of Hindi and cash awards were given to the winners of last year's scheme. With a view to develop proper mental environment for the successful implementation of Official Language Policy, 'Rajbasha Week' was celebrated during the month of September 1998. A Hindi Essay Competition and a Hindi Debate Competition were organised during the week.

10

National Commission for Women

The National Commission for Women (NCW) was constituted by the Government of India on 31st January 1992 as a high-powered autonomous body at national level in pursuance of National Commission for Women Act 1990. The Commission was constituted to safeguard the interest of women, gaining for them equality in status and elimination of any discrimination against them. The Commission consists of a Chairperson, five Members an one Member Secretary.

During the period under report, Ms. V. Mohini Giri was Chairperson of the Commission till 20th July, 1998 thereafter Ms. Vibha Parthasarathy took over as Chairperson of the Commission from 18th January, 1999. Ms. Indira Basavaraj, Ms. Sukeshi Oram, Ms. Syeda Saiyidain Hameed and Ms. Binoo Sen continued to be Members and Member Secretary respectively of the Commission whereas Ms. Vijay Daksh and Ms. Poornima Advani took over as Members of the Commission in place of Ms. Kokila Vyas who expired and Ms. Kailash Pati who completed her tenure as Member.

In order to review the strength and weaknesses of the NCW and assess its contribution, a conference "Crossing the Bridge" was organised. The Chief Guest at the conference was Smt. Suman Krishan Kant. The key note address was delivered by Smt. Margaret Alva, who emphasised the need for NCW to have financial autonomy and status equivalent to NHRC. She was also of the view that NCW should be free from bureaucratic control; there was also a need to have transparency in selection of

Chairperson and Members, which should be free from political considerations.

Activities of the commission

The Commission took extensive tours in various states, in order to acquire a first hand knowledge of the problems and plight of socially and economically oppressed groups of women, women in custody, women belonging to SC/ ST and other special groups. A number of seminars, conferences and workshops were organised or sponsored to deliberate on various socioeconomic and legal issues relating to women's empowerment.

During the period under report, the Commission concentrated on consolidation of the activities initiated in the preceding year. A resume of the main activities of the Commission undertaken during the period, 1st April 1998 to 31st December, 1998 is given below:

Safeguarding Women's Rights

The main function of the Commission, according to the NCW Act, is to safeguard the rights of women in the country. The Commission noted with great concern that the women were increasingly being denied their rights. With a view to make women aware on this aspect, the NCW has initiated a multi-pronged strategy consisting of:

i) Legal Awareness Programme

A country wide legal awareness programme for women has been initiated by the Commission aiming at dissemination of the knowledge of legal rights and safeguards provided to them in law. The Commission sponsors NGC)s and women's colleges conducting the programme. During the period under report 10 legal awareness generation programmes were held.

ii) Complaints, Prellitigation and Counselling Cell

The functions of the Complaints and Prelitigation Cell are to look into complaints and take suo-moto notice of matters relating to (i) deprivation of women's rights, (ii) non- implementation of laws enacted to provide protection to women and also to achieve the objective of equality and development, (iii)non-compliance of policy decisions, guidelines or instructions aimed at mitigating hardships and ensuring welfare and (iv) providing relief to women and taking up issues arising out of such matters with appropriate authorities, which include the law enforcing agencies and police departments.

During the period under report, nearly 1752 complaints had been lodged with the NCW.

In certain specific cases, the Commission investigates the complaints under section 10(l)(4) of the Act for the purpose of summoning and enforcing the attendance of any person against whom the complaint has been lodged, for the purpose of making an in-depth enquiry into the allegations made by the complainant. As per the provision, the Commission made the following enquiries and investigations regarding atrocities on women:

Reports were received from Gundupatti village at Kodaikanal in Tamil Nadu, regarding unleashing of violence by the police on women and children as a sequel to abstinence from voting by the villagers. The villagers were protesting against the Government for not providing them basic necessities. The inquiry report of the Commission was forwarded to the State Government of Tamil Nadu and also to the Inquiry Committee set up by the Government for their consideration. On receiving a report that the village health nurses of Perambalur District of Tamil Nadu were being harassed by the doctor of the Primary Health Centre at Poyyur, the Commission inquired into the incident and submitted its report to the State Government. In their recommendation, the NCW suggested that the doctor who was guilty of harassing the nurses should immediately be transferred to the General Hospital; also, the Supreme Court judgement regarding Sexual Harassment to Women at Work Place, be translated into Tamil and pasted on the notice board of all the primary health centres to prevent innocent women from being victimised.

During their visit to Madhya Pradesh, the NCW team were approached by several women's organisations to look into the indiscriminate violence unleashed at villagers, and molestation of women by police. The women were peacefully demonstrating as part of the "Narmada Bachao Andolan" against the Makeshwar Hydra Project in Khargaon District. One of the Members of the Commission, alongwith an investigating team, visited the areas, carried out investigations and forwarded their recommendations to the Madhya Pradesh Government. The Commission also urged the State Government to stop all construction at the Maheshwar Hydra Project until the task force constituted to look into the grievances of the villagers, submitted its report.

iii) Sexual Harassment of Women, at Work Place

The Commission sponsored a study on "Sexual Harassment of Women at Work Place". For this study, a survey was conducted in States of Andhra Pradesh, Maharashtra, Madhya Pradesh, Uttar Pradesh and West Bengal, covering a sample of 1,211 women. It was found that 50 percent of the women in the sample faced sexual harassment. Among these, 85 percent were not even aware of the Supreme Court Judgement regarding protection of women from sexual harassment at work place. More problems are reported from women in the unorganised sector compared to those in the organised sector.

The Commission also formulated a code of conduct in accordance with the directions given by Supreme Court Judgement on Sexual Harassment to be implemented at Work Place. According to this code, all organisations, both government and private, are required to set up "complaint committees" for investigating charges of sexual harassment. These committees should investigate the charges within a limited period of time. The code has been widely circulated to Central and State Commissions, public sector organisations, banks, media and apex bodies of private sector like FICCI, CII, etc.

iv) Parivarik Mahilla Lok Adallats

The fact of hundreds of cases remaining pending with courts, causing undue delay in justice delivery and sometimes no justice at all, had been a cause of anguish for the Commission. The desire to provide speedy justice to women led to the development of the innovative concept of Parivarik Mahila Lok Adalats (PMLAs) by the NCW. These adalats are organised on the lines of the Lok Adalats with the help of NGOs and the Legal Aid Boards at state and district levels. The effort has been very successful in getting justice delivered to women in respect of family disputes. The types of cases which are handled by the PMLAs are : pending cases, prelitigation cases, legal advice in respect of legal/judicial matters such as matrimonial disputes, criminal cases, labour, motor accident cases and dowry harassment, etc.

v) Review of Laws and Legislative Measures

The Union Government had referred a list of 39 legislations which have a direct bearing on women, for review by the National Commission for Women. During the year under report, the Commission reviewed the following 11 legislations and forwarded their comments to the Government for consideration.

1. Amendment to the Commission of Sati (Prevention) Act.
2. Amendment to the Dowry Prohibition Act.
3. Amendment to the Hindu Marriage Act.
4. Medical termination of pregnancy Act.
5. Child Marriage Restraint Act, 1929 (19 of 1929)
6. Family Courts Act, 1984 (66 of 1984)
7. Foreign Marriage Act, 1969 (A of 1969)
8. Guardian and Wards Act, 1869 (A of 1869)
9. Indian Succession Act, 1925 (39 of 1925)
10. Immoral Traffic Prevention Act, 1986
11. Indecent Representation of Women (Prohibition) Amendment Bill, 1998

New Bills/Laws prepared by NCW

During the year under report, the NCW proposed 2 new Bills for the consideration of the Government of India. These are:-

— Draft SAARC Regional Convention on Prevention and Combating Trafficking in Women and Children.

— Framing of rules under Section 9(b) and Section 10 of the Dowry Prohibition Act 1961.

Activities Reguarding Legal Rights

Campaign against gender based violence in south Asia

The NCW was a partner in the Indian context to the 16

days global campaign launched by the UN Development Fund for Women and other UN agencies, NGC)s and educational institutions. The beginning of the campaign coincided with the International Day for Elimination of Violence Against Women, November 25. Various awareness building programmes for people formed a part of the campaign. The campaign culminated in a Global March on 10th December, 1998 which coincided with the Human Rights Day.

Dahei Mukti Abhiyan

The NCW has launched the Dahei Mukti Abhiyan so that the country marches into the 21st century without the social stigma of dowry. For bringing about awareness even at the formative stages, essay, painting and poster competitions would be organised through State Governments for different age groups from 6 years to 25 years.

Abuse of the girl child

A public inquiry was sponsored by the Commission on "Sexual Abuse of Girl Children in Kanyakumari District", Tamil Nadu. This event was organised by All India Democratic Women's Association at Nagarcoil. Eleven cases of child rape were presented before the jury during the inquiry. It was noted that all the victims belonged to the working class and were extremely poor. During the hearing, the DSP and the District Collector were also present.

A Some of the recommendations made by the NCW, adopted at the end of the hearing are :

— Child rape cases should be covered by a separate law ;

— The definition of child rape should be widened to involve a wide range of sexual abuse and violence.

— Minimum punishment for child rape should be 10 years.
— Child rape cases should be disposed of within a period of six months.
— A special fund for rehabilitation of rape victims should be created.

Special social groups

Carrying forward the activities undertaken for the Special Social Groups like widows, women in custody, and the mentally ill women, the Commission took up the issue of the development of these groups. The important activities undertaken by the Commission in this regard are as follows

i) Women Belonging to Muslim Community

During their visits to cities like Kolhapur, Jabalpur, Aligarh, etc., the Commission met groups of Muslim women who had expressed a number of grievances and requested for the following:

— Divorced women should start getting maintenance as in the past under the Criminal Procedure Code 125.
— A law should be enacted for disallowing oral one sided divorce.
— The single wife law applicable to Hindus should be extended to Muslims also.
— A Commission should be established for rehabilitation of divorced women and their children.

Taking note of the above, the Commission decided to study the problems of minority communities in greater depth. An Expert Committee was set up by the Commission to study the problems of the development of women belonging to minorities. The Expert Committee came to the following conclusions regarding the problems of Muslim women and ways of resolving them:

— Effort should be made to win the confidence of Muslim women and work should be done through these women for their own benefit.

— Priority was necessary for educational development of Muslim women.

— There was a need to organise seminars and conferences, etc., to generate awareness among Muslim women.

— Dialogue may be initiated with Muslim Personal Law Board to bring about reforms.

— Public hearings may be arranged at the regional level to bring to the fore, the grievances of Muslim women.

— A standard Nikahnama may be prescribed for marriages.

The Commission participated in a Seminar on Muslim Personal Law organised by the Centre for Study of Society and Secularism and the Institute of Islamic Studies. At this seminar, two major problems were identified viz. : Muslim Personal Law (Triple Talaq) and multiple marriages.

On the basis of the recommendations of the Expert Committee, public hearings were organised at different places to hear the grievances of minority women. Such hearings were held at Chennai, Mumbai, Lucknow, Hyderabad and Jabalpur.

During a discussion between the Commission and the Muslim Personal Law Board, it emerged that there is no religion which accords as much rights to women as Islam. The Muslims, in fact, extrapolate from it only that which is convenient or useful to maintain men's superiority over women. The question is how to change the mindset and how to show the Muslims that this mindset is harming their image.

The public hearing for minority women, sponsored by NCW and organised by the Jabalpur Centre of the All India Womens Conference was attended by more than 300 women including Muslims, activists and other minority communities. Some of the important suggestions made at this event are:

— Divorce of Muslim women should be registered with some recognised Muslim organisations so that influential persons can intervene and settle family disputes,
— Maintenance should be increased to Rs. 3000/-p.m.
— A woman should have the right to file the case at the place of her choice.

ii) Scheduled Caste/Scheduled Tribe Women

The Commission has been deeply concerned about the empowerment of women belonging to SC/ST communities. The Commission visited a number of states and the tribal areas therein to study the problems faced by tribal women. The Commission visited the State of Orissa and attended a Parivarik Mahila Lok Adalat (PMLA) held at the Angul TD area. The Commission also visited the Tribal Research Institute in Orissa and viewed the research work done by the Institute relating to tribal women. The Institute has done complete ethnographic studies of 12 out of 62 tribes in the state.

During the Commission's visit to Kodaikanal in Tamil Nadu, the Commission interacted with a group of women who came to attend the Adivasi and the Dalit Women's Conference organised by one of the NGOs. Addressing the group of women, the chairperson pleaded for formation of micro level groups at all villages in the area. Such core groups will ensure total empowerment of women particularly Adivasi and Dalit women and make them economically independent. The women in the gathering narrated their suffering to the Commission and submitted petitions. The Commission requested the State Commission to form a two member committee to study their problems and submit a report.

The Commission during their tour of Andhra Pradesh visited a housing colony developed at Guntur, by one of the NGOs, with the cooperation of HUDCO. Women belonging to this colony were being provided with training in vocations like stitching, leather work, etc., apart from literacy. A dairy' unit was inaugurated by the Commission in the colony.

A conference of the Directors of Tribal Research Institutes in various states was organised by the Commission to discuss the ways and means of evolving an institutionalised mechanism for generating comprehensive data and information regarding tribal women and fill the existing gaps.

The above conference was followed by a conference of State Tribal Commissioners to deliberate on implementation of women specific programmes within the Tribal Sub Plan and orientation of general programmes to suit the needs of the female population in tribal areas.

iii) Mentally ill women

The Commission sponsored a documentary film on mental health of women. The film was made by Counter Point. It portrays the conditions prevailing and services provided in various institutions in the country providing mental health care.

The report of a study of mentally disabled women who have been separated or divorced, which was sponsored by the Commission in the preceding year and conducted by Schizophrenia Research Foundation in India, Chennai was released at the "Regional Conference on Rehabilitation and After Care of Women Mental Patients" organised by Indian Women Council for Social Affairs at Chennai.

iv) women in Custody

Under section 100)(k) of the NCW Act 1990, the Commission is required to inspect or cause to be inspected a jail, remand home, women's institutions or other places of custody and take up with the concerned authorities remedial action. Accordingly, the Commission inspected a number of jails and took up the emerging issues with the concerned authorities. During the period under report the Chairperson and Members of the Commission visited nine jails in five states viz. Bihar, Karnataka, Madhya Pradesh, Orissa and Uttar Pradesh.

The general observations in these jails were :

— Most of the prisoners were undertrials in cases related to dowry.

— The prisoners were not produced in the courts for long periods for various reasons causing prolonged detention.

— Majority of the undertrials had no work to do.

— Generally the food provided was not according to the required norms.

At Bellary, the Commission met three women prisoners who had murdered their husbands under grave provocation. The Chairperson requested the jail authorities to release them.

Apart from the prisons, the Commission visited other custodial institutions. One of the important institutions thus visited was Liluah Home in Calcutta. The Home appeared to be overcrowded and lacked medical facilities. The Commission found inhuman conditions in the Home which accommodated as many as

715 inmates though it had capacity for only 350. The Commission wrote a letter to the Chief Justice of Calcutta High Court who treated this letter as a writ petition. The Court issued notice to the Judicial Secretary and the Secretary to the West Bengal Social Welfare Department to show cause as to why appropriate direction should not be issued for the release of these inmates and why compensation should not be paid to those who might have been illegally detained.

After a hearing, a Division Bench of the Calcutta High Court ordered setting up of a five member committee to examine the conditions of the undertrials in the Liluah Home. The report of the Committee is awaited.

The Commission also met, wherever necessary, the Governors of States in connection with problems faced by women prisoners languishing in jails.

Interaction with NGOs and Masses

Apart from the women of special groups and the custodial institutions, the Commission interacted with a number of NGOs and groups of men and women during their state visits. During these meetings, fruitful discussions were held regarding various women's issues and ways of tackling them.

During their tour of Bihar, a visit was paid to A.N. Sinha Institute at Patna, where a prolonged discussion with a gathering of 500 women, including a number of NGOs, took place regarding the strategies of empowerment of women. A meeting with Bihar Women Lawyers' Association brought out a number of legal issues facing the women in the state. The Chairperson of the Commission was also the Chief Guest at the meeting of the Bihar Chamber of Commerce. She also participated in a meeting of police officers and emphasised in her speech the need for their sensitisation regarding the problems of women. She also addressed a gathering of women and men lawyers of the Bar Council in Patna. One of the Members of the Commission paid a visit to 'Aditi, an NGO in Bihar and appraised herself of the work done by the organisation, particularly in regard to female foeticide in Sitamarhi and Katihar.

The Commission also met Officer of Dalmia Cement where the labourers were suffering immensely on account of a lock out. The Commission and the Labour Officers had received a number of complaints from the women, who were particularly suffering due to the lock out.

During the state visit to Maharashtra, the Commission visited the Maharashtra Council of Agricultural and Educational Research (MCAER), which is an apex Institution coordinating six agricultural universities in the State. It was noted that the MCAER had taken a decision and reserved 33 percent seats for rural girls for courses of agriculture graduation, since most of the women are involved in agricultural work. The Research Institute has also developed a training module on single window system for sensitising senior level officers of Agricultural Department. Each topic in this module has a gender component.

The Commission had a discussion with the DCP, Pune, who looks after the women's cell and discussed the need for sensitisation of police personnel. The chairperson also paid a visit to the Maharashtra Women's Development Corporation. A fruitful discussion with Pune Shramik Patrakar Sangh was held by the Joint Secretary, during the course of which some important issues were suggested to be taken up by NCW such as improvement of facilities in women's railway coaches and for undertrials in jails; study of family courts, etc.

The Commission during a visit to Ranchi in Bihar, had a meeting with district officials. It was noted that community mobilisation through Self-Help Groups was quite successful in the State. The minority community in the State had also developed Self-Help Groups engaged in economic empowerment of women and improvement of basic services as well as availability of credit for women. Major social problems were witchcraft, lack of land rights for women, domestic violence and alcoholism.

Sensitisation of police officials

The National Commission for Women conducted the first in a series of sensitisation programmes for police officials from the IG to the ASI level in Ranchi and Hazaribagh. At the request of the DGP, the NCW prepared a special module and conducted the first workshop on 'Gender Sensitisation' for nearly 200 police officials at Ranchi and a similar workshop at Hazaribagh. The DIGs and Dy.Commissioners of Police right upto the level of Sub-Inspector and Asstt. Sub-inspectors, and members of the Judiciary participated in the workshop. The sensitisation programme was welcomed by the police officials which emphasised the need for the law enforcement agencies to have a human face, for creating confidence in the community.

Voluntary agencies came forward with offers to help the police in curbing violence against women and to help in tackling social problems. The police in turn came up with deep insights into the reasons which led to atrocities against women such as witchcraft.

Political participation

The NCW sponsored a National Project on "Women in Panchayati Rai", coordinated by Professor Susheela Kaushik, which covered States of Madhya Pradesh, Orissa, Rajasthan, Tamil Nadu and Uttar Pradesh. During the study information was gathered on :

— The extent of political awareness of the elected women based on family background, their notions on politics and Panchayati Rai, on political structure of the village community and identification of the community needs and priorities.

— Their self-image as women's power and limitations,

— Their views on women's development and rights.

The Commission organised workshops "Listen to Women Vote" in Jaipur, Mumbai, Chennai and Chandigarh jointly with the British Council. The keynote address was given by the Chairperson, National Commission for Women. The main issues discussed were public accountability of politicians and strategies to raise women's awareness. It was noticed that the women wanted a change in the culture of politics. They do not want politics of war, but politics to resolve conflict.

The NCW has set up a Core Committee on "politics and women" which met on 1 6th and 20th July and on 9th September, 1998. The Committee discussed the constitutional aspects of the 84th Amendment Bill and also the strategies to generate awareness among people. The Committee was of the opinion that:-

— There should not be any dilution of the Bill

— Indian women should not be divided on the lines of religion, caste, etc. It was decided that:

— Efforts for mobilisation of women and masses in general, to demand introduction of the Bill in the Lok Sabha should be intensified.

— Regional conferences should be held in Gujarat, Guwahati, Hyderabad, Chandigarh, and Chennai for raising awareness on the issue of reservation for women in the Parliament.

— A rail yatra may be organised to mobilise public opinion.

As per the decision of the Core Group, the NCW supported and encouraged the "Rail Chetna Yatra" financed by the CSWB and the Joint Action Front for Women. The main objectives of the yatra were :

— To mobilise public opinion in support of Reservation Bill

— To prevent violence against women

— To make women aware of their rights

The Yatra passed through nine states viz. Delhi, Haryana, Uttar Pradesh, Maharashtra, Madhya Pradesh, Andhra Pradesh, Tamil Nadu, Kerala and Karnataka, creating mass contact with passengers, meeting people at stations and several women activist groups *en route*. Regional conferences were arranged by the state commissions, State Social Welfare Boards and NGOs at Ernakulam and Chennai..

The campaign succeeded in reaching out to the people on issues of growing violence on women and girl children. The goal of obtaining a million signatures from supporters of the Women Bill on a 100 yard long cloth was achieved after discussion with the signatories and going through the pamphlets.

A delegation of the NCW met the Minister for Parliamentary Affairs regarding the Women's Reservation Bill and pleaded for introduction of the Bill in the Winter Session of the Parliament. The bill was finally introduced in Parliament on 14 December 1998.

The Commission also sponsored various seminars/ workshops relating to women, girl child, family, etc. during the year under report.